TOWARD A European Nation?

POLITICAL TRENDS IN EUROPE
East and West, Center and Periphery

Working in concert for the first time, scholars from across Europe examine current processes of integration and disintegration at the level of individual national and federal states; regions; and the European center and periphery. The twelve chapters have been organized into three parts, treating, respectively: (1) trends in Western Europe; (2) developments in Eastern Europe; and (3) European integration overall. The contributions are based on papers originally presented at the First European Conference of Sociology held in Vienna in 1992, which brought together social scientists from every part of post-Soviet Europe.

TOWARD A European Nation?

POLITICAL TRENDS IN EUROPE
East and West, Center and Periphery

Edited by

Max Haller
and
Rudolph Richter

M.E. Sharpe
Armonk, New York
London, England

Library of Congress Cataloging-in-Publication Data

Toward a European nation? : political trends in Europe—east and west, center and periphery / edited by Max Haller and Rudolf Richter.
p. cm.
"Papers collected in this volume were first presented at the First European Conference of Sociology, held in Vienna, August 26–29, 1992."
"Published also as v. 24, nos. 1–3 of the International journal of sociology."
ISBN 1-56324-384-9.
1. Europe—Social conditions—Congresses. 2. Europe, Eastern—Politics and government—1989—Congresses. 3. Nationalism—Europe—Congresses. I. Haller, Max, Dr., II. Richter, Rudolf, 1952– III. European Conference of Sociology (1st : 1992 : Vienna, Austria)
HN372.T69 1994
306'.094—dc20 93-48346
CIP

Printed in the United States of America

The paper used in this publication meets the minimum requirements of American National Standard for Information Sciences—Permanence of Paper for Printed Library Materials, ANSI Z 39.48-1984.

∞

BM (c) 10 9 8 7 6 5 4 3 2 1

Contents

About the Editors and Contributors

Max Haller, professor of sociology at the University of Graz, received his Dr.phil. from the University of Vienna and his Dr.phil.habil. from the University of Mannheim (1984). His main research area is comparative social research on social structures and values. In 1986–89 he acted as president of the Austrian Sociological Association and in Vienna in 1992 he was a cochair of the Program Committee of the First European Conference of Sociology. He has published many articles in international social science journals, and his recent books include *Klassenstrukturen und Mobilität in fortgeschrittenen Gesellschaften* (Frankfurt/New York, 1989) and *Class Structure in Europe,* (Armonk, 1990).

Rudolf Richter is professor and chair of the department at the Institute of Sociology, University of Vienna. His main research areas include life-style research, political sociology (political participation in environmental affairs), and family sociology, especially the changing of values and youth. In 1992 he was the chair of the Organizing Committee of the First European Conference of Sociology, and in 1990–93 he was the president of the Austrian Sociological Association. His recent publications include *Familien in Wien und Budapest*, ed. with L. Cseh-Szombathy (Vienna, 1993) and a series, Current Trends in European Sociology, published in *Innovation in the Social Sciences.*

Maurizio Bach is associate professor of sociology at the University of Constance, Germany.

Ivan Bernik is associate professor at the Faculty of Social Sciences at the University of Ljubljana, Slovenia.

Volker Bornschier is professor of sociology at the Institute of Sociology, University of Zurich.

Mattei Dogan is a professor at the Centre National de la Recherche Scientifique in Paris.

Jap Dronkers is a professor at the University of Amsterdam.

Attila Eralp is associate professor at the Department of International Relations, Middle East Technical University, Ankara, Turkey.

Peter Ester is professor of sociology and director of IVA, Institute for Social Research, Tilburg University, the Netherlands.

Johan Galtung is professor of peace studies currently residing in Paris.

Salvador Giner is a professor at the Institute of Advanced Social Studies in Barcelona.

Loek Halman is a research fellow at IVA, Institute for Social Research, Tilburg University, the Netherlands.

Jiří Musil is professor of sociology at the Czech Academy of Sciences and director of the Central European University Foundation in Prague.

Dominique Schnapper is a professor at Ecole des Haute Etudes en Sciences Sociales in Paris.

Wlodzimierz Wesolowski is a professor at the Institute of Philosophy and Sociology, Polish Academy of Sciences in Warsaw.

Preface

The papers collected here were originally presented at the First European Conference of Sociology, held in Vienna, August 26–29, 1992, under the title "Sociological Perspectives on a Changing Europe: Paradoxes of Socioeconomic, Political, and Cultural Transformation." The idea for this conference was originally developed by Max Haller (Graz) and David Lane (Cambridge) in the aftermath of an annual conference of the Austrian Sociological Association in Graz in 1987—that is, even before the revolutions in Eastern Europe and the opening of the borders between East and West. In cooperation with about two dozen European national sociological associations, an international program committee was formed, with Giandomenico Amendola (Bari), Thomas P. Boje (Roskilde), Ayse Günes-Ayata (Ankara), Michal Illner (Prague), Wladyslaw Kwasniewicz (Cracow), and Rudolf Richter (Vienna) as members, David Lane and Max Haller as cochairs. The committee met several times to discuss the structure of the conference. The Austrian Sociological Association, under its then president, Rudolf Richter, offered to host the conference and a local organization committee was formed, with Eva Cyba, Elisabeth Jandl-Jager, Max Haller, Helga Nowotny, and Ronald Pohoryles as members and Rudolf Richter as chair.

The conference was a considerable success. It was attended by around 650 participants from 27 European nations; more than 130 papers were presented. Sociologists from the smaller European nations were well represented at the conference, as were sociologists from Eastern Europe, including the Baltic states and Russia (thanks to funding support from the city and the Tourist Association of Vienna, the Austrian ministries of Science and Research and of Labor and Social Affairs, and the European Community).

We thus achieved one of our central aims, which was to promote scientific communication among European sociologists. The conference was also the starting point for the founding of a European sociological association, which is now under way.

The present volume includes outstanding papers from the conference that are related to the issue of changing national and supranational loyalties and identities in Europe. Most were presented as plenary lectures. A second volume of papers from the conference under the editorship of Thomas P. Boje focuses on socioeconomic issues.

As organizers of the conference, we wish to express our thanks to the colleagues who helped to plan the conference, to the participants and speakers who made it a great success, and especially to Sylvia Supper, who for two years was engaged in the organization of the conference. As editors of the present volume, we would like to thank the authors, who revised their contributions, and Patricia A. Kolb, executive editor at M.E. Sharpe. Without their cooperation and efforts, this volume could not have been produced.

Max Haller and Rudolf Richter
Graz and Vienna

TOWARD A European Nation?

MAX HALLER AND RUDOLF RICHTER

Introduction

Within the past few years we have witnessed a fundamental transformation of Europe. The region's communist regimes broke down in the late 1980s and, with them, the generations-old Iron Curtain between West and East. For three decades, Western Europe has experienced an unprecedented process of economic integration and growth within the European Community. Now the politically neutral states of Austria, Switzerland, Sweden, and Finland are applying for membership in the Community as well. Before long, postcommunist East-Central European nations including Poland, the Czech Republic, and Hungary may also become members, thus creating a totally new political landscape in Europe.

What, then, can we say of Europe's prospects? Will it, in fact, complete the century-long process of centralization that has brought a continual reduction in the number of independent states? What are the social, political, and cultural preconditions for a "United Europe"? What would be the implications of such an outcome for Europe itself, for neighboring macroregions, and indeed for the world as a whole? Might a new Community of Europe become the model for a series of other large regional unions of nations, just as America became a model for postcolonial states of the non-European world?

These are some of the questions discussed in the present volume. In this introduction, we give an overview of the contributions. In the epilogue, we develop a more comprehensive framework within which some of the strengths and weaknesses of the contributions can be systematically evaluated.

Let us begin with a short overview of the historical changes in Europe during the last half-century.

The Transformation of Europe Since World War II

The second half of the twentieth century led to fundamental and massive changes in the political landscapes of Europe. Most dramatic and consequential was the division of Europe into a larger Western, liberal-democratic, and market-oriented capitalist part and an Eastern, state-socialist bloc. But within Western Europe itself, another significant division persisted for a considerable time, until the mid 1970s. While the Western, Northern, and Central European countries now all had democratic, parliamentary political systems, two countries in the South (Spain and Portugal) remained under dictatorial, fascist rule. Nevertheless, elements of historically new, reintegrating processes were evident even decades ago. Beginning with the Montan-Union in the early 1950s and the establishment of the European Economic Community (EEC) with the Treaty of Rome in 1957, which was signed by Belgium, the Federal Republic of Germany, France, Italy, Luxembourg, and the Netherlands, a dynamic process of economic integration was at work. This process culminated in the 1992 Maastricht Treaty among the twelve members of the European Community, which projected an economic and political community with its own currency, economic and social policy, and perhaps even military forces.

Fundamental transformations in the social and political landscape of Eastern Europe were also taking place in the late 1980s as the power of the communist regimes seemingly evaporated. In the context of a massive and rapid emigration from some of the smaller East-Central European countries to the West and a "revolution from above" initiated by President Mikhail S. Gorbachev in the Soviet Union, a succession of peaceful ("velvet") revolutions swept away the communist regimes of more than half a dozen countries, including the Soviet Union itself. The next stage of this dramatic transformation brought the dissolution of several multinational states—the Soviet Union, Yugoslavia, and Czechoslovakia. Unfortunately, the breakdown of Yugoslavia unleashed terrible fighting, bloodshed, and atrocities, and there is the bleak prospect of violence on an even wider scale in the former Soviet Union.

These historic transformations pose an extreme and provocative challenge for the social sciences.

All the contributions to the present volume investigate, in one way or another, the question of whether and to what degree we are moving toward a "European nation." When we compare developments in Western and Eastern Europe, it becomes evident how important and acute this question is. In both the West and the East, the issue of ethnicity and the nation as a significant base for social and political transformations has come to the forefront in recent times. In the East, not only have multinational federations been dissolved, but even in ethnically homogeneous states such as the German Democratic Republic and Poland, nationalist ideology and sentiments have played an important role in delegitimating communist regimes.

It is important that we not overlook trends toward decentralization or even disintegration of national states in Western Europe. We need only think of the secessionist and autonomist movements among the Northern Irish, the Scots, the Basques, and the Catalans in Britain, France, and Spain, or the strong new regional movements in Italy, or the recently enacted constitution in the multinational state of Belgium that virtually brought into existence three largely independent substates.

In this light, it is the more surprising that, despite accelerating disintegration processes at national levels, a potent process of reintegration is operating at the European level. This is especially evident in the West.

Trends Toward Unity and Integration in the West

In the first essay in this volume, Salvador Giner reflects on "The Advent of a European Society." Giner points to two paradoxical facts in the present-day advent of Europe "as a unit," as a society with an identity of its own. First, the uniqueness of Europe as a distinct civilization in its own right has become debatable in the context of worldwide "Westernization." According to Giner, current processes of globalization demand the creation of "larger societies" all over the world, in which case Europe may be playing a pioneering role. Giner makes a second point, that the high level of internal heterogeneity and fragmentation of Europe does not preclude the possibility of seeing it as a "unity."

"Nationalism is still the most significant basic political value in the contemporary world, but not in Western Europe." This is the thesis put forward by Mattei Dogan in his contribution, "The Erosion of Nationalism in the West European Community." To substantiate his thesis, Dogan adduces a number of well-established facts and trends. He shows that after the Second World War a strong erosion of nationalistic sentiment took place all over Western Europe as was evident in the decreasing hostility among various European nations. His data chart the blossoming of a "European consciousness," with two-thirds to three-quarters of citizens in the European Community now generally approving of the unification process. The long-term continuity and persistence of these trends is confirmed by the fact that they are more clearly observable among both the young and more highly educated people. This trend toward European integration and the development of a true "European society," according to Dogan, is found not only in the economic, social-structural, and cultural dimensions, but also in the political dimension, where supranational legislation is nourishing supranational loyalties.

What are the main forces behind these fundamental trends? An answer is given by Volker Bornschier in his contribution, "The Rise of the European

Community." Bornschier begins by asking why, after a considerable period of paralyzation of the integration process, the European Community was able to inject a new momentum into this process in the mid-1980s. Bornschier argues that, during the 1970s and 1980s, the economic and political elites in Europe began to feel a new economic threat from the United States and Japan, which had set about putting Europe in economic third place. This threat, he argues, emerged because there is a "world market for protection" (social order), produced by territorially based governments and sold by them to capitalist enterprises and to citizens. This is made much easier if supranational institutional preconditions are present. Exactly such a precondition has been set up by the institutions of the European Community, and particularly by its independent Commission.

In Bornschier's view, transnational corporations have been the main driving force behind the unification process. They "demanded that the political entrepreneurs in Europe provide them with the combined advantages their rivals were enjoying in the United States and Japan," and focused on the creation of a large homogeneous market combined with strategic planning, particularly with regard to factory technology. European integration, seen from this point of view, cannot be explained as a struggle for a new European hegemony in the world economy, but rather as a necessary emergency measure in order to remain "a player at the core." To achieve this, Europe would have to remove its neocorporatist crusts as well as its centralist legacies and develop a "lean state" without abandoning the strategic advantage of a legitimizing welfare state. Its future prospects might then be good in economic (and political?) terms; in cultural terms, the attractive EC project could even take the lead over the other two competitors on the world scene, the United States and Japan.

Maurizio Bach, in his essay, "Technocratic Regime Building," gives an acute analysis of the actual structure and workings of these new supranational institutions at the level of the European Community. He shows that a truly "supranational, quasi-étatist political institutional order with its own legitimacy and sovereignty" already exists today. Three features are relevant in this regard. The first is a legal order, which is wholly new insofar as Community law has clear primacy over the law of the individual nation-states. The second is a new corporate order that brings bureaucracy to the Community and the real power and authority in the processes of integration to the Commission. This is so because the Commission has a monopoly on information and commands both legislative and executive powers. Third, the resulting "Eurocracy" represents a totally new type of public administration, composed of many relatively small, highly specialized groups of experts working with great informality and fluidity. Myriads of commissions, committees, and advisory boards—whose members travel from their national capitals to Brussels throughout the year—have increased tenfold the comparatively small core of the permanent "Eurocracy" (comprised of some thirty or thirty-five thousand public officials). Thus a really new "transnational governmental elite" has been created, which effectively routinizes transnational cooperation at the European level.

But how does Europe look if we consider postcommunist East-Central and Eastern Europe? Here, a totally different situation is evident, as will be shown in the next group of essays.

The Difficult Transition to Democracy and Civil Society in the East

The euphoria of the revolutionary years 1989 and 1990, sustained by the assumption that the demise of communist regimes would create fertile ground for democracy and for rapid economic and social change, was rather soon replaced by anxiety concerning the future of these regions. In his contribution, "Integration and Disintegration Models," Jiří Musil starts from the observation that, at present, political and social trends in Western and Eastern Europe differ fundamentally: In the West, integration processes clearly prevail, but in the East, disintegration processes are much stronger. He discusses two general theories of integration that could help to explain this paradox and provide guidelines for shaping the future. A functional theory holds that political integration processes are a necessary concomitant of the development of advanced industrial societies. According to Musil, this model dominates the present West European integration process. For European integration to become successful in the long run, a more encompassing model of integration, one based on "generic rationality," is indispensable. Such a model must focus on the values of communication, cohesion, and cooperation; an integration process evolving from this model would also make the development of feelings of loyalty necessary to the emerging supranational community. This would mean that there must develop not only a consensus in Europe based on common values and ideas, common interests, common advantages, and common dangers, but also a set of "common ideas expressing the core values of European culture."

Essentially, it is Musil's argument that even the present disintegration processes in postcommunist Eastern Europe have to be looked at differently. Referring to the Czech social scientist and politician Thomas Masaryk, who lived in a period with astonishing parallels to the present-day situation (the collapse of the Hapsburg monarchy), Musil argues that the dismemberment of several East European states that had been united under communist rule might even be a necessary precondition for a new process of unification and integration at the European level. The fate of Czechoslovakia has been paradigmatic of this argument. In this case, even considerable sociostructural similarities were not sufficient to maintain the unity of the state; obviously lacking were shared values and feelings of common identity and mutual solidarity. As Masaryk put it two or three generations ago, "A real federation of nations will emerge only when the nations are free and unite of their own will. This is the direction of Europe's future."

In his contribution, "Postcommunist Transition to Democracy," Wlodzimierz Wesolowski is concerned with these fundamental issues. He starts from a classical sociological distinction between two basic forms of social relationship, "associative ties" and "communal ties." "Associative ties" are typical of developed democratic and market-oriented societies. They are entered into freely and rely on sociopolitical discourse; a society based on them can be designated as a "union of unions." An opposite type of relationship is designated as "communal ties." One typically belongs to these by birth; they are underlined by strong common symbols and values. Societies based on such relationships usually show strong internal cohesiveness. In addition to these two forms, Wesolowski designates a third type of social relationship that he calls "communitarian ties." These combine characteristic features of both the former types: freedom of access on the one side, and a set of common core values on the other side. Both Catholicism (in a modernized, liberal form) as well as social democracy can be considered as examples of communitarian ties.

What happened after the successful revolution was a disastrous splitting up of ideas and values, a proliferation of political parties and partisan factions unable to find compromises among several deeply divisive issues. Neither communal nor associative ties could serve as a basis for a new civil society. Wesolowski argues that, in this situation, only through a reinforcement of communitarian ties will a solution come in sight.

The difficult birth of civil societies in the postcommunist states of Eastern Europe is also Ivan Bernik's main theme in his contribution, "Politics and Society in Postsocialism." Following a system-theoretical logic, Bernik starts from the observation that, in all these societies, politics dominates the other spheres of society, thus preventing the formation of autonomous subsystems. This is a paradox, since it was "society," as distinct from authoritarian politics, that was the decisive force in the liberation from communism. Supplementing the analyses of Musil and Wesolowski, Bernik elaborates the role different elites have played in the revolutionary process. The main actors in the first stage of the transformation process were intellectuals (more exactly, a subgroup of "marginalized nonconformist intellectuals"), but they were no longer successful in the postrevolutionary process.

According to Bernik, this was so because their ideology was that of "civil society pure"—that is, to give voice to "society at large" and not only to particularistic interests; they, in fact, perceived their actions as "antipolitics."

The new, more successful postrevolutionary elites were "political newcomers" who simply promised to abolish the old order. But when their attempts to restructure the economy did not result in the improvement of the economic well-being of large parts of the population, democratization did not lead to a pacification of these societies. Today, these new governing elites face the difficult task of the "management of mass disappointment," and they are no longer legitimized by the historical task of the abolishment of the old order. Bernik's conclusion is that the transition to democracy is far from being completed in Eastern Europe, and that it is also not irreversible.

The Persistence of Structural Diversity

In the Netherlands, not only bi- but even trilingualism has been common among educated people for generations (German and English in addition to Dutch). Recently, increasing numbers of parents in this country are sending their children to high schools and universities that teach exclusively in English. Is this the model trend for Europe as a whole? This highly relevant question is investigated by Jap Dronkers in his contribution, "The Causes of Growth of English Education in the Netherlands." He clearly shows that the tendency toward full bilingualism in the Netherlands is restricted to a specific segment of the educated upper classes. Thus it can be said that the increasing cohesion among the economies of the European nations will lead toward an increasingly stronger international orientation in the Dutch elite. If this is true for other countries as well, one can say that European integration will contribute to an increasing sociocultural inequality within the single European societies and their national elites.

A much stronger case for a traditional but still relevant dimension by which Europe can be seen—at least at first sight—as a cultural unity is religion. Dominique Schnapper deals with the significance of ethnoreligious studies. She argues that the "disenchantment" of the world has to be analyzed as a dialectic between the principles of rationality in personal and political relationships and the social realities that remain in many aspects of the *Gemeinschaftsidee.* In analyzing ethnic revival, one should at least distinguish the cases of Eastern and Western Europe. In Eastern Europe, it sometimes arises from premodern ethnic identities; in Western Europe, from contradictions in modernity itself. Schnapper concludes that we might be witnessing a decrease in the diversity and autonomy of the various domains of social life and the creation of an "ethnoreligious" field.

Peter Ester and Loek Halman, in "Empirical Trends in Religious and Moral Beliefs in Western Europe," show that the differentiation in Christianity within Europe is not of decreasing importance, even in our age of secularization. By comparing data on religious practices, social permissiveness, and civic morality from the European Value Study in 1981 and 1990, they find that the various West European countries did not converge. Rather, in several instances the differences became even greater.

But defining Europe on the basis of Christianity would lead to the exclusion of non-Christian regions, especially predominantly Islamic nations. A highly relevant case in point is Turkey. In his essay, "Turkey and the European Community," Attila Eralp shows that such processes of social exclusion have already been at work in the recent history of European integration. It seems quite evident that it was concomitant to the redefinition of Europe along historical-cultural lines, invoking ancient Greece and Christianity as its ideological foundation, that "Turkishness" became increasingly to be defined as something alien to European culture. The consequences of this were considerable for Turkey, which was constrained to adopt "Turkishness" gradually as a constituent element of its own national identity. This, in consequence, led to a serious weakening of liberal, democratic, and progressive forces within Turkey and to a strengthening of those forces that successfully tried to redefine its geopolitical role as a leader for the Turk peoples in the new independent successor states of the Soviet Union in the South and in Central Asia. Ironically, this redefinition of its role in world political affairs brought Turkey closer to the United States and its power politics in these regions of the world. This quite dramatic shift, we can conclude, did in fact imply that Europe has overlooked one quite important occasion for implementing a new kind of peaceful regional neighborhood politics.

Johan Galtung, in "The Emerging European Supernationalism," is arguing in a historical-cultural way. He focuses more on the borders in the mind among the European nations than on unity. The diversification in Europe can be shown in frontier lines—to the Islamic South and to Russia in the East—between "good" countries and "bad" countries. From this, it seems possible to foresee the coming conflicts and especially to warn of European supernationalism with suprainstitutions.

Thus we could say that the increasing unification of Europe in political terms is dominated by West European countries now already in the Community. When they will "focus all attention on writing history acceptable to all European nations and on improving relations among old enemies," then a new superpower may emerge. From such a view it follows that the decrease of single-state nationalisms within Europe by no means must imply a general decline of nationalism. On the contrary, it would be quite compatible with an increasing European supranationalism as described by Galtung.

In the epilogue by Max Haller, the contributions are evaluated and integrated under the question of whether we are moving toward a new "European Nation." A review of persistent and newly arising structural and cultural differences within Europe, relations between populations and elites, leading actors and interests, and a changing world constellation all lead to the conclusion that Europe should not aim to become a nation in the classic sense, but a historically new type of "Community of Nations."

Part I

Trends, Forces, and Patterns of Integration in Western Europe

SALVADOR GINER

The Advent of a European Society

I

Nowadays, more people than ever before speculate about the nature of European society. Europe's culture, economy, political constitution, unity, diversity, prospects, and destiny are scrutinized and pondered from every conceivable angle. Taken to extremes, the endeavor can be a thankless one. For when people muse endlessly over the possible "essence" of an entity as elusive as a society, we may be fairly confident that something crucial is missing from it. The endemically missing component is usually that which, were it present, would account for the very essence that is being looked for. This is, indeed, a painful paradox, and it arises all too often in the frequent and stubborn search for the nature of European society.[1]

Europe invites constant speculation because it cannot be taken for granted. It is never obviously or wholly there. It is an essentially problematic entity. Most of us appear to cherish it but are unable to define it properly. For many of its citizens, "European" is the widest possible social identity, beyond occupation, locality, and nation; it is the ultimate frame of social reference in terms of education, taste, ethics, belief, and public and private conduct. Yet its cultural and even physical boundaries are never clear. Until recently, Europe has been only a shared notion, albeit a crucial one, for a set of Western peoples.

The contemporary search for the precise features of European society is at the core of the very plight which now confronts the polities, the cultures, and the economies of Europe's peoples.[2] It is also part and parcel of the current obsession with "identity." Over the last decades, the search for uniqueness, roots, distinctiveness, difference—in short, for identity—has become one of the chief themes of our age, both in Europe and abroad. As a preoccupation, the search for identity has invaded and colored all our speculations about Europe, including, first and foremost, our often unavowed anxieties about her future at this decisive moment of her history. Sociological enquiry is supposedly detached from such metaphysical concerns, but it has been far from immune to the enticements of that search. Hence the need for us to be aware of the powerful presence of this contemporary inclination. We ought to be aware that, in the end, a relentless search for identity leads nowhere; it is the quintessential Sisyphean task. As sociologists, we ought to know better than to look for the ultimate, at least in this elusive matter: Roots and final identities are best left where they belong, in the realm of mystery, lest they be used and abused by ideologies, whether providentialist, nationalist, or any other ilk. Let then sociology not enter the hallowed realm of the mysterious. Identity is averse to rational analysis, though religion, art, and poetry may sometimes convey it superbly.

The endemic difficulties inherent in any search for the identity of a complex and varied society have been compounded in Europe's case by two very different things: her own projection upon the rest of the world, and the once prevalent Eurocentric and providentialist conception of history. The world expansion of European culture, variously carried to every corner of the earth—by a handful of seaborn Western European empires, toward the East by the Russians, and then everywhere else by the United States—has, in the end, undermined its own uniqueness and blurred its frontiers. The very worldly success of the "European cultural formula" (the combination of rationalism, political pluralism, individualism, citizenship, and technical growth)[3] has meant its contemporary demise as a specifically European phenomenon.

Meanwhile, the philosophies of history that narrated the story of our core traditions and claimed to foretell their triumphant future and destiny have been either disgraced or substantially discredited. There seems to be no way in which comparable *Weltgeschichtliche* constructs as those of our recent past could be put forward today and receive a wide and serious audience. It looks as though any interpretation of such grandiloquence and ambition that still may dare to appear will be given short shrift by some of us and laughed out of court by the rest. Grand futuristic conceptions (in the past often linked to cosmogonies and philosophies of history) have also been discredited. On a practical level, however, Europeans—like all Westerners as well as all other peoples who have substantially assimilated elements of our culture—continue to be futuristic. With all due caution, it can be said that futurism is our very condition as creatures of modernity: Economists, politicians, industrialists, educators, ecologists, physicists, architects, scientists, sociologists, must all "plan ahead" and forecast. They must, by trade, imagine and wish a future that is different from the present. This is the legacy of the powerful belief in progress that characterized one crucial and easily identifiable trait of our culture from the age of the Enlightenment until yesterday. Such faith in its original shape may have all but disappeared, but it has left us with a need, or compulsion, to plan the time ahead. It has left us with the imperative to be futuristic. It is, nevertheless, a residual futurism. We are now futurists without a grand design.

No particular identity can be established, then, from either the structure and culture of European society or any specific theory of our history and foreseeable future. Yet, looking back on our common history (insofar as it is common) we can at least agree that we have often been united to a considerable extent by what has been termed a *Schicksalgemeinschaft.* This seems to be true both for our distant and recent past and for our own time, and it includes contemporary trends and the difficult rise, at long last, of a united Europe. Solemn though the expression may sound, it conveys an evident fact: The lives and destinies of the European peoples have been inextricably intertwined for a long time indeed, and no emphasis on internal varieties and variations can ever disguise the fact that the continent has had one single civilization over the centuries. Under Rome, Medieval Christendom, the Renaissance and Reformation, the Enlightenment, and the Democratic and Industrial Revolutions, it is a civilization that has been wholly, though unevenly, shared by nearly all the peoples of the continent. Some of Europe's former colonies have also shared a substantial part of the experience during the last centuries.

The question that now arises, however, is one of continuity—or, rather, of discontinuity. There is now a distinct possibility that the "shared destiny" that affected Europeans in different but always important senses and degrees may cease to exist over the next decades. Europe may be trying to unite precisely at the moment when its distinctiveness is more problematic than ever. Faced with growing cosmopolitanism, massive immigration from the rest of the world, the relentless spread of the culturally syncretic mass media, telecommunications, global interdependence and the globalization of social relationships, demographic and ecological imbalances, world trade and industry, and transnational social inequalities, specifically European characteristics may become even more blurred than they already are. Europe's particular traits may become less distinct. This could happen not because our nations will have suffered the inroads of alien cultures, but because they will have had to confront the consequences of their very own projection upon the world—the echo, as it were, of their own voices.

Herein lies the paradox: Europe may lose much of her identity when confronted with the consequences and ramifications of her own historical dynamics as recast, perfected, or transformed by the peoples who once upon a time fell under her spell or were the direct offshoots of her relentless global expansion. The "Europeanization" of the world has weakened the distinctiveness of Europe herself.

Globalization, about which sociologists have had so much to say in recent times,[4] was a characteristically European creature during its early stages. Regardless of whether Europeans intended to export modernization (and many colonialists and imperialists clearly did not), capitalism, technology, instrumental reason, the desire for social equality, and the appeal to democracy were innovations that often traveled well. They were easily wrested from Europe's hands, when they were not preached by the Europeans themselves. They naturally found other homes and soon ceased to be our preserve. European society can no longer be defined only in terms of its traditional civilization, for it now belongs to any people of the earth.

II

General considerations such as these about the nature and present condition of European civilization may turn out to be quite relevant for any rigorous analysis of the possible rise, today, of a single European society. For the advent of Europe as a political, economic, and transnational unit, whose demarcation lines are relatively well clear-cut, and whose nation-states share important traits in their internal structures and dynamics, is taking place precisely when, for the first time in history, her uniqueness as a distinct civilization begins to be questioned. It is likely that both apparently contradictory events are more closely related to each other than they may appear at first sight.

Clearly, the process of economic, political, and cultural unification begun with the 1957 Treaty of Rome was set in motion only after the severe loss of imperial hegemony by several of the European nation-states. Formal steps toward unification also began well after social trends and a diffuse but remarkable political movement, the European Movement, had created the necessary preconditions. The long unification process has not yet been completed, and it is not likely to run its course easily, as the troubled aftermath of the Maastricht agreements of 1991 plainly shows. It was the states' weaknesses, then, not their strengths, that forced many politicians, economic interest groups, and social movements to move willy-nilly in the direction of unity. Looking back on the last decades, it is obvious that the many undercurrents and social trends that had been leading toward the rise of one single European society for a long time, and are now clearly beginning to come to the fore,[5] would not have triggered, by themselves, the incipient moves toward real integration and loss of sovereignty that are under way today. There were also the shared plights of relative national smallness, loss of competitiveness against external powers, military weakness, the Soviet threat in the decades after World War II, and other similarly powerful factors that managed to weaken the seemingly inexhaustible moral and political resources of the defenders of the nation-states. Yet the militant foes of unification stood their ground and made unification a very tough task indeed. They had countless allies among their respective citizenries, for the established nation-states of Europe commanded, and continue to command, enormous emotional resources from their loyal citizens. Even today, hardly any Dane, Italian, German, Frenchman, Scot, Spaniard, or Pole will call Europe his or her motherland, which lends credence to the wrong notion that a strong, federal Europe is inimical to nationhood.

Despite the hard facts of nationalism and national attachments, the diminution of European specificity and independence as a civilization has certainly been a cause of integration. Though not as easily identifiable as other factors, it must be counted alongside the other currents that have broken or undermined well-entrenched resistances against the creation of the single society on this continent. Just as the anxiety over a threat to ethnic identity reinforces nationalism, the loss of European distinctiveness (identity) has given rise to a widespread preoccupation—at least among certain European elites—with its survival. That anxiety has, in turn, spurred the development of "European nationalism," or "Europeanism," as a new form of collective identification. Though milder and less demanding than "national" nationalism, "Europeanism" claims—just as any other form of nationalism—its own public pieties, sacred symbols, and loyalties. It also demands its embodiment in political structures.

To these forces, another one must be added. If the globalization and Westernization (that is, "Europeanization") of the world often require the formation of large markets and political units throughout the globe, they also require, in the end, larger societies. Europe herself is one of them, albeit still in the making. In fact, Europe is the first "larger society" to appear in our times. "State-building" and "nation-building," those two creatures of modernization, first developed within European civilization. Large-scale "society-building" has also begun within its framework, at least in modern times. America, however, might be the first historical example of the simultaneous development of the three closely related processes of nation-building, state-building, and large-scale society-building. But on European soil, the phenomenon began to develop in the aftermath of World War II, which saw the downfall of the penultimate internal European empire, the Third Reich. The collapse of the last internal European empire, the Russian, between 1988 and 1991, has opened the way to further steps toward societal, not just political, unification. (Empires are often good means to keep a congeries of peoples under one rule and one *pax*, though they do not always manage to beat them into one single social structure and culture.) The dissolution of Soviet power has indeed left in its wake much disarray and turbulence on its western frontiers, especially in the Balkans, but as intra-European empires go, it looks as though these might be the very last of such turbulences. As a consequence, Europe, East and West, North and South, is now much more ready for peaceful forms of unity among her nations and for greater integration among the diverse interests of her regions, social classes, and groups than it ever was.

The acceleration of a wide variety of European unification processes has been quite recent, however. In fact, trends toward convergence were so slow, and political and violent confrontations between states so acute, that social scientists often were blind to any kind of convergence. Thus the often-heard notion that social scientists notice and react to events only when they have come to fruition or, if they pose some sort of threat, only after it is already too late to do anything about them, rang somewhat true. Yet this familiar harsh judgment is not entirely fair. It is true that, for the most part, European social scientists have preferred to work within the framework of their national societies: They were, in every sense, more easily accessible to them as clearly bound units of observation. There was linguistic unity; and statistical material, already gathered data, and research funds were readily available for territories under one single administration. However, it is no less true that many social scientists have been engaged in work of a truly European scope for a long time. It is a work which, over a number of decades, has scarcely ignored the economic, political, and cultural trends that have been leading toward the rise of this complex but nevertheless single European society that is now only beginning to take shape.[6]

A "European vision" and a European standpoint have not been absent in the recent past from the preoccupations of sociologists. Trans-European migrations, economic integration, the rise of Community law, transnational social inequality, welfare-state provisions throughout Western Europe, the consolidation of democracy in entire regions of the continent, the fluctuations of the labor market, and the nature of industrial conflict in different countries, as well as many other trends, have been amply and often successfully analyzed across Europe and as specifically European phenomena by social scientists for quite a long time. Meanwhile, political, economic, and cultural history has been steadily losing its former nationalistic undertones. Despite the revival of nationalist feelings in many parts of Europe, historians have been recovering (all too slowly in some cases) from nationalistic biases and ethnocentric assumptions.

The uneven political development of Western Europe has been a serious hindrance to the growth of what one may strictly call a common European consciousness. (This consciousness, especially when free from excessive "Euronationalism," may be a prerequisite for looking at European society in a sociologically fruitful manner.) The rise of one single democratic territorial continuum throughout the northern, western, and southern regions of the European continent has been a strenuous process lasting at least from 1945, when the fascist regimes in Germany and Italy fell, until 1974, when Portugal, Greece, and Spain began their respective transitions to democracy. For its part, the eastern half of the continent had become suddenly and forcibly cut off from the rest of Europe by the Soviet empire and in the name of ideology. It was an ideology that, interestingly but unfortunately, was based on the awful distortion of the specifically European traditions of equality, emancipation, solidarity, and progress. With the breakdown in rapid succession of the Stalinist dictatorships and police states of the East over the last few years, further barriers to future social confluence have been brought down. The beginning of societal convergence (save for that already begun in earnest in a unified Germany) between these two halves of Europe is not apparent yet. But chances are that it will eventually happen. Or, to be more precise, that it will happen in the complex, ambivalent, slow, and tortuous way in which such phenomena usually take place in Europe.

III

To be convincing, any vision of Europe as a single society must be grounded on an awareness of the various facets, nuances, and dimensions of what a "society" of such size, intricacy, and richness might mean. Above all, it must stand on an awareness of how easy it is to deny that a European society really exists. Those who doubt the existence of a European society move, conceptually, on fairly firm ground. Their argument goes that Europe has always been a mere geographical expression, whose shared cultural features were never strong enough to turn her into a real unit. The widespread feeling today that Europe has materialized before our eyes is no more than the unexpected and fortuitous coincidence of a series of political and economic events upon the European stage that merely give that impression. Who is to say that the current situation is to last? Why should Europe not revert eventually to her traditional and normal condition of political disunity and acute social diversity?

Despite opinions such as these, a belief in the existence of a solid European universe rising over and beyond the deep cleavages and confrontations that have divided her peoples has been quite strong among scholars and thinkers, even among those whose analyses have given the nation-state its considerable due.[7] Weber, Simmel, and Pareto shared such conviction. After them, from Karl Mannheim to Raymond Aron and Norbert Elias, the voice for consideration of Europe as more than a mere cultural unit continued to make itself heard. Theirs was not only an opinion but also a method for analyzing European culture, politics, and social structure as the expression of the same universe. In their hands, it was undeniably a fruitful approach. For these and other sociologists, many social structures clearly differed from nation to nation, but more in degree than in kind. Most obviously, religious, scientific, political, and economic developments diverged from, or collided with, each other. Yet as a single civilization and culture as well as a community of fate, Europe was a fact of life. It was true that such community of destiny shared by Europe's peoples had to contend with various centrifugal forces—such as religious schism, nationalist politics, war, and ideology. That certainly posed a problem, but it did not manage to obliterate the ultimate unity of European society. Given the massive strength of the nation-state in modern times, however, the notion of a single European society for these social theorists was more a civilizational fact than anything else. But it was also a moral one, something to be upheld and defended. Thus, reflecting on the horrors of the "suicidal destruction of European values" amid the unprecedented slaughter of the Great War, Georg Simmel said: "It is not enough that the idea of Europe cannot die: we also want it to live."[8]

Perhaps not all observers who doubted the existence of a European society in the face of the endless confrontations between states were sufficiently aware of the fact that political, class, and ideological struggles were often as bitter within nations as among them. And those struggles did not deny the existence of nations. Significantly, they were struggles over the same values. None of the sources of European divisiveness or forms of conflict could be confined to one single country: they were shared by most countries of Europe. Thus, for a very long time liberalism, socialism, capitalism, citizenship and civil society, a comparatively open class structure, and other characteristically European features affected practically all the European peoples (and were practically restricted to them and to some areas peopled by Europeans). Although the strongly uneven distribution of these distinctive traits across the European continent posed important analytical problems, it did not undermine the ultimate "unity" of European society. It was a unity built not only on a degree of cohesiveness but also and paradoxically on the nature of the inner cleavages and confrontations within each country.

Thus the class struggles and the confrontations generated by industrialism, capitalism, nationalism, and the rise of the bureaucratic state produced parallel (though never identical) episodes in every European society. Some countries possessed a weaker civil society than others (Italy, and even more so, Portugal) while others (England and Scandinavia) had stronger ones. Some (Switzerland, France, and Germany) became vastly more prosperous than others (Greece, Poland, and Spain). Yet all were evolving along a broadly similar historical path. In some countries socialism was stronger; in a few others, anarchism. Fascism, when it came, was nearly omnipresent, greatly so in Italy, Austria, and Germany, very powerfully in Spain, and limited but causing a great deal of harm in Portugal, Greece, Belgium, and Romania. Several more and equally important examples of shared political and ideological movements (both good and evil) could be added. They have all shaped our common experience.

IV

Over the last decades, the bitter internal confrontations inherited from the past have undergone a severe attenuation in Western Europe. This may have helped some to understand (more or less dimly, more or less without apprehension) that different nations may partly or even wholly belong to the same society, and not only to the same state (a home truth to which most nationalists are understandably blind). Nation-states existed, of course, and they were by definition "societies." Stateless nations existed too, either openly recognized as such or, more frequently, denied existence. In both cases, they often belonged to larger units. But societies, increasingly spanning more and more states, and nations were not so easily perceived save perhaps incipiently in their economic dimension. Thus many foes of the mere idea of a single European society are nevertheless friends of the Common Market or of the European Economic Community. Is it possible, however, to belong for long to one economy and to keep the other dimensions of social life wholly separate?

Developments such as these—internal peace and the growth of social interpenetration beyond state and ethnic boundaries—have allowed the pace of political, economic, and cultural unification to gather sufficient speed to force a substantial number of intellectuals and social scientists to address themselves to the implications of the possible rise of one single economy, one single polity, and even one single society within Europe. Among the implications involved in that process must be counted those which are of a somewhat theoretical nature. As theory in this case does matter, it must now be evoked.

The "convergence/divergence" issue, both in its European context and on a world perspective, is the one paramount theoretical problem that requires our attention. One's approach to the issue is bound to color the results we obtain from the data as well as our interpretation of the entire question of European unity.

Essentially, "convergence" has two different meanings. First, it may refer to the confluence of several societies into one single society. This entails a process of fusion and interpenetration, though not necessarily at all levels. Thus there are distinct ethnic or cultural communities that can hardly be analyzed as separate societies, as they are inextricably bound, economically, politically, and sociostructurally, to larger units. By the same token, internal differences between regions (which are not necessarily distinct linguistically, ethnically, or politically) can be great without any threat to the overall unity of the society, although observers may then metaphorically speak of different societies existing under one political order whose people define themselves as fellow citizens and countrymen.

A second, quite different though closely related meaning is that which refers to the development of parallel or similar structures in several distinct societies. The growth of capitalism, industrialism, and the modern state has provided many examples of this phenomenon at the macro level. Even more numerous are the cases at the micro or individual levels of convergence; that is, the rise of similitudes in the areas of social intercourse, personality patterns, and individual attitudes and beliefs.

"Full convergence" occurs only when there is both confluence and similitude (macro and micro) among societies.

Convergence and divergence are, ultimately, matters of "de-differentiation" and differentiation, of homogeneity and heterogeneity. These are phenomena to which sociology, from the work of Herbert Spencer and Emile Durkheim onward, has devoted much attention, especially when tackling one of its favorite themes, modernization. In that framework, the rise of a single, though internally well differentiated, European society, could be understood as the latest phase of modernization on the very continent that saw its historical inception.[9]

This is not the place for a discussion of the debate (often heated) that has surrounded the convergence/divergence issue over the last decades. Suffice it to say that traditional theories of modernization (for instance, of industrialization, or of the supposedly irresistible spread of the capitalist mode of production throughout the world) tended to assume a progressive though often unsteady convergence of all societies that fell under the "Western dynamics" or civilizational pattern. Some of these theories went even further than that. Such was the notorious case of the "industrial-man" notion, which posited the rise of one human type whose overriding presence was a concomitant of all advanced industrial societies regardless of certain other traits such as national tradition and local moral or religious values; or the once all-important divide between state socialism and Western capitalism. The "industrial-man" thesis, together with a supposedly necessary attitudinal complex made up of individualism, a thirst for personal achievement, and other (essentially Western?) anthropological traits, also brought psychological interpretation into the picture. The notion of an inevitable convergence of all European, and by extension, Western, societies under the ever-expanding logic of industrialism, capitalism, liberal democracy, and achieving individualism thus became popular at the macro, the micro, and the individual levels of discourse. Under continued modernization, their unimpeded progress to every corner of the earth was foreseeable.

Serious criticism of these assumptions (which became quite widespread in the 1950s and 1960s in the United States and North and West European countries) came first from those Marxist and neo-Marxist scholars who had opted, instead, for various theories of "uneven development," "dependent development," the "capitalist world system," and such like. Many anthropologists and sociologists of persuasions other than Marxism also questioned the universal convergence thesis. In the case of Europe, the growth of intra-European comparative analysis of social classes, cultural attitudes, politics, and the economy showed, from the mid-1960s onward, that vast disparities existed among national societies but also within them. Italian social scientists, for instance, were quick to insist not only on the persistence—under conditions of intense economic growth—of the North–South divide in their own country, but also on the actual increase of both traditional and new nation-specific inner disparities. Comparative research across Europe showed that, due to the uneven destinations of migration flows, different welfare-state policies, ethnic loyalties, and other equally powerful factors, no undifferentiated single society could be said to be rising in Europe. Moves toward a common market and greater political unity were, obviously, not enough. For quite a long time it looked as though the old "convergence" thesis had become untenable, even within a small continent with the characteristics of ours. Suddenly the assertion of progressive convergence seemed naive, even unintelligent.

Stubbornly, however, many indicators continued to point toward significant forms of convergence. Data about the most diverse phenomena have been pointing in that direction for a very long time indeed. The rise in life expectancy, the growth and diversification of the middle classes, the development of an international youth culture, changes in family patterns, the reduction of gender inequality, secularization, the rise of a new class of employees and a roughly corresponding decline in the number of the industrial workers, the development of welfare capitalism, the demise of the peasantry, the growth of higher education, and many more trends, have all occurred in every Western European country. The pace and rhythm at which these trends have taken place has varied from country to country; and the path followed has not been the same: The countries of Northern and Western Europe have followed one set of related routes, none of them identical; those of Southern Europe, another set of routes;[10] the East, still another. Both on a European scale and within each of these regions, then, no two countries have reached the same identical destination. (To complicate things further, some of these trends have also been taking place elsewhere in the world, as part of modernization and globalization currents.) Yet only someone bent on an obsessive cult of difference will assert that no common ground has arisen out of the modernization process. Today, countries as diverse as Italy, England, Germany, Spain, Austria, and Sweden have reached, albeit in different degrees, a world of democracy, secularism, corporate interest, class structure, and prosperity that is sufficiently common to all of them for us to conceive of them, more than at any other time in history, as part of one single universe. This is particularly so if we consider the growing and unprecedented degree of interpenetration and social intercourse that takes place in Europe today.

The key questions related to convergence refuse to go away. If sociologists, with their often refined questions and their understandable fear of generalizations, do not ask them, other people will. It is obvious that politicians, either pressing for a greater degree of equality among European nations and regions, or else fearful of the costs to their own taxpayers of any serious redistribution of resources, have become keenly aware of the implications of the rise of European society. Yet over and beyond their opposite specific interests and ideological inclinations, it is social scientists who must continue to ask themselves the elementary questions about the matter at hand: Have the societies of Europe become more similar to each other? Have they grown more dependent on each other? Have their frontiers become more blurred and has a new, single European society begun to rise?

There is plenty of evidence that the task of responding to these questions has already begun, and that, as could be expected, scientific debate has immediately followed.[11] This is not the place to go into its episodes and ramifications. Suffice it to say, however, that no one seems ultimately to challenge the existence of powerful convergent trends (often alongside divergent ones) covering most of the European continent. Obviously, no one can ignore important setbacks to further convergence, such as the fall of the standard of living in Eastern Europe after 1990, or political resistances to further unification (the Danish referendum of 1992, endemic British reticence, and so forth). Nor can all sociologists agree as to the relative significance of each transnational trend. Yet the overall picture is that of a considerable degree of consensus that the incipient advent of a European society is clearly in sight.

V

There is always a danger of complacency for those who join a consensual opinion. It is therefore important to remind ourselves that the fairly general agreement about the current rise of the rudiments of a European society does not entail a parallel agreement about its desirability or, indeed, about its goodness. Widespread poverty amid plenty, an incapacity to stifle war within the continent of Europe itself, the growth of racial hatred and xenophobia, the inability to reduce unemployment, the permanence of organized crime, the halting of the advance of democracy and freedom, and the lack of solidarity with other parts of the world are just some of the quite worrisome features of the new Europe. Europeans also grow more alike in ways that are disgraceful and unworthy of their civilization.

Convergence was often seen by many as, implicitly, a step forward, a confirmation that some progress was possible. One single European society was to be intrinsically better than congeries of European societies. Yet as we begin to approach unity in more than the juridical, political, and economic senses, we also begin to realize that, in some important ways, the result is not always better than what we already had.

Our current sense of frustration is to a considerable extent the result of the fact that the advent of one single society in Europe is the consequence of a deliberate intention on the part of many Europeans. No matter how deterministic we may be, it is obvious that a united Europe is not only the result of blind social and historical processes, but also of a widespread desire to make it happen. The passions of localism, nationalism, and regional and national politics, as well as vested interests of all sorts and age-old institutions whose prosperity and continued well-being may be compromised by any erosion of their privileges, are mighty obstacles that stand in the way of the federal solution and further integration. For that reason, it would be hard to prove that a fully fledged European society, should it ever come to fruition, would be the sole result of anonymous historical processes.[12]

A good many "European movements" and individual wills and convictions stand behind the rise of European society, helping history along its way—a history that many of us understand in quite humble terms, immune as we are to the slightest Hegelian weakness. Yet the deliberate building of a single European society has always been anchored in a belief in progress and democracy. It is precisely because the result is all too often meager, or even dismal, that we now look at it with a certain melancholy.[13] It is a melancholy that could lead to cynicism and despair, were we to forget Max Weber's warning about the nature of social trends: Their triumph is always incomplete and often produces outcomes that are the precise opposite of what was originally intended. We have been forewarned, then, by the wisdom of our discipline.

Being aware of the Weberian paradox does not mean that we must accept imperfection as final or inevitable. On the contrary, sociology, as an art and a practice that cannot possibly sever its links with ethics,[14] ought to be able to help Europeans to widen their citizenship without losing their profound attachments to their homelands and ethnogeny. It can, and must, teach people about the unending quest for public virtue and the development of a decent society. Sociology knows better than perhaps any other discipline that there are unintended consequences of any kind of human will and action. Sociology could help us understand why our current preoccupations and troubles should not lead to despondency. They should simply be tackled with the same determination with which others began to build Europe under quite difficult circumstances half a century ago out of the ruins of our last internal and savage conflagration, so that it could never happen again on the soil of this ancient and miraculous civilization. As a unique creature of the European enlightened mind, sociology ought not to be absent from the continued effort to create one single Europe.

Notes

1. Throughout this essay, reference is made to "European society," the possible rise of "one single society" within Europe, "convergence" into one kind of "society," and other similar expressions. I am, however, fully aware of the difficulties inherent in the use of the term "society," which is far from unproblematic even when it refers to relatively well bounded entities such as "national societies" are supposed to be. "Society," then, is used here only for reasons of expediency. About the problems and dangers involved in the abuse of the term, see G. Busino (1991).

2. The literature on the nature and chief characteristics of what constitutes Europe is considerable. Some references are Dahrendorf (1990), Díez del Corral (1974), Morin (1987), Pomian (1990), and Veneziani (1990).

3. The "formula" as expressed here in an oversimplified manner was never "exported" equally and as such by each expanding European nation. Each emphasized different aspects of it. But even areas of the world colonized by nations historically not much inclined to pluralism or secularism (the Russians, the Spaniards) have suffered "Europeanization" in every other sense and have also been exposed (albeit to a lesser extent) to those aspects of the "formula" that were originally feebly transmitted by the metropolis.

4. Although interest in the sociological analysis of globalization (beginning with "world systems" theory, with I. Wallerstein and others in the 1970s) is relatively recent, its roots in Marx's theory of the world dynamics of capitalism are of course much older.

5. H. Kaelble (1987).

6. Cf. for instance, R. Dahrendorf (1964); M.S. Archer and S. Giner, eds. (1971); S. Giner and M.S. Archer, eds. (1978); R. Hudson and J. Lewis, eds. (1985).

7. R. Pahl (1991).

8. G. Simmel, *Der Krieg und die Geistigen Etscheidungen* (Leipzig: Duncker & Humboldt, 1917), trans. in P.A. Lawrence (1975), p. 270.

9. G. Therborn (1992) may be taken as a example of this approach.

10. For the Southern European route to modernity and convergence, see S. Giner (1986).

11. See, for instance, M. Haller (1989, 1990, and 1991) and B. Hamm (1991).

12. J. Baechler (1992).

13. P. Bruckner (1990).

14. S. Giner (1987).

References

Archer, M.S., and S. Giner. 1971. *Contemporary Europe: Class, Status and Power.* London: Weidenfeld and Nicolson.

Baechler, J. 1992. "L'utopia di una federazione europea," *Mondoperaio*, vol. 45, no. 7 (July), pp. 82–89.

Berting, J. 1991. "Social Inequality and Social Justice in Europe." First European Social Science Conference, multicopied paper, UNESCO National Commissions of Europe.

Bruckner, P. 1990. *La mélancholie démocratique: Comment vivre sans ennemis?* Paris: Seuil.

Busino, G. 1991. "Société: une notion à repenser," *Revue européenne de sciences sociales*, vol. XXIX, no. 89, pp. 199–247, reprinted in his *La sociologie sens dessus dessous*. Geneva and Paris: Droz, 1992, pp. 19–64.

Dahrendorf, R. 1964. "Recent Changes in the Class Structure of European Societies," in S.R. Graubard, ed. *A New Europe?* Boston: Houghton Mifflin.

———. 1990. *Betrachtungen über die Revolution in Europa*. Stuttgart: Deutsche Verlags-Anstalt.

———. 1992. "Europa am Anfang der neunziger Jahre," *Der moderne soziale Konflikt*. Stuttgart: Deutsche Verlags-Anstalt, pp. 245–57.

Díez Del Corral. 1974. *El rapto de Europa*. Madrid: Alianza Editorial.

Giner, S. 1986. "Political Economy, Legitimation and the State in Southern Europe," in G. O'Donnell, P. Schmitter, and L. Whitehead, eds. *Transitions from Authoritarian Rule*. Baltimore and London: The Johns Hopkins Univerity Press, pp. 11–44.

———. 1987. "Sociology and Moral Philosophy," *Revue Internationale de Sociologie/International Journal of Sociology*, no. 3, pp. 47–86.

Giner, S., and M.S. Archer, eds. 1978. *Contemporary Europe: Social Structures and Cultural Patterns*. London: Routledge & Kegan Paul.

Haller, M. 1989. "European Class Structure: Does It Exist?" in M. Haller, ed., "Class Structure in Europe, Part I: Class and Social Structures in Europe," *International Journal of Sociology* (Summer), vol. 19, no. 2.

———. 1990. "The Challenge for Comparative Sociology in the Transformation of Europe," *International Sociology*, vol. 5, no. 2 (June), pp. 183–204.

———. 1991. "Reply to Bernd Hamm's Critique of 'The Transformation of Europe as a Challenge to Camparative Sociology,' " *International Sociology*, vol. 6, no. 1 (March), pp. 117–22.

Hamm, B. 1991. "Comparative versus Evolutionary Approaches to European Society," *International Sociology*, vol. 6, no. 1 (March), pp. 111–17.

———. 1992. "Europe, a Challenge to the Social Sciences," *International Social Science Journal*, no. 131 (February), pp. 3–22 (issue devoted to "Europe in the Making").

Hudson, R., and J. Lewis, eds. 1985. *Uneven Development in Southern Europe*. London: Methuen.

Kaelble, H. 1987. *Auf dem Weg zu einer europäischen Geselschaft: Eine Sozialgeschichte Westeuropas, 1880–1980*. Munich: C.H. Beck.

Lawrence, P.A. 1975. *Georg Simmel: Sociologist and European*. London: Nelson.

Morin, E. 1987. *Penser l'Europe*. Paris: Gallimard.

Pahl, R. 1991. "The Search for Social Cohesion," *Archives europeennes de sociologie*, vol. XXXII, no. 2, pp. 345–60.

Pomian, K. 1990. *L'Europe et ses nations*. Paris: Gallimard.

Therborn, G. 1992. "Social Modernity in Europe," in W. Barber et al., eds. *Storia d'Europa*. Turin: Einaudi, vol. I, pp. 1–146.

Veneziani, M. 1990. *Processo all'occidente: la società globale e i suoui nemici*. Milan: SugarCo.

MATTEI DOGAN

The Erosion of Nationalism in the West European Community

The West European countries achieved their national integration a long time ago. They find themselves today in a postnationalistic phase, aspiring to supranational cooperation as a consequence of their profound processes of economic, social, cultural, and political interpenetration. In each West European country, the nationalistic attitude toward other West European countries is in a phase of erosion in the sense that it no longer appears as a basic characteristic of the civic culture. Nationalism is still the most significant basic political value in the contemporary world, but not in Western Europe.

I shall focus my analysis on the perception that each West European country has of other West European countries and on the decline of nationalistic tendencies *within* Western Europe, neglecting the attitudes that these nations may have toward other regions of the world except the United States and Japan.

What can be said about the erosion of nationalism in Western Europe obviously cannot be extrapolated to Eastern Europe.

Ethnicity and nationalism are obviously different notions, and I consequently exclude movements of ethnic regional identity from the analysis. The concept of nationalism is not the most appropriate for characterizing such movements. For instance, there is no incompatibility between the revival of regional identities in Spain and the decline of nationalistic attitudes of Spaniards toward other European nations.

I also exclude from the analysis racist reactions against non-European immigrants. Racism and nationalism are different phenomena—they overlap only marginally. There is no contradiction, in the minds of some people, between a decline of nationalistic attitudes toward other Europeans and a simultaneous maintenance and even increase of racist hostility toward immigrants from Africa and South Asia. An important literature is dedicated to these racist attitudes.

What Is Meant by Decline? Compared to When?

The ideal point of departure for a longitudinal analysis would be the 1930s, at the apogee of the totalitarian regimes in six European countries and the rise of extreme rightist movements in others. In 1938, among the twenty-two countries of Western and Central Europe, eleven were dictatorships and most of the others witnessed the development of significant nationalistic parties. But at that time, survey research was unknown or in its infancy.

It may be that in 1939 young people were not all enthusiastic about getting into war. They were not consulted; they obeyed collectively. Today, democratic governments would not secure such obedience if they did not first succeed at convincing the citizens that they are called to fight for a moral cause. The socialization of young people was quite different in the 1930s. We do not have surveys based on national samples for that period, but we do have a wealth of historical research about mass beliefs, which stress the importance of the nationalistic context and indoctrination in that time. Hundreds of books published in every European country before the war or after provide an impressive testimony to those mass beliefs. Longitudinal analyses covering the last half century would be impoverished if they were reduced exclusively to survey research. For instance, we do not need survey data in order to admit a decline of Italian nationalism toward Austria after the collapse of the Austrian empire. On this point we may trust Italian historians.

Content analyses of popular media, elitist media, and the textbooks for elementary and high schools in the 1930s and in the 1980s are also meaningful sources of information about the state of the public mind at these times. A comparative analysis of the messages transmitted by the various vectors of the socialization processes of youth in many countries in the 1930s and in the 1980s (such as speeches of schoolteachers in Italy, Spain, France, or Germany) underline changes in national values, stereotypes, and prejudices. The capacity of veterans' leagues to mobilize enormous masses in the streets (for instance, in Italy in 1922), the circulation of their literature, and the content of their media in the 1930s contrast with the relative discretion of veterans after World War II. The predominance of certain ideologies in the 1930s leaves no doubt about the intensity of nationalistic feelings that filled millions of people at that time. That in Western Europe the 1930s marked the high tide of nationalistic *Weltanschauung* is not merely an assumption: its reality is attested to by many historians. On this apogee of nationalistic feeling there is a general consensus among European social scientists (Hobsbawn 1970).

Another possible point of the slope is 1945. Since then, there has been a trend that we can perceive at certain moments by survey research.

What we try to observe is the declivity of a long process, a trend over several generations. Ideally, we would wish to have empirical evidence for many countries at two points in time, at a distance of thirty to forty years, because basic values change slowly. However, the available survey data sufficiently cover only the recent period. Part of the empirical evidence that I shall present is based on a secondary analysis of a survey conducted by the European Value Systems Study Group in nine European countries in 1981, which was later expanded to include a few other countries, particularly the United States and Japan. A new survey, adopting the same questionnaire (with a few exceptions), was repeated in 1990–91 in more than twenty European countries. For most basic values, the second survey confirms the findings of the first, with differences in percentages being rarely significant. Given the relatively short period between the two surveys, we found, as expected, more analogies than differences. Another part of the empirical evidence comes from the *Eurobarometer* of the European Community, for the period 1971 to 1991, as well as from the publications of various institutes of public opinion research in France, Britain, Germany, and Italy.

All available survey data should be taken into consideration, but this kind of data is not an exclusive source, and certainly not a sufficient one. The work of historians is of primary importance. For such an analysis of change over time, the comparative approach is a necessity.

Five Indicators of Nationalism

Erosion does not mean eradication. Nationalism obviously has not disappeared in Western Europe. Decline should not be confounded with decadence: never in its history has Europe enjoyed greater wealth, culture, freedom, and civic rights than today. All West European countries today are pluralist democracies. Thus, only a rigid and superficial moralist could deduce that the decline of nationalism in Western Europe reflects a decline of moral standards.

Most of the data presented here take on clearer significance if placed in historical perspective, but only in a few cases can we sail upstream.

When we consider the recent trends in nationalism, five indicators seem particularly significant: the feeling of national pride; the degree of confidence in one's national army; the willingness or reluctance to fight for one's country in the event of war; the trust or mistrust of neighboring countries; and the feeling of belonging to the European Community. These indicators of nationalism are correlated, but they are not interchangeable. Some people may be proud of their country without being willing to fight for it in a war.

Some identify themselves with the nation but are not necessarily very proud of it. Nevertheless, these variables constitute meaningful psychological configurations confirming that we are dealing with a profound trend.

Mitigated National Pride

"To be or not to be proud of my country is a question that I cannot understand." So replied one in every three French respondents interviewed by SOFRES in 1977. Since Almond and Verba's *Civic Culture*, pride in one's nation is, nevertheless, a recurring item in surveys on basic values. This feeling has been investigated by the International Values Survey in 1981–82, the European Value Systems Study Group in 1981 and again in 1990–91, by a European Community survey in 1970, by the Eurobarometer in 1983, 1985, and 1988, and by research institutes of public opinion in various countries, particularly Germany, Britain, and France.

A wealth of empirical data on national pride has been collected, but it is not easy to derive a clear picture from it. Too much ambiguity is implied in the vague question "Would you say you are very proud, quite proud, not very proud, or not at all proud to be [a given nationality]"? In only three countries—Greece, Ireland, and Spain—did the absolute majority of people respond with "very proud" in at least four surveys between 1981 and 1991. All three of these countries had a turbulent national history that was still present in the collective memory. In Britain, too, the absolute majority responded with "very proud" in 1981, 1982, 1983, and 1985, but in 1988 and 1991 only a plurality responded this way. For five countries—Germany, France, Italy, Belgium, and the Netherlands—it is possible to observe the change over a longer period. We found in all of them a drop in the number of "very proud" respondents between 1970 and 1981.

There is a strong relationship between national pride and the position on the left–right dimension. Among the most leftist oriented Europeans, 29 percent were "very proud" of their nationality in 1981; among the most rightist oriented, 60 percent (Harding et al. 1986, p. 61).

People might be proud of their country for a variety of reasons: its economic performance or sound democratic institutions. The Portuguese are proud of their "historical heritage" and not of their standard of living; many Italians rate "natural beauty of the country" and "their artistic treasures" highest.

National pride is not incompatible with the perception that one's country is stagnating. The Greeks, for instance, are "very proud" of their country (70 percent "very proud" and 20 percent "rather proud"), but at the same time 45 percent admitted in 1987 that their country was following a downward trend, and only 34 percent perceived their country as still prosperous. The Greeks' high national pride, particularly in Cyprus, should be interpreted in recent historical perspective. Contrary to a certain image, Greece is a young nation-state, having achieved its national independence only in 1830, after four centuries of Turkish occupation.

Nor does the level of national pride depend on the size of the country: Iceland, Ireland, and Greece show the highest national pride. But within countries, it varies according to the educational level of individuals. For instance, Martinussen reported that in Norway "in all age groups with high education a high national pride is infrequent."

Germany, Italy, Japan, and Belgium are the countries in which we found the lowest levels of national pride in 1981: only 35 percent of Germans, 28 percent of Italians, 25 percent of Belgians, and 22 percent of the Japanese responded with "very proud." For these countries, the proportion of "very proud" people remained low during the entire following decade. Germany could be considered here as a clinical case. It seems that the syndrome of defeat has had lasting effects on the population. "Rather than being strongest immediately after the end of the war, the effect seems to take hold over a lengthy period of time" (Noelle-Neumann 1985, p. 2). The cultural debates that took place in Germany over the last four decades preceding the reunification certainly contributed to the diffusion of such mitigated feelings. As for Belgium, the reason for such a low level of national pride may be found in the deep division between the Flemish and the Walloons.

The proportion of those "not proud" of their country has significantly increased during the 1980s in Britain and Belgium and remained relatively high in Germany (between 29 percent and 31 percent), Italy (15 percent), and France (19 percent). But it is quite possible that the national pride of the Germans has risen since reunification and the collapse of the Eastern colossus.

In a few countries, certain people evidently experience a kind of "negative identification." Pertinent questions allow for the detection of such a feeling: "In which country would you have wished to have been born?" "In which country would you like to live?" Responses to questions asked thirty years ago in Italy or in Britain about the desire to emigrate to the United States suggested the existence of a small minority with eradicable roots. Such a desire has declined seriously over the past two decades.

Examining survey data on fifteen countries, one finds that in the modern world there is a weak relationship between the level of national pride and the economic or cultural achievements of these countries. But it would be wiser to abstain here from making comments about the most obvious discrepancies.

Level of Confidence in the Army

The level of confidence in a nation's army can be interpreted in the light of a military history that apologetic historians prefer not to remember. What is involved is the country's real capacity to resist and win in the event of war, and not necessarily the competence of the military staff.

In terms of national military experience and national collective memory, there is an essential difference between the prewar generation and the postwar generation. Parents and grandparents of the present German generations have lost the war twice; Italy began its involvement in World War II in one camp and ended it in the other; after losing the battle in June 1940, France was occupied for four years; the military forces of Belgium, the Netherlands, Denmark, and Norway succumbed in 1940; the Greek army was not able to maintain its country's independence, not even in the islands; Polish soldiers were crushed in 1939; the Romanian army was tossed between the Wehrmacht and the Red Army; the Spanish army fought not against foreign enemies but against half of the Spanish people in 1936–38; the Portuguese army was humiliated one generation later in colonial wars. The most notorious European case is Czechoslovakia, which "capitulated" three times without trying or having a chance to fight: in 1937, in 1948, and in 1968. But under similar circumstances, small Finland chose to fight and did so successfully. Only the British army, protected by the channel, has been fully victorious—but war accelerated Britain's economic decline. The truth is that without the massive help of the American army, Europe would not have been liberated from totalitarianism—brown or red—in spite of the abnegation and heroism of millions of European soldiers and fighting resistants. In order to explain today's defeatist temptations, it is necessary to recall these important historical facts.

The specter of the Red Army played an important role in lowering the level of confidence in West European armies. For four decades, European peoples and their leaders lived with this fear. Soon after the armistice, half of all French citizens believed that "a new world war would blow up in the following years" (*Sondages* 1948, p. 91). In most countries, this fear oscillated between 35 percent and 45 percent during the Cold War. In the presence of such danger, European military officers and politicians realized that "their" armies had become "too small." The old rivalries within Europe entered into "old history." Every European country ceased to be militarily independent, and this loss of independence was soon perceived by the masses (ibid., p. 92).

Western Europe consists of five large countries and ten small ones. The size of the country is not a significant parameter in determining its citizens' degree of confidence in the army. In 1981, 57 percent of the Dutch, 59 percent of the Danish, and 53 percent of the Belgians had no confidence in their armies. Even the larger countries, which spent a significant part of their national resources on their armies over a long period, did not show themselves to be much more confident: 44 percent of the French, 48 percent of Germans, 45 percent of Italians, and 36 percent of Spaniards had no confidence in their armies. Only the British (who no doubt have a vivid collective memory of the winter of 1940) showed themselves, four decades after the war, confident of their army and their insularity, with only 20 percent doubting the capacity of their army. The Finns, in the shadow of the Eastern colossus, manifested confidence (68 percent) in their small army. At the same moment, 64 percent of the Japanese had no confidence; among all advanced democracies, Japan appears to be the most antimilitaristic.

Between 1981 and 1990–91, the average proportion of people in the twelve countries of the European Community with a "great deal of confidence" in their armies dropped from 20 percent to 13 percent, and the proportion of those not having confidence increased from 38 percent to 48 percent. Such was the feeling before the implosion of the Soviet empire.

A military career has lost most of its traditional prestige. A reliable symptom in France is the fact that the graduates of the Ecole Polytechnique, an old selective military school, no longer choose to become military officers as they did before 1940; excepting a few who belong to ancestral military families, they opt for civilian positions in the state apparatus.

There is a strong relationship between confidence in the army and religious beliefs in all countries. Most agnostics do not have confidence in the army (87 percent in Germany, 77 percent in Spain and Ireland, 71 percent in France), while the majority of religious persons do have confidence in the army.

Simultaneous with the decline of confidence in the national army was the growth of the idea of a multinational army. One of the most important and passionate debates took place in the French parliament in 1954 on the proposal for a "European army." At that time, the majority of the French were not ready to accept "the rearmament of the hereditary enemy." Deputies rejected the project 319 to 264, reflecting public opinion: one-third for, one-third against, one-third hesitating (*Sondages* 1954, p. 16). One generation later, in December 1990, 66 percent of French adults who were surveyed said they were favorable to a "common European defense." In the entire European community, seven out of ten adults favored one (*Eurobarometer*, December 1990). The idea required one-third of a century to mature!

Low confidence in the army goes hand in hand with dislike of the military draft. Pecheron reported that only one-third of French adults surveyed severely condemned attempts to escape the draft by cheating (42 percent of practicing Catholics, 27 percent of agnostics). Only one out of every five youths directly concerned (between 18 and 24 years of age) saw a serious moral problem with such behavior. The same phenomenon has been observed in other European countries, particularly in Italy and the Netherlands. But it is in Germany that this "hate of militarism" has been the most pronounced, as periodically illustrated by mass demonstrations of young people in the largest cities there. Already in 1955, only 40 percent of Germans were in favor of the reconstitution of a new German army (Noelle and Neumann 1957, p. 295). Interviewed in 1990 about investment priorities of the state, Germans ranked the army last among sixteen items, showing preferences for expenditures in health, housing, and schools.

Having lost the war, Germany and Japan passed from extreme militarism to strong antimilitarism in one generation. The irony of history is that these two countries have succeeded in obtaining by technological superiority and economic expansion what they failed to achieve by military aggression: to become the second and third economic powers in the world.

Thus one of the traditional components of nationalism—the capacity of military defense of individual countries—seems to be fading.

One does not need to be a prophet to foresee that, after tomorrow, either there will be a professional European army based on some kind of proportionality, or European integration will become an aborted ideal.

Reluctance to Fight for One's Country: Defeatism

Another indication of the decline of nationalism is the reluctance shown by an important part of the population to fight for one's country. In the 1981 European survey on values, it was asked, "Are you willing to fight for your country?" The question did not specify under which circumstances or against whom. But in the political climate of that time, there was no doubt in the minds of those interviewed that the Soviet Union was the implied enemy. For all nine European countries, an average of 43 percent said in 1981 they were willing to fight, and 40 percent said they were not (17 percent did not reply or gave unclear responses).

These averages had not changed significantly between 1981 and 1990–91; and they had not been expected to change, because the political and military context had remained the same. It is with the prewar situation that the comparison should be made. If such a question had been asked in 1930, the social pressure would have been so strong that relatively few people would have given a nonconformist reply, which in Germany, Italy, Spain, Portugal, Austria, France, and Belgium could have been considered as a criminal offense. It may be that what is involved here is only a verbal reaction, and not the expression of an intimate feeling. But verbal behavior is a sociological fact, confirmed by comparative analysis.

Who were those willing to fight, and who were the defeatists? For the entire European sample, the willingness to fight was found more frequently among farmers than among industrial workers, among religious people than among agnostics, among those on the right than those on the left, among those who gave more importance to freedom than to equality, and among owners more than tenants. Politically, "these people who would fight for their country allow a higher priority to the goal of maintaining order in the nation, they have more confidence in the armed forces, the police, the parliament, the institutions in general, they favor more free enterprise and have a greater respect for authority" (Stoetzel 1988, p. 169).

Responses differed significantly among the countries. In Germany, only 35 percent of the respondents showed themselves willing to fight; in Italy, 31 percent; in Belgium, 27 percent; and in Japan, 19 percent, in contrast with 83 percent in Norway. The number of undecided persons was particularly high in Germany (23 percent), Belgium (23 percent), and Japan (35 percent). For Germans in 1981, a war appeared to be fratricide, as reflected in the slogan *Besser rot als tot* (Better red than dead).

The relationship between defeatism and absence of national pride or mitigated pride was highly significant. Among the French willing to fight for their country, 49 percent were "proud" of their country as opposed to 18 percent who were "not proud"; in Spain, the figures were 57 percent and 31 percent; in Italy, 31 percent and 19 percent; and in England, 66 percent and 39 percent (Rose 1985, p. 94). There is also a significant relationship between the low level of confidence in the army and reluctance to fight.

In a *Eurobarometer* survey conducted in November 1989, interviewees were asked to choose one of twelve "great causes" worth fighting for. Considering the twelve countries together, "defense of the country" was ranked seventh after "human rights," "peace," "protection of nature," "fight against poverty," "freedom of the individual," and "fight against racism." "Defense of the country," nevertheless, ranked higher than "defense of religious faith." Maybe there is a logic to this: defense of the country is a collective endeavor, whereas religious faith is an individual issue.

In France and Italy, the proportion of defeatists among those who did not believe in "life after death" was higher than among those who did believe (France, 51 percent to 38 percent; Italy, 61 percent to 48 percent). For other countries, the difference is less significant.

Today, Japan seems to be the most defeatist among the advanced democracies. Surveys conducted in 1980 and 1981 indicated that almost half the

Japanese would be likely either to desert (21 percent) or to surrender to their enemy without a fight (23 percent) if their territory were invaded. Only 31 percent of the Japanese sample declared themselves willing to fight. This proportion was even smaller when the question specified "at risk to one's life."

The psychological aspect should not be neglected. The technology of contemporary weapons has important psychological impacts on fighting capabilities. For one out of every four American soldiers evacuated from the front during World War II, the cause was psychological trauma.

Before World War I, all young German, French, Italian, and Spanish men were drafted into the army for three years. It was the supreme national obligation: deserters were deprived of civil rights. Today, a democratic government could not obtain such a sacrifice in peace time. The mentality has changed drastically at all levels of the political pyramid; the military technology, too.

No doubt, in the event of a real war, the behavior may be very different from the verbal reactions in the survey, but it is important to stress here that the opinions expressed on a variety of issues are consentient with these responses.

Mutual Confidence Among West European Nations

Another indication of the decline of nationalism is the trust that European nations show toward their neighbors, as revealed by *Eurobarometer* surveys sponsored by the Commission of the European Communities and carried out in 1970, 1976, 1980, 1982, 1986, and 1990. Over the course of these twenty years, the results of the surveys have varied but have not reversed the basic findings. It is unnecessary to display here the many statistical tables. I will concentrate the analysis on the survey conducted in October 1980, the most detailed of the six. The questions asked did not make any distinction among trust of people as individuals, trust of the country as a collective body, or trust of rulers in power at the moment of the survey. Only by such distinctions could clear interpretations become possible. The available data carry various stereotypes. In the replies of some of the French about Italians, the stereotype was "the knife in the back," driven forty years earlier by Fascist rulers. The stereotype of the United States is "capitalism," "imperialism." It does not refer to Americans as individuals. It is well known that American and European businessmen trust Japanese and Chinese businessmen, even if they do not have any particular reason to trust Japan and China as nations. In practice, it is difficult to obtain "aseptic" data.

The absolute majority of all Europeans polled in 1980 had confidence in nine of the thirteen European countries considered. Only four countries—Italy, Greece, Spain, and Portugal—were perceived as trustworthy by less than half of the Europeans in the other nine countries.

After several generations of nationalistic antagonism between France and Germany, three wars, and a tenacious collective memory full of prejudices, an important turning point has taken place in European history: Today, the majority of Germans have confidence in the French, and vice versa. In surveys conducted in France and Germany in May 1983 and October 1988, in response to the question, "Among the following countries which are the two that you consider as friends of your country?" France was at the top of the list in German samples, and Germany in French samples (SOFRES 1990, p. 145). A miraculous change, would say those who glean in the archives.

In July 1954, one of every two of the 2,562 French included in a national sample told the interviewers that he or she was a "victim" of the war with Germany in 1914–18 or 1939–45, having lost a family member or been injured or had their house destroyed (*Sondages* 1958, I, p. 54). In February 1955, 30 percent of the French believed that Germany represented a "danger," while 40 percent feared mostly the Soviet Union. From November 1954 to May 1956, the proportion of French people who had "a bad or very bad opinion of the Germans" fluctuated through six surveys, from 26 percent to 31 percent; only in May 1957 did the proportion fall to 18 percent, and seven months later to 15 percent (*Sondages* 1958, I, p. 46). In September 1952 and again in December 1955, one out of every three of the French who were surveyed believed that in case of a war with the Soviet Union, France could not trust Germany, and only 9 percent had confidence in their former enemy. In the same survey, Britain and the United States were highly trusted without reserve (*Sondages* 1958, I, p. 50). In 1954, only 24 percent of the French would have had confidence in a treaty with Germany, against 43 percent who did not trust such a treaty (*Sondages* 1958, I, p. 64). At the same time, old stereotypes continued to flourish: "The German people fundamentally like wars," responded one of every two of the French who were surveyed in 1954; "the German mentality has not changed"; "it would be better for France if Germany remains divided" (*Sondages* 1958, I, p. 74). The same person who at age 25 in 1954 carried such stereotypes may have changed his mind by 1983 at the age of 54 and admitted that Germany was France's best ally.

In 1980, the majority of the French showed confidence in the English, but the feeling was not reciprocal (there was, perhaps, residual resentment due to the Gaullist policy of keeping Britain out of the Common Market).

British people trusted the Germans more than they trusted the French: 60 percent to 34 percent. Similarly, the French tended to rank their former enemy higher than their former ally: 60 percent to 53 percent. World wars belong to history; European unification represents the future.

The majority of Italians surveyed had confidence in the French and Germans, but a smaller proportion of both French and Germans trusted Italians. There was a strong affinity between Belgians and the Dutch. Curiously enough, the majority of the Irish trusted Britain, and vice versa.

A significant proportion of Greeks surveyed did not have confidence in Americans (53 percent), Germans (45 percent), Italians (45 percent), or the British (42 percent). They were paid in return: one-third of all Europeans did not trust Greeks (with 27 percent not responding). Not only did many other Europeans not trust Greeks, but even one out of every four Greeks did not trust their own fellow citizens. The country that inspires the most confidence in Greeks is France (58 percent), without doubt for historical reasons dating from the nineteenth century.

The most interesting case is Italy. In 1980, one out of every two Europeans surveyed had no confidence in Italians, especially Germans (64 percent). At the same time, Italians did not trust their Mediterranean neighbors, in particular Greeks (45 percent)—no doubt due to residual memory of the Italian–Greek War of 1941—but also Spaniards (45 percent) and the Portuguese (42 percent).

Should we see the persistence of xenophobic tendencies in Italy in this data? Or should we take into consideration a feature of Italian political culture, especially in the Mezzogiorno, which results from a thousand-year history: the mistrust of all others, even compatriots, except for one's family. This low level of mutual trust has been noticed by a host of Italian writers and was confirmed in the 1950s by a survey on prejudices. Edward Banfield labeled it "amoral familism." A survey in 12 European countries in 1986 showed that Italy was the country where mistrust of compatriots was highest (35 percent), as opposed to 25 percent in Greece, 17 percent in Portugal, 16 percent in Spain, 17 percent in France, 14 percent in Ireland and Belgium, and 11 percent in Britain and the Netherlands. Such mistrust is a cultural feature that should not be confused with nationalism and xenophobia, because it refers to compatriots. The geographical distribution of this phenomenon, much more common in southern Italy than in the center or the north, confirms such an interpretation (*Doxa* 1986, p. 164).

The absence of trust in Italians by many Europeans dates back to World War II, when the Italian army did not show a great enthusiasm for fighting. This is quite likely a misinterpretation because, in the minds of many Italian soldiers, a great combative spirit would have signified support for the Fascist regime.

It is difficult to rank the countries according to the degree of confidence that they enjoy in the minds of their neighbors, because too many respondents failed to express any opinion about the smaller countries: these seemed to ignore each other and to gravitate toward the largest ones. For instance, 54 percent of the Irish surveyed did not have any opinion about the Greeks; and reciprocally, 42 percent of the Greeks did not know what to think of Irish people. A large proportion of the Irish did not express any opinion about the other smaller European countries: 48 percent had "no opinion" about Belgians; 46 percent had none about Danes; 40 percent had none about the Dutch; 53 percent had none about Luxembourgers—but only 7 percent had no clear opinion about the British. Similarly, many Greeks responded with "no opinion" about the other smaller countries: Belgians (37 percent), Danes (36 percent), and Dutch (33 percent). One-third of Belgians did not know if the Portuguese or Greeks are or are not trustworthy. One-third of the French and 44 percent of Italians had the same hesitation about the Irish. It seems that some "small peripheral" countries—Ireland, Portugal, Greece—were not really integrated into the European consciousness. Other "small" countries—Switzerland, Belgium, the Netherlands—were among the most trusted; very few people mistrusted them because, being small, they were not perceived as a possible threat.

Between 1976 and 1990, the level of mutual trust increased for all countries except Britain. Already high in 1976, the confidence in the four small northern countries (Belgium, Denmark, the Netherlands, and Luxembourg) continued to rise. A substantial increase in trust was noticeable for Italy, Spain, and France. Between 1986 and 1990, Italy reached the level of trust enjoyed by the other major countries. Ireland also improved its image between 1976 and 1990, as did Portugal and Greece. Only for Britain was there a perceptible decrease of trust between 1980 and 1990—the "slow coach"—but this country nevertheless remains one of the most trusted by the Europeans. The salience to Europeans of the smaller countries has improved between 1986 and 1990 (Hofrichter and Niedermayer 1991, pp. 13–19).

Briefly, only a small minority of West Europeans do not trust other West Europeans, but the majority show trust unencumbered by nationalism. It is not difficult to imagine what the results would have been of a similar survey conducted in the 1930s in France, Germany, Britain, or Italy. Today, all West European countries are pluralist democracies; as Michael Doyle argues, liberal states do not tend to fight one another.

Mutual confidence among peoples in Western Europe contrasts with the absence of such confidence in Eastern Europe. The figures convey their full meaning when compared to those concerning Eastern Europe. In a survey conducted in October 1990, the majority of Poles declared that they "do not trust very much" or "not at all" the Russians (69 percent), Ukrainians (75 percent), Belarusians (63 percent), Romanians (64 percent), Bulgarians (56 percent), and Czechs (61 percent). Only 2 percent of Poles "have a lot of trust" in Russians, Ukrainians, or Belarusians. Americans, British, French, Italians, and the Swiss are the only ones to be "trusted a lot" by at least 10 percent of Poles. The collective memory is still alive 45 years after the end of the war: 70 percent of Poles mistrust Germans (*Eurobarometer*, December 1990, p. A47). We must conclude that, at the time of the survey, the majority of Poles felt that they lived in a hostile environment. Such a feeling can only nourish strong nationalism.

Czechs also seem to believe in a hostile environment. The majority of Czechs did not trust Russians (62 percent), Poles (77 percent), Romanians (77 percent), Hungarians (67 percent), or Bulgarians (64 percent); but only 44 percent of them did not trust Germans. One particularly interesting finding is that a significant minority of Czechs did not trust the Slovaks (ibid.).

The Blossoming of a European Consciousness

As we have seen, many Europeans express a limited national pride, are not fully confident in their country's army, and are unwilling to fight for their own country, but trust their neighbors. These four indicators are related to multiple parameters, but have a combined cumulative effect that counteracts the secular trend of nationalism.

Three questions formulated by *Eurobarometer* generated empirical evidence of the blossoming of a European consciousness. The first question asked whether people were in favor, indifferent, or against European unification; it was asked again 31 times between 1952 and 1990 in France, Britain, West Germany, Italy, and Belgium. Other countries were included in the survey at a later stage (the Netherlands, in 1962; Denmark, in 1973; Greece, in 1980; Portugal, in 1981). In all these countries, a favorable attitude toward unification has increased (even in Britain, from 58 percent to 74 percent). The average of favorable responses for ten countries went from 63 percent in 1973 to 80 percent in 1990.

The second question asked if the membership in the Common Market was "a good thing, a bad thing, or neither good nor bad" for the country of the person interviewed, and was asked again 37 times between 1973 and 1990 in most countries (in Spain, Portugal, and Greece since 1980). The results indicate a significant increase of positive judgments in all countries without exception. For the entire Community, the average of favorable responses grew from 56 percent in 1973 to 68 percent in 1990.

The third question asked, "Taking everything into consideration, would you say that your country has on balance benefited or not from being a member of the European Community?" Through seventeen surveys, there was a slight decline in positive replies between 1983 and 1990 in Italy and the Netherlands, and a strong increase in the four countries that have benefited the most from the redistribution of the Community's revenues: Spain, Portugal, Ireland, and Greece, the least wealthy of the 12 countries. On the whole, the favorable replies rose from an average of 46 percent in 1986 to 59 percent in 1990 (*Eurobarometer*, special issue, "Trends 1974–90").

How does one explain such a trend? Nationalism is declining in Western Europe because a supranational consciousness is rising out of a progressive interaction at several levels: economic, military, social, cultural, and political.

The consequences of the interpenetration of European economies are obvious and decisive. Each country needs to trade with other countries and, above all, with its immediate neighbors. For most countries, about one-half of their GNP is based on foreign trade, mostly within Europe. West European economies interpenetrate each other. They are undoubtedly in competition but also show reciprocal dependency. Considering current technological performance, no European country—not even Germany, France, or Britain—is a viable economic space in itself. This interdependency engenders a supranational market, detrimental to old-fashioned economic isolationism or protectionism.

Certainly, economic rivalries within Western Europe persist, particularly at the regional level, but these rivalries are relegated to a secondary level by the advantages offered by the Common Market in the economic competition with the other two powers, the United States and particularly Japan. A kind of economic nationalism is already visible in Japan. The reaction to such an external economic nationalism nourishes the erosion of classical nationalism *within* Western Europe.

Second, at a military level, four decades of the Cold War during the age of missiles, under the protection of the American atomic umbrella, convinced many people as early as the 1960s that no European nation could resist an attack from the Eastern giant, who, in turn, may have had the same reaction to the Atlantic alliance. The nation-state, having already been for several decades too weak to protect its citizens against the Eastern superpower, has lost part of its military function. It is significant that the military establishments in West European countries are no longer nationalistic. Today, no European democracy could claim to be militarily independent: Nationalism has lost its military foundation. Military dependence and economic interdependence have combined their effects.

In parallel, the frontiers between the old states of Western Europe have received, so to speak, the seal of perpetuity. A war between these countries is inconceivable today, except perhaps in Northern Ireland. Consequently, nationalism in Western Europe, in contrast to that in Eastern Europe, can no longer nourish itself on territorial disputes.

The increasing complexity of social stratification is another important aspect of this trend toward a European consciousness. Every European country is characterized by considerable internal diversity, and there is a striking cross-national similarity between these intranational diversities. There are more similarities between a French and a British bourgeois than there are between a British middle-class person and a British manual worker, or between a French lawyer and a French farmer. There are more social differences within each country than among the countries, at all levels: birth rates, divorce rates, growth of some sectors of the economy and decay of other sectors, unemployment rates, financial crisis of the social security system, and so on (Dogan and Pelassy 1987).

At the cultural level, European consciousness has progressed enormously during the past decades. Numerous surveys give evidence of the rapid internationalization of national cultures. People, ideas, and goods circulate freely today in the European community. More Europeans have crossed the frontiers within Europe during the last four decades than during the previous eight centuries. Every summer, millions migrate from northern lands to southern seas. Television ignores national barriers; Eurotelevision is already a reality. In spite of linguistic diversity, cultures become less and less national and more and more mixed—among young people more than among their elders. Of course, the mixing of cultures does not occur equally everywhere. The number of foreign tourists that Spain and Italy receive every year is greater than their adult populations. The majority of Dutch teenagers are familiar with two foreign languages.

It is possible to rank the countries according to the level of their "pro-European feelings." *Eurobarometer* has repeatedly measured the proportion of people favoring European integration. From 1973 to 1990, the levels of favorable attitudes were the highest in three kinds of countries. First, the countries whose economic performance depends largely on foreign trade—particularly the Netherlands, Belgium, and Luxembourg—showed the highest pro-European feelings. Second were the countries for which the European Community was a protecting institution: the German Federal Republic before the fall of the Berlin Wall and Greece. Third came a few countries that believe they could resolve their national problems more efficiently by delegating some power to the European superstructure. Many Italians believe that the efficiency of Italy's administration could be improved in some areas if some decisions were made in Brussels instead of Rome. Belgians also see the European Community as a source of legitimacy for their "tribal system." In France, when there is a conflict between a national-level regulation and a European-level one, the regulation made at the European level generally prevails. Slowly but surely, the European parliament increases its domain of intervention. The *Eurobarometers* periodically indicate in which spheres the population is willing to accept common regulations and the "harmonization" of laws.

In most countries, the nationalist extreme right-wing parties represent a negligible fraction of the electorate. France and Austria are the only European countries where right-wing extremists received more than one-tenth of the vote in the 1980s, and that was principally an expression of hostility toward non-European immigration rather than hostility against other European countries. A content analysis of the neofascist ideology of the National Front movement in France shows that it is racist rather than nationalistic in the traditional sense. Virulently against immigrants from former French colonies in Africa, this rightist movement does not exhibit open hostility toward other European nations, because its leaders know that such hostility has no propaganda value. "Immigration" is their only effective issue at the electoral level at a time when one-tenth of the male active population is unemployed. The deteriorating support for traditional extreme right-wing parties in West European countries is a consequence of the decline of nationalism. Extreme rightist activist groups may attract the attention of mass media by their violence, but they are too small to appear significantly in national samples.

The International Dynamic of the Decline of Nationalism

The decline of nationalism will probably continue; it is inherent in the demographic pyramid. Surveys conducted in almost all European countries show that nationalistic tendencies are less common among the upcoming generation than they are among the aging generation. Mountains of statistics attest to this dynamic.

A comparison of the results of surveys conducted by the European Values Systems Study Group in 1981 and in 1990–91 in nine countries shows an increasing gap between the youngest and the oldest adults in each of these countries over the course of only ten years. While the oldest people have not returned to more traditional values, the youngest are more numerous and hence their adoption of nonconformist values, particularly in the realms of nationhood and religion, looms larger in the surveys.

Another way to observe the potential trend according to generations is to group the individual respondents in the national samples by age. In order to obtain a sufficient number of individuals for each grouping, two *Eurobarometer* surveys were combined (April 1982 and April 1983). The first grouping is comprised of those born before 1915; the second, of those born between 1916 and 1920 and so on in five-year increments; the last grouping is comprised of the cohort born between 1954 and 1958 (*Eurobarometer*, June 1983, pp. 55–57). An index was constructed, showing a significant relationship between age-group and the level of national pride in 1982–83. The proportion of "proud" people is higher among older cohorts, particularly in France, the Netherlands, and Belgium.

In the six countries for which comparison is possible, the feeling of national pride diminished between 1970 and 1982: the index declined by 10 percent (*Eurobarometer*, June 1982, p. 28).

In a 1988 special survey of young people between 15 and 24 years old in ten European countries, the young were "very proud" of their nationality less frequently than were their elders (26 percent to 40 percent). In 1970, an almost identical survey had been carried out in five countries. It is thus possible to compare the opinions of the same group (born in 1946–50) at different ages—when they were 21 to 24 years old in 1970, and when they were 33 to 36 in 1982. Two findings are significant. First, the feeling of national pride was higher among older people than among younger people at both moments. Second, the level of national pride declined for all age groups between 1970 and 1982. The shape of the curves according to age varies slightly from country to country between the two dates—the strongest decline having occurred in Belgium, and the weakest in Germany, for which the level of pride was already very low in 1970 (*Eurobarometer*, December 1982, pp. 87–90).

The generational gaps are confirmed by a survey conducted in April 1983. The proportion of people in ten European countries who were "very proud" of their country was much lower among the young than among the old: 29 percent of those aged 15–24 years; 35 percent among those aged 25–34 years; 39 percent among those aged 45–54 years; 52 percent among those aged 55–64 years; and 54 percent among those aged 65 years or more (*Eurobarometer*, June 1983).

In a 1982 ten-country survey of youth between the ages of 15 and 24 about "causes worth doing something about," two traditional "causes"—"my country's defense" and "my religious faith"—were the least chosen of the nine proposed causes, which included "human rights," "struggle against poverty," and "world peace" (*Eurobarometer*, April 1982).

The same questions were asked of the entire adult population in July 1989 (*Eurobarometer*, November 1989). A comparison of the results of the two surveys shows significant differences between the attitudes of the very young and those of the mature population in all ten countries.

As basic values are forged by socialization processes early in life, what teenagers and very young adults believe today is a good indication of what their beliefs will be tomorrow. In response to a question asked about the importance of *patrie* (mother country) in 1977 in France, only 28 percent of the entire sample responded that it was less important today than it was in the past, and 48 percent responded that it remained equally important. But among young people under 25 years, about half said that they attached less importance to the idea of *patrie* (SOFRES 1984, pp. 151–52).

Does military service have more positive or more negative consequences in generating patriotic feelings among youth? Survey results reported by Duhamel show that military service had a negative influence for 61 percent of those under 25; for 46 percent of people between 25 and 34 years; for 32 percent of those between 35 and 49; for 37 percent of those between 50 and 64; and for 24 percent of people aged more than 65 years.

Only 7 percent of French youths between 18 and 25 years of age would agree to "risk their lives" in the event of an invasion of French territory by a foreign army, under any circumstances, whatever the cause of war; 56 percent would do so only if they were certain that their country "defended a just cause." Patriotism is no longer unconditional, unrelated to ideological or moral principles; many people no longer believe that what is good for the country is *a priori* moral and just.

A similar question, "Suppose France is in danger of a foreign invasion, what would be your reaction?" was asked by SOFRES in a June 1987 national survey. The proportion of French people who stated that they "would not sacrifice their life for their country" increased by generations: from 25 percent among those older than 65, to 44 percent among those aged 18 to 24 years.

Half the surveyed French youth between 18 and 25 years of age admitted in 1977 that they felt closer to a foreigner of his or her social class than they did to a French person from a different class; and more than half (58 percent) felt closer to a foreigner of their own age than they did to French people of their parents' age. Clearly, there is generational and class solidarity across nations.

In Germany, to a question asked by Emnid in 1987 about the importance of the flag as a national symbol, the proportion of those responding that "it is unnecessary" varied strongly according to age: only 15 percent among those aged 65 or more said it was unnecessary; 19 percent of those aged 50–54 years; 25 percent of those aged 30–39 years; 49 percent of those aged 20–29 years; and 46 percent of those under 19 years (this referred to the West German flag) (Hastings and Hastings 1987, p. 478). It is quite probable that the attitude toward the flag as a symbol of united Germany is quite different.

The public is aware of these differences of attitude among generations. In Britain, the majority of people under the age of 34 responded in March 1988 that they were less patriotic than their elders (Hastings and Hastings 1987–88). Similar attitudes have been found in other European countries.

Even in Ireland—the most traditionalist country in Europe—the generational dynamics are at work: The proportion of those who have no confidence in the army, or not very much, is significantly higher among younger people than it is among older people (40 percent for those between 18 and 24 years of age, to 11 percent for those more than 65 years of age). The youngest are less frequently proud of being Irish than the older people (Fogarty et al. 1984, pp. 161, 251).

The decline of nationalism is more apparent in the most educated strata in all European countries. It was the opposite at the apogee of nationalism, around 1848, when it was the intellectual elite that carried the patriotic torch in Europe. The fact that citizens with more education tend to be less nationalistic, in the old sense of the word, has important potential consequences. As Richard Rose (1985, p. 89) comments, "Governments spending large sums of money to raise the level of education of their citizens may find that their actions have the unintended consequence of reducing the national pride of younger citizens as they become better educated." In fact, the youngest and oldest parts of the population are not socially identical. This phenomenon is apparent in all countries, without exception.

There is a strong relationship between religiosity and nationalistic beliefs: The youngest, less attached to religious values, also rank relatively low on the scale of nationalistic attitudes.

In sum, there are obvious important differences between younger and older people everywhere across national frontiers. What is the real meaning of these gaps? Two theoretical interpretations are possible: We are dealing either with age groups or with generations. In the first case, what is involved is a life cycle, and the youths of today are adopting the same attitudes as their parents had held at the same age; the young of today will later adopt the same opinions as older people now hold.

The most famous example of the age phenomenon is the political role of students. The twentieth century is punctuated by political movements started by students in fifty countries, from Cairo to Tiananmen Square. The political eruption of students has taken the most diverse forms, from the extreme right to the extreme left. It appeared first in Europe at the beginning of the century, but spread to all other continents before and after the independence of numerous countries in Asia and Africa, the Middle East, and the Far East. In 1968, it spread like an epidemic through ten countries. Here we obviously have an age phenomenon—explained by the privileged place that students enjoy in society—periodically renewed. It is not a generational phenomenon.

In the second case, we are observing a generational effect. According to this interpretation, the youth of today have been influenced by a series of factors specific to contemporary historical circumstances, to such a degree that their beliefs can be explained better by historical experiences and the changes of society as a whole than by the fact that they are young.

The first interpretation has to be excluded without hesitation for an obvious reason: There is a real contrast between the beliefs of contemporary youth and the beliefs of youth thirty or forty years ago. We can demonstrate this contrast empirically because there is sufficient survey data for the 1950s, when the fathers and mothers of contemporary youth were themselves young. In addition, as we have already noticed, the younger generation and older generation are today sociologically quite different in terms of education and religious orientation. Certainly, some young people might change their attitudes as they mature. Nevertheless, we are in the presence not only of age differences but also of a generational change. A large part of today's youth will continue to carry with them the new values they have forged about religion, freedom, equality, the work ethic, sexuality, and nationalism. The older generation looks like a rear guard defending traditional values against the younger generation that is advocating nonconformist values.

Concluding Remarks

The decline of nationalism results from a multiplicity of factors, one of which is of extreme importance but difficult to capture with empirical data: the perception of the role of Europe in world affairs yesterday and today. No West European nation is large. All are middle-sized or small countries and two are ministates. But all together they represent a demographic, economic, cultural, scientific, military, and political potential that could show up Oswald Spengler as a false prophet.

Western Europe has experienced more social changes since 1945 than it had during the previous two centuries, in the level of education among others. Of all the variables influencing nationalistic feelings, education has everywhere proved to be one of the most important. Thus we can stress the following relationship: The higher the level of education, the lower the level of nationalistic attitudes. This relationship is also valid for longitudinal analyses. When we compare the people who were young in the 1930s with those who were young in the 1980s, we compare age per se only partially. We are dealing in fact with different kinds of populations, with two different generations.

That liberal states do not tend to fight one another seems to be an accepted proposition. Thus, the decline of nationalism could also be related to the fact that today all West European countries are liberal states and have repudiated the dictatorships that many of them experienced before World War II.

The two large countries that have achieved the greatest economic growth since World War II, Germany and Japan, are also the ones that have exhibited the highest degree of antimilitaristic attitudes during the last decades. Are they antimilitaristic because of their vivid collective memory of defeat, or, as Richard Rosecrance suggests, because they are now successful "trading states"? Are the German and Japanese peoples aware of the fact that the economic growth of their country has been largely favored by the low military allocations in their national budgets? How much rationality is involved in their antimilitarism?

A significant aspect of this longitudinal and cross-national comparison is the ubiquity of the same basic trends, all countries moving in the same direction even if the speed of change differs here and there.

Another lesson to be drawn concerns the concept of civic culture. If basic values can change so much from one generation to the next, should we not reconsider the pertinence of the concepts of civic culture and national character that have seduced so many scholars since 1963?

One of the most important findings of this analysis may be the fact that, in the distribution of basic values, the differences *within* nations are greater than differences *between* countries. The heterogeneity of each nation is more significant than the diversity among nations.

The specter of the Red Army intervened as a catalyst in the blossoming of the West European consciousness at the mass and the elite levels, as attested to by content analysis of parliamentary debates and the autobiographies of many leaders. With the implosion of the Soviet Union, this threat has disappeared, but meanwhile European integration has achieved a decisive advance, and nationalism *within* the countries of Western Europe has experienced an unprecedent decline. There is no way to compare pacifist feelings among the Western peoples with those in the Soviet Union at the same moment. But the phenomenon of implosion can nourish retrospective speculations.

The level of national loyalty and supranational consciousness varies significantly from country to country and among social categories. During the last three decades, the Netherlands has been the most Europeanist, Britain the least, for a variety of reasons among which economic ones predominate. People involved in agricultural activities tend to be more protective of their regional interests than are people in the tertiary sector. The opinion of urban workers varies according to the competitiveness of their industrial sector. Men are better informed than women about the issues of the Common Market and are more willing to take a position, favorable or unfavorable. But the most important distinction is the generational one. The national averages of survey results conceal these intranational diversities.

This essay has focused on attitudes, values, and feelings of citizens, without giving consideration to the institutional aspects, an analysis of which would require a different approach. It is nevertheless obvious that nations are organized in states, and that we are dealing in fact with nation-states, with complex societies heavily penetrated and regulated by state administrations. European integration involves not only the changing balance between national loyalty and supranational orientation, but also what is called the "harmonization" of laws and rules. The European Parliament, Council, Commission, and bureaucracy are taking initiatives and decisions that will result in a diminution of national sovereignties. This transfer of power from the national level to the supranational level is rarely spectacular, but it is consistent and effective. There is already impressive European regulation in various domains, affecting the daily life of people. Surveys conducted periodically at the national and at the European levels indicate how far and how rapidly the "Eurocrats" can or should advance. Supranational loyalty is constantly nourished by supranational legislation. The sovereignty of the nation-states is slowly but progressively reduced by a kind of loose confederal sovereignty, called vaguely "Community." Citizens react increasingly to the substance of European policy and express opinions on many economic and social issues rather than on basic national values.

References

Abrams, Mark, David Gerard, and Noel Timms, eds. (1985). *Values and Social Change in Britain*. London: Macmillan.

Calvaruso, Claudio, and Salvatore Abbruzzese (1985). *Indagine sui Valori in Italia*. Torino: Editoria Internazionale.

Demoskopie (Institut für) (1981). *Einge Generation Später, Bundesrepublik Deutschland 1953–1979*. Allensbach: Institut für Demoskopie.

Dogan, Mattei, ed. (1988). *Comparing Pluralist Democracies: Strains on Legitimacy*. Boulder, CO: Westview Press.

Dogan, Mattei, and Dominique Pelassy (1987). *Le Moloch en Europe: Etatisation et Corporatisation*. Paris: Economica.

Doxa (Bollettino della) (1946 and onward). Milan: Istituto per l'Analisi dell'Opinione Pubblica.

Eurobarometer: Public Opinion in the European Community (1971–1993). Commission of the European Community, issues 1 to 33.

Eurobarometer (1980). "Special Issue on Trust in other Nationalities," December.

Eurobarometer (1989). "Special Issue on Racism and Xenophobia," November.

Eurobarometer (1991). "Special Issue on Trends 1974–90," March.

Fogarty, Michael, Liam Ryan, and Joseph Lee (1984). *Irish Values and Attitudes*. Dublin: Dominican Publications.

Halman L., F. Heunks, R. de Moor, and H. Zanders (1987). *Traditie, secularisatie en individualisering. Een studie naar de waarden van de Nederlanders in een Europese context.* Tilburg: Tilburg University Press.

Harding, Stephen, David Phillips, and Michael Fogarty (1986). *Contrasting Values in Western Europe*. London: MacMillan.

Hastings, E.H., and P.K. Hastings, eds. (1981, 1982, 1987). *Index to International Public Opinion*. Westport, CT: Greenwood Press.

Hobsbawn, Eric (1970). *Nations and Nationalism since 1870*. Cambridge: Cambridge University Press.

Hofrichter, Jürgen, and Oskar Niedermayer (1991). *Cross-border Social European Integration: Trust between the Peoples of the European Community*. Zentrum für Europäische Umfragenalysen und Studien (mimeo).

Noelle, Elisabeth, and E.P. Neumann (1957). *Jahrbuch der Offentlichen Meinung*. Allensbach: Verlag für Demoskopie.

Noelle-Neumann, Elisabeth (1983). "Who Needs a Flag? Thoughts on German Attitudes," *Encounter*, LX, pp. 72–80.

Noelle-Neumann, Elisabeth (1985). "National Identity and Self Esteem." Paper presented to the World Congress of Political Science in Paris.

Noelle-Neumann, Elisabeth (1990). *Nationalgefühl als Historishes Ereignis*. Allensbach: Institut für Demoskopie.

Noelle-Neumann, E., and Renate Köcher (1987). *Die Verletzte Nation*. Stuttgart: Deutsche Verlags.

Orizo, Francisco A. (1983). *Espana entre la Apatia et il Cambio Social*. Madrid: Mapfre.

Rezsohazy, Rudolf, and Jan Kerkhofs (1984). *L'univers des Belges, Valeurs Anciennes et Valeurs nouvelles dans les années 80*. Louvain: Ciaco.

Rose, Richard (1985). "National Pride in Cross-National Perspective," *International Social Science Journal,* 37, pp. 85–96.

Rosecrance, Richard. *The Rise of the Trading State: Commerce and Conquest in the Modern World* (1987).

SOFRES (1984). *Opinion Publique. Enquêtes et Commentaires*. Paris: Gallimard.

Sondages, Revue Française de l'Opinion Publique (1944–78). Paris: IFOP.

Stoetzel, Jean (1983). *Les valeurs du temps présent: une enquête européenne*. Paris: Presses Universitaires de France.

Stoetzel, Jean (1988). "Defeatism in Western Europe: Reluctance to Fight for the Country." In Dogan, *Comparing Pluralist Democracies*, pp. 169–80.

Turner, C. Frederick (1988). "Basic Values: Religion, Patriotism and Equality." In Dogan, *Comparing Pluralist Democracies*, pp. 181–200.

VOLKER BORNSCHIER

The Rise of the European Community

Grasping Toward Hegemony? Or Therapy Against National Decline?

A considerable phase of stagnation—so-called Eurosclerosis—preceded the launching of the Single European Act in 1986. This revitalization of the European Community (EC) is a telling example of discontinuous social transition. In this article we point to the factors that might explain the remarkable move in the West European politicoeconomic regime. Most of the long-term goals of the EC were agreed upon in the Treaty of Rome, which was signed in 1957 by the then six member-states. However, the project did not develop smoothly. The question of why the original goals were pursued with varying strength at different times therefore becomes important. This is why we stress the timing of events and the social forces behind the relaunch of the 1980s.

In the first section we introduce and clarify theoretical concepts that we think are important for an understanding and explanation. First, we show briefly how transnational interactions, together with interstate or suprastate regimes, form the world political economy. Then we introduce the theoretical suggestions of the cycles of hegemony, or long cycles of world leadership, and their links with regime theory through the hegemonic stability theorem. We argue that a satisfactory explanation of the relaunch can be reached only by introducing the economically motivated behavior of political entrepreneurs and the demand they face. This is modeled in the "world-market-for-protection" argument.

In the second section we pose and suggest answers to the following question: Why—almost three decades after the first EC agreement in Rome—did integration suddenly gather momentum in the 1980s, as manifested by the Single European Act of 1986? We shall discuss several explanations and suggest integrating them.

The third section evaluates the position of the European Community vis-à-vis the United States and Japan. Europe's shortcomings in technology are contrasted with possible future competitive edges as a result of the greater ease with which it can form a politicoeconomic regime—a "lean state"—that may underpin "lean production," the new management philosophy of the emergent information-and-communication–based technological style.

There are several important events in the transformation of Europe which we do not address in this paper—the end of the Cold War, German reunification, and the breakdown of Soviet rule over significant parts of Europe following the events of 1989. Since we focus on the relaunch of the European Community that gathered momentum in the early 1980s, we do not touch these issues here.

The EC in the World Political Economy: Theoretical Perspectives

What has the European Community to do with questions of the world political economy? In theoretical terms, a first answer seems not too difficult. The EC has both altered and been shaped by the world economy. More precisely, since its beginning in 1958, the EC has regulated transnational links by adding a set of regimes to the world political economy, that is, a supranational one, which was considerably recast in 1986 under the banner of "Europe 1992."

The EC—recently enlarged by the agreement in Luxembourg with six European Free Trade Association (EFTA) member-states to the European Economic Area (EEA)[1]—together with its new "outer rim" commands more than 30 percent of the world product and has a share of more than 40 percent in world trade, while its population forms by far the largest single market in the world economy with about 370 million inhabitants (although this respectable figure represented only 7 percent of the world's population in 1990). Yet a narrow economic analysis is inadequate for understanding the dynamics of the world political economy and the changing role of the EC in the global system. This becomes clear from a booklet distributed at Seville's 1992 Universal Exposition wherein the Community presented itself to the world community:[2]

> Now an economic giant, the Community is striving to consolidate the single market into an economic and monetary union and to put in place political structures that will give it a *prime* role in helping define the post–Cold War world order (Commission of the EC 1992, p. 2; emphasis added).

The self-presentation admits that the EC is only part of the so-called triad: "The community is one of the three pillars, along with the United States of America and Japan, on which the system of pluralist democracy and market economy is built" (ibid.). At the same time, the EC's claim of a *prime* role signals hegemonic rivalry.

A study of the EC in such a perspective needs a clarification of concepts and an evaluation of different approaches. For the reader who wants to go first to substantial issues of the EC, we briefly outline what we are doing in section 1. We first develop an understanding of the notion of world political economy, of which the EC is part. The concept of international regimes then becomes relevant. These are interstate manifestations of politicoeconomic regimes and represent sets of institutions. In institutional economics, institutions are addressed as transaction-cost–reducing devices. This leaves aside the question of who creates such economically valuable goods. The macrosociological theory of the world market for protection introduces two kinds of "enterprises," states and firms, and suggests a framework that integrates supply and demand. The political science–based regime school explains international regimes on the basis of either functionalism or neorealism (power interests of states). Another body of theory relevant for our question consists in the approaches of hegemony or leadership cycles. There exists a link to international regimes via the hegemonic stability theorem. International-regime as well as hegemonic-cycle approaches have shortcomings insofar as they focus on the nation-state as the relevant unit. The perspective of the world market for protection may overcome some of these shortcomings. Together with the idea of the rise and decay of societal models—to which we will come in the second section of this article—this approach seems promising, especially when we focus on questions of timing and of protagonists behind the relaunch.

The World Political Economy

Theoretically, the EC is located at the intersection between transnational and international relationships (more correctly, "interstate relationships"). Transnational (economic) and interstate (political) phenomena define the necessarily political character of the world economy (Bornschier and Suter 1990; 1992). In a multistate system, transnational and interstate spheres can be intersected in three ways: (1) The individual state can determine the permeability of its borders with regard to economic transactions. For example, it regulates trade, intervenes in capital and financial flows, and controls the migration of labor. (2) The state creates social order within its territory through its constitution and political regulation, thereby creating public goods extending only over its territory. As examples there are the education system, the social security system, and redistributive measures or technology policy. (3) Finally, states can affect social order beyond their frontiers through international regimes, which they agree upon or which are imposed by a hegemonic power. Through this cooperation, or hegemonic constellation, transnational public goods are created. One example is the GATT regime, which has affected world trade since its formation in 1947 (Bornschier 1990).

Regarding the EC, the third area mentioned is obvious, but it is not the only important one; the coordination between member-states regarding industrial or common agricultural policy pertains to the second area; and common trade policy toward third parties belongs to the first area. The EC is then a manifestation of a *set* of "international regimes" covering the three areas and providing public goods at the suprastate level.

International Regimes

International regimes can be understood as manifestations of social institutions (Young 1986, p. 106). This opens access to the views of transaction-cost analysis and the theory of the world market for protection. According to institutional economics, the main goal of any economic institution is saving transaction costs (Williamson 1985, p. 21f.). The frictions of transactions in the division of labor are addressed by this viewpoint, and what Kenneth Arrow terms "operating costs of the economy" are not neglected anymore. Thus it becomes possible to gain a more realistic view.

The concept of the world market for protection (Bornschier 1988; 1989) also considers regulatory institutions as a precondition for any form of economy. The naive idea of the market as a natural order is thereby refuted. The example of GATT shows clearly that, if no regulation existed, in no way would the so-called free market be the result. In another connection, Karl Polanyi used the phrase "laissez-faire was planned."

Contrary to transaction-cost analysis, which merely explains the demand side for social institutions by focusing on cost savings, the protection-rent theorem introduced by Lane is also able to address the "production" of social institutions. The relevant framework is that states compete with each other as producers of institutional regulation, but can also cooperate. Economic competition between states arises not simply because capital—and, to a much smaller degree, labor—is internationally mobile, but because states as "producers" of social order, as well as creators and guarantors of institutions, introduce a production factor into the world economy. States are therefore subject to an encroaching economic logic since varying economic long-term successes also stem from different qualities of social order and their costs (Bornschier 1988; 1989).

The regime school proposes different explanations of how international regimes as institutions are created (Krasner 1983; Bornschier 1988, p. 125; Effinger et al. 1990). Two opposing lines of argument, whose contrasting positions recently have become closer, can be mentioned here. The functionalist, or institutionalist, theory suggests that increasing international interdependence and growing density of interaction in the international system will result in more need for international cooperation. In contrast, realists, or structuralists, view the creation and continuation of international regimes as dependent on the power interests of states and on hegemony. An integration of both lines is suggested by neorealists (Krasner 1983; Waltz 1979; Gilpin 1975). Although state behavior is still seen as rooted in national interests, it is at the same time embedded in an encompassing system with already existing values, normative theories, and institutions. Apparently, these views have the shortcoming that they are not able in their current formulation to account for transnationally and supranationally initiated integration, as the focus is the national government.

Hegemonic Stability

A link between regime theories and hegemonic-cycle theories has been suggested by the hegemonic stability theory (Kindleberger 1973; Keohane 1984; Gilpin 1987). This theory belongs to the power-structure line of argument. It originally claimed that international cooperation requires a hegemon. The neorealist position in Keohane's formulation (1984, p. 32) modified this argument. Although the establishment of influential regimes is dependent on hegemony, their survival is nevertheless possible even after hegemonic decline. With regard to the political world economy, the thesis of hegemonic stability connects the problem of order with hegemonic- or leadership-cycle theories (Bornschier and Suter 1990; 1992).

The rise and decline of nations, which is addressed by hegemonic- or leadership-cycle theories, offers one factor to explain the accelerated EC integration, proposed already by Sandholtz and Zysman (1989). Such a frame of reference is also shared by transnational business and supranational political entrepreneurs, as demonstrated by spokesmen's statements. Hegemonic or world leadership theories, however, can hardly do justice to the actual global politicoeconomic constellation as represented by the triad United States of America, the European Community, and Japan; and the multicultural project of EC integration contradicts present formulations of hegemony or world leadership theory in that each of these posits national states in such a role.

The rise and decline of states in the world system may explain power shifts with the resulting dissolution of order and challenges to players in the global power game. However, this change as such does not explain integration and its characteristics at the suprastate level. Further, theoretical views and arguments need to be taken into account. We suggest the protection-rent theorem, which Bornschier (1988; 1989, pp. 216–19) extended to the idea of a world market for social order.

World Market for Protection

The theory underlying the "world-market-for-protection" argument emphasizes that "social order," what we also term *protection,* is a public utility, although a territorially bounded one. Thus, protection should be built in as an argument in the national function of economic production. Governments—which can be understood as political undertakings (Otto Hintze, see below)—produce "order" and sell this public utility to capitalist enterprises, as well as to their citizens. The postwar societal model can be conceived of as a step in the evolution of the outcome of "world market for protection." Either governments were forced to behave according to the requirements of a capitalist state in order to compete in the world system, or they were economically punished in the long run.

The ideas underlying the notion of the "world market for protection" as a regulatory mechanism build on prior theoretical work (Bornschier 1988, chap. 14; 1989, pp. 216–19). Max Weber's conceptualization of a distinction between *economic* and *economically motivated* behavior was seminal. According to him, the continuous, formally peaceful or belligerent struggle between competing states provided the most excellent opportunities for modern capitalism. A given state had to compete for the free-flowing capital that dictated the conditions under which it was willing to help state power develop. The idea of two kinds of interdependent "enterprises"—a political undertaking alongside the economic one—was first formulated by Otto Hintze to account for modern state formation and capitalism. In Frederic C. Lane's (1979) work on protection rent these ideas reappear.

The theorem of the protection rent can be stated from the point of view of states or capitalist enterprises: (1) a state will be the strongest if it can combine moderate taxing with effective support favorable to innovation and investment; and (2) a capitalist enterprise will prosper most if it can choose, or is fortunately situated in a network of, economic transactions effectively protected at low cost. Advantages thus accrue to both sides: higher returns due to lower protection costs provide rents for capitalists and enhance their accumulation of capital; and for the state, accumulation and higher returns provide a larger resource base for its strength. What we add to this is that the capitalist state per se is not the one most favorable to economic success, but the one that reconciles the capitalist profit logic with the claims for legitimacy from its citizens, which are based on demands for security, equality, and efficiency. This is what we term the *extended* protection-rent theorem, which forms the core of the idea of the world market for protection.

The idea of a world market for protection enriches the theoretical apparatus in one important point. The economic motive of political undertakings (even stronger: the thus implied view that states are producers of economically valuable goods) can plausibly explain why states may even be willing to give up their sovereignty and merge. Such mergers happen much more easily if supranational institutional preconditions are present and available for initiative and political entrepreneurship. A case in point is the EC Commission. Its independent role was already stipulated in the Treaty of Rome.

Integration of the outlined theoretical perspectives may eventually lead to mergers of political undertakings, which can be conceptualized as specializing in establishing and maintaining relevant social institutions. This is what actually happened in the course of EC integration. Jean Monnet, the all-important figure in the launching of the EC project after the war, obviously disliked the term at that time. In an idealistic statement, he proclaimed, "We are not merging States, we are uniting men" (Commission of the EC 1992, p. 1).

The Revitalization of Europe: Reasons for the Relaunch in the Eighties

Under the flag with the magic inscription "Europe 92," Western Europe has started to transform itself economically and politically. With the internal market and the project for unity, the EC integration in a way continues the 500-year-old European state-building process, its main characteristic having been the concentration of politicoterritorial rule (Norbert Elias)—an implosion of what originally were 500 statelike structures to only two dozen (Charles Tilly). On the other hand, it is a social innovation in at least two respects. The process will mean the end of a multistate balance of power in Western Europe. Furthermore, the project for unity does not conform to two crucial characteristics of state-building that are so far present in the model of Western Europe (Stein Rokkan). As far as can be ascertained today, the future union will not be characterized by a prominent central authority or by a standard culture; thus the nation-state model will not be continued.

The Single European Act

The impetus for this reform, represented in the Single European Act, came from world political transformations. For decades, Europe has not been the center of the political world economy. After World War I, the European powers had to relinquish this role to the United States, which actually assumed the role only from World War II on. The European powers took their place behind the United States after World War II as number two and were startled when, due to the hegemonic decline of the United States, the usual stability of the world economic structure was no longer guaranteed and the impressive rise of Japan thrust even the most powerful among them down to number three in the world.

It is not our intention to cover all aspects of the European unification process. Our purpose, rather, is to emphasize the need to explain the new upswing of the 1980s, after years of Europessimism and so-called Eurosclerosis. A few indicators are sufficient to make clear the characteristics of the acceleration of the unification process. The relaunching in the middle of the 1980s is manifested in two EC documents: the White Paper of the Commission to the European Council of Ministers on the completion of the Internal Market (Weissbuch 1985), and the Single European Act (SEA). While the White Paper was a political initiative of the Commission, the SEA represents decisive supplements to the EC agreements, which are of supranational character, as they in part directly affect national law.

The White Paper, published June 6, 1985, suggests the target of "Europe 1992," with the main aim being the completion of the EC Internal Market. The first part of the document mentions the areas that prevent a truly integrated market. Possibilities are suggested as to how these obstacles can be removed. The second part lists approximately 300 legal measures that are necessary to create a truly Internal Market and that should be made into national law by the EC member-states according to a two-step timetable (1985–86 and 1987–92). The goal is the complete elimination of nontariff barriers to the trade of goods and services within the EC and the adoption of the "four freedoms" so that goods, people, services, and capital can move freely within the area of the EC. Although the White Paper wrongly creates the impression that the idea of the Internal Market is entirely new, it actually revitalizes the goals of the 1950s that led to the Treaty of Rome in 1957. While customs duties and quantity restrictions had been eliminated 18 months earlier than scheduled, that is, in 1968, the nontariff barriers increased in the 1970s during the decline of the Western societal model.

While the White Paper was the initiative of the Commission, the SEA, to which the Council agreed, is the important legal and institutional base. Three points should be stressed: (1) According to Paragraph 13 of the SEA (Paragraph 8A of the Treaty of Rome), the EC organs are called upon to take all measures necessary for the realization of the Internal Market by the end of 1992. (2) The SEA decreed that decisions regarding regulations and guidelines would no longer have to be unanimous, but could be decided by qualified majority voting to rescind the compromise of Luxembourg of 1966 for decision making (see below). (3) The SEA introduced a new supranational procedure for the creation of law. Different national laws and standards were now no longer harmonized, but the common legal realm expanded by the mutual acceptance of national laws and standards. Even if mutual acceptance instead of adaptation is still at various stages of development (Fifth Report 1990: Appendix V), the resulting acceleration of the integration is immense.

The momentum, which reaches from the White Paper to the contractual agreement in the Single European Act and its subsequent implementations, has decisively broadened in more recent times. The Community heads of government agreed in December 1989 to begin the process of economic and monetary union (EMU). Half a year later, they gave the go-ahead for negotiations on political union as well. At the EC summit in Maastricht (December 1991), the European Union was agreed upon which one currency, the ecu, should be used and that cohesion funds make possible the convergence of the four poorest members. The EC has embarked on its way to full statehood:

> The Community needed a political dimension to match its new economic strength and responsibilities. The key external dimension of political union centres on a common foreign and security policy. The second focus of political union is the revision of the Community's institutional structures, notably by extending the power of the European Parliament, and expanding still further the scope of the Rome Treaty (Commission of the EC 1992, p. 4).

Looking back to the 1980s, we observe an immense acceleration in recasting the EC. The drive is not only impressive, but gains new contours against the setbacks of the late 1960s and the 1970s. But obviously, this process will not continue without further setbacks, as the Danish referendum rejecting the Treaty of Maastricht demonstrated at the beginning of June 1992.

Eurosnobbery

Is the relaunch a grasp at hegemony, as Eurosnobs among top politicians and Eurobureaucrats would have us believe? At a press conference in Washington in May 1990, German Chancellor Helmut Kohl proclaimed that Europe, and not Japan and America, would be the dynamic force of the 1990s. Patronizingly, he added that it would be important for America to participate in this miracle of the strongest economic area in the world (Schenk 1990, p. 41).

Jacques Attali, adviser to French president François Mitterrand and president of the European Bank for Reconstruction and Development, presents another version of this Eurosnobbery in his book *Lignes d'horizon*. Attali describes an EC that rules not only Europe, including Russia, but also the Pacific apart from the United States. "If Western Europe understands that the Eastern part of the continent must participate in its future, then it can claim to be the heart of the world economy, and its most densely populated, richest and most creative area" (Attali 1990, p. 75).

The political Euroentrepreneur, Jacques Delors, who from 1981 to 1984 was Socialist minister for industry and finance in Paris and assumed the presidency of the EC Commission in Brussels on January 6, 1985, sees things more moderately. For years, he brought impetus into a Community paralyzed by lethargy and budget squabbling; recently, he declared in an interview: "Out of the dynamic economic and commercial power which we already are, a great political power must develop" (Delors 1991, p. 20). He explains this as a "historical responsibility" and feels it would be a sad development if "the Europeans of the year 2010 . . . were degraded to spectators of history" (ibid., p. 21). The anxiety about saving Europe's brilliance into the future appears in Delors's warning:

> We must move quickly otherwise Europe will become an archaeological excavation place, where Americans and the Japanese search for lost thoughts and ways of life (Delors 1991, p. 21).

The Challenge of the World Political Economy

The rather moderate view of Delors—who understands that the acceleration of integration is the answer to the Japanese–American challenge, a competition that is not completely without prospects for the EC—is also typical of the European business elite. In an address in Madrid in 1989, Clemente Signorini, senior executive of FIAT, declares: "The final goal of the European 'Dream' is to transform Europe into an integrated economic continent with its specific role, weight and responsibility on the international scenario vis-à-vis the U.S. and Japan" (Signorini 1989, p. 6). Rainer E. Gut, president of the board of directors of Credit Swiss (who despite Switzerland's nonmembership in the Community pushes forward his bank's European positions) brings the view of the business elite to another sobering conclusion: "The EC is aiming to strengthen its competitiveness compared to the two economic regions of North America and the Far East" (Gut 1991, p. 7).

These comments demonstrate that, when speaking of changes in Europe, the transnational and supranational actors express themselves in terms of an answer to the power struggle and challenge. The explanation of regime change and integration from the realistic, structural viewpoint covers such viewpoints as well.

The Functionalist Explanation

Let us turn for a moment to the alternative explanation. The functionalist integration and regime theories mentioned earlier predict integration to take place when governments have realized that certain economic policies can no longer be accomplished by national means. This could lead national governments to cooperate in creating supranational institutions, which then develop on their own, determined by inner laws of spin-offs and spill-overs.[3] Sandholtz and Zysman (1989) consider this interpretation and then reject it. Their argument is that the stop-and-go character of previous European unification efforts contradicts that claim, as does the observation that in the 1970s national options for problem solving were more often adopted than EC options.

As with the Bretton-Woods agreement or with GATT, the EC is not the result of interlacing and growing interdependence, but rather was established by political decisions that then led to further interlacing. Core world economy agreements and rules, if they bunch together, represent a new societal deal that is agreed upon in times of extreme crisis (for example, 1941–44, from the Atlantic Charter to the Bretton-Woods agreement; Bornschier 1990, p. 29 ff). Again, the thrust toward unity in the EC in 1985 stands at the end of a long crisis, namely, the dissolution of the neocorporatist-Keynesian societal model that prevailed in the West for decades.

The Rise and Decay of Societal Models

In *Westliche Gesellschaft im Wandel* (1988), I suggested a cyclical explanation for societal change. A societal model that consists of a combination of visions connected with normative theories, a technological style, and a politicoeconomic regime is likely to emerge at the end of a profound and enduring societal crisis; it gains acceptance, eventually leads to growing tension in the course of its later development, and disintegrates.

The Western societal model disintegrated toward the end of the 1970s. Former hegemonic societal doctrines like Keynesianism were replaced by monetarist and supply-side ones after the World Summit Conference in Bonn in 1978. In 1982, the new doctrine was anchored in the OECD paradigm for a new economic policy in the West. The technological style, characterized by the Fordist mass-production paradigm, already had reached its limits in the early 1970s. The political shifts at the verge of the 1980s destroyed the unquestioned position of postwar politicoeconomic regimes. By this approach, recasting the EC can be explained as a move toward the vision of a renewed social contract in Western Europe. There are many statements by EC commissioners that are in line with such a view. A statement by Karel Van Miert, member of the European Commission, is one example:

> Truly "1992" will mean a transformation of society. Mentalities and habits will change. Everywhere the key players in the economy realize that the future lies in the fullest sense in Europe (Commission of the EC 1992, p. 8).

The explanation we suggest is supported by several facts. We already have pointed out that the Internal Market project is not entirely new. It dates back to the 1957 Treaty of Rome. While tariffs and quantitative barriers had been eliminated earlier than scheduled, the nontariff barriers to intracommunity trade remained an ever-growing problem in the 1970s. This rather cyclical movement corresponds to the rise and decay of the Western societal model at large. Popular opinion incorrectly holds that the procedural reform of qualified majority voting is new. In Article 148 of the original treaty, the Council of Ministers already provided for the fact that most decisions would be made by a qualified majority vote and, after a transitional period that would end in 1965, decision making would be made in a much wider area by qualified majority voting. In 1966, Charles de Gaulle forced the already mentioned "Luxembourg Compromise," to which the remaining five members had to agree in order to keep France in the Community (Leonard 1989, p. 42). The decisive paragraph speaks only of the application of the clause in instances of vital interest. Actually, this paragraph was interpreted much more restrictively. The necessity for unanimity, which then became practice, paralyzed integration for about two decades. Again, we suggest an explanation for this regression by referring to the societal model. The growing dissent in the disintegration phase of the societal model is manifested in sharply increasing conflict within Western societies as well as among Western states (Bornschier 1988, chap. 7).

The argument of Sandholtz and Zysman (1989), that the significant ideological shifts within member states do not explain the momentum of integration on a *higher* system level, needs reformulation. The point to be considered is that the replacement of the former political and economic doctrines throughout the West was a transnational phenomenon, as became apparent in the new OECD paradigm for economic policy in 1982 as mentioned above. Of course, the transnational character of the new doctrines itself does not explain supranational integration. The relaunch of the EC must also be seen as an answer to contradictions inherent in the interventionist role of the state—a cornerstone of the neocorporatist-Keynesian societal model. Economic interventions are free of only major interstate conflicts if they are embedded in and curbed by international regimes.

One important pillar of this coordination was the U.S.-dollar–gold exchange regime of Bretton Woods. The United States, which had established this system, was no longer in a position to defend the dollar in 1971. From an institutional viewpoint, this hegemonic power was relinquished just at the time when the United States gave up the exchange system it had once created by "suspending" the obligation to maintain the U.S.-dollar–gold parity. By 1973, as the European countries were forced to switch to floating exchange rates, the system of fixed exchange rates completely broke apart, and the disciplinary pillar of coordinated economic policies no longer existed. The important, seemingly irrevocable clasp had broken, because—as hegemonic stability theory would argue—no country was in a position or was willing to guarantee the international exchange system. The economic decline of the United States and the disintegration of the societal model, which was dependent on interstate coordination of economic policy, are mutually linked. Both viewpoints can be combined for an explanation of the momentum of EC integration.

The explanation outlined so far still has at least one major shortcoming. *Who* were the actors who gave initial thrust to the relaunch? This question appears to be neglected in the fascination of the discussion of the spectacular rise of the EC itself that followed the years of crisis. For certain, a new beginning necessarily had to be launched beyond the nation-state level in order for policy coordination to be regained. But who were the protagonists behind it? Without a consideration of the impetus, we shall find no satisfactory explanation for the revitalization.

Transnational Corporations in Search of a Political Entrepreneur

As already suggested by Sandholtz and Zysman (1989), one necessary condition for the acceleration of integration in the 1980s was the independence of the EC Commission—certainly an institutional precondition for political entrepreneurship. Acknowledging this still gives us little information about to whom this political entrepreneur was most receptive.

In their work, Sandholtz and Zysman (ibid.) point to agreements between the European business elite and the Commission. The Round Table of European Industrialists—a meeting of representatives from large European corporations—was founded in 1983 with the help of Etienne Davignon, a member of the EC Commission (ibid., p. 117). This seems to suggest that the interests of the European corporations already had been formed when Jacques Delors invited business in 1985 to support "his" vision by stating, "We count on business leaders for support" (Krause 1988, p. 24).

The competitive disadvantages of Europe as an industrial site were first felt directly by the transnational corporations. After the economic crisis of the 1970s, the United States as well as Japan recovered much easier than Europe did. Despite its decline in competitiveness, the United States was able to take advantage of its own huge and rather homogeneous internal market; and Japan enjoyed the advantage of elaborate strategic planning, which already had been essential for Japan's extraordinary rise. It was the (albeit mild and flexible) "planned economy," indeed tied to capitalistically inspired business and oriented to long-term strategic goals that made Japan big, and not laissez-faire principles.

The argument of the protection-rent theory then reads as follows: The European corporations[4] directly and indirectly demanded that the political entrepreneurs in Europe provide them with the combined advantages their rivals were enjoying in the United States and Japan. This demand created the start of a new state project along the following lines: a large homogeneous market combined with strategic planning, particularly with regard to the ever more important production factor, technology.[5] From at least 1983 on, this project was discussed in a quasicorporatist arrangement, without employee representation, with the EC Commission under the presidency of Jacques Delors since 1985, and eventually it was agreed upon. From 1985 on, the Commission started to popularize the deal and underpinned the project with scientific expertise that certified savings of transaction costs (compare the Cecchini Report of 1988). Thus we have included and emphasized a "demand-side" explanation for the starting point of the relaunch, one which overcomes the shortcomings of a "supply-side" explanation that stresses only the autonomy of the Commission as political entrepreneur.

The evidence so far available of European cooperation in high technology indicates that collaboration between big corporations and the Commission already had begun in the first half of the 1980s. This cooperation between transnational corporations and the supranational EC Commission culminated in various programs. Among them were ESPRIT (European Strategical Research and Development program, since 1984) and RACE (Research and Development on Advanced Communication Technologies in Europe, since 1985).[6] "In telematics, European collaboration emerged when the Commission, under the leadership of Etienne Davignon, struck an alliance with the 12 major electronic companies in the EC" (ibid., p. 113). The reasoning is given in a publication of the Commission itself: "In consideration of the fast technological transition, Europe can no longer afford the luxury of increasing costly duplication in R&D" (Commission of the EC 1991, p. 32).[7]

Much more comprehensive collaboration among European industrialists preceded the initiative of Jacques Delors in 1985. The Round Table of European Industrialists began to form in 1983 under the presidency of Pehr Gyllenhammar of Volvo. Sandholtz and Zysman (1989, p. 117) mention that Etienne Davignon, a Belgian member of the EC Commission, participated actively in the recruitment of its members. Certainly, the Commission was the catalyst. But the members of Delors's cabinet were aware of the power of the industrialists. It is reported that one member of Delors's cabinet commented, "These men are very powerful and dynamic. . . . When necessary they can ring up their own prime ministers and make their case" (van Tulder and Junne 1988, p. 214ff; Sandholtz and Zysman 1989, p. 117). And as we have already mentioned, Jacques Delors himself referred to the power center when he was launching his initiative.

Strategic Planning and Protection

What does strategic planning as an element of the new role of the EC have to do with protection? The EC justifies its planning procedure on the grounds that there are pressures to be more competitive, but there are insufficient funds for research and development in information technologies (Commission of the EC 1991, p. 8). "The Community therefore developed a global strategy in the first half of the 1980s in close collaboration with industry and with research institutions" (ibid., p. 10). This is followed by a list of different elements, the support of business as well as measures against undesirable side effects, and a vision:

> preparation of the transition to a society in which information is seen as a raw material, which is used in agreement with the social partners *[Sozialpartner]* and on the basis of the corresponding offers for education and training" (ibid.).

It is not only protection inside the EC that is included in these assignments. In the words of the Commission, "Considering the growing challenges in the area of ICT (Information and Communication Technologies), the Community must prove its joint action towards third-party states. This applies to the bilateral relationship of the EC to the United States and to Japan, as well as in international institutions like GATT (General Agreement on Tariffs and Trade), ISO (International Standards Organisation) or ITU (International Telecommunications Union)" (ibid. p. 71).

According to the EC, even after completion of the Common Market there should be no "fortress Europe" but, in the words of the president of the Commission, Jacques Delors, Europe should not be anyone's easy prey (ibid., p. 71). Japan is warned from the "European viewpoint," among other things, to reduce its strong export orientation and concentrate its economy more on internal demand (ibid.). The EC protested against the semiconductor deal of 1986 between the United States and Japan, and their claim was backed by the GATT enquiry commission in 1988.

The role that protection already plays and will play in the future in the world political economy is demonstrated by the example of HDTV (high-definition television). In 1986, Japan offered a proposal in 1986 for standardization and compatibility of this completely new medium with its own transmitting channels, which would have required exchanging all traditional receiving apparatus as well as the setting up of additional networks. The EC reacted:

> The European countries have expressed themselves against the Japanese concept. The Commission therefore supported early on a European initiative for a worldwide production standard with the parameters 1250/50. In December 1989 the EC Ministers decided to make a united attack in favor of the European standard. At the conference of May 23rd, 1990, in Düsseldorf, the CCIR (International Advisory Committee for Broadcasting) decided on 23 of the total of 34 parameters necessary for the complete definition of the new HDTV standard. The CCIR thereby unrestrictedly followed the European recommendations (ibid., p. 27).

With its global strategy of 1989, the EC wanted to ensure that European industry will be able to produce the necessary hardware in time; that the European standard for production and exchange of HDTV programs becomes the worldwide standard; and that the Community can advertise the use of the European HDTV systems in the world market (ibid., p. 28). This example concerns an area of industry—information-and-communication technology—that today already represents 5 percent of the gross domestic product worldwide and 8 percent of that of industrial countries. The ICT area can be considered as one of the key elements of the emerging new technological style.

Discussion

Sandholtz and Zysman (1989) have already pointed to the transformation of the world economy as a necessary condition for the revival of the European project. The second necessary condition we introduce concerns the cyclical career of societal models. A sufficient explanation is offered in this article by the theory of protection rent. It suggests the motive of the leading corporations and political entrepreneurs to want a pact. The fact that the EC commission as a political entrepreneur has relative autonomy is certainly important in the sense that it can act innovatively and make the idea of a merger of their state services attractive to national governments. This institutional precondition was, however, not a creation of the 1980s; it had existed since the beginning of the EC.

Our emphasis is on timing. At the verge of the 1980s, certain constellations were apparent. The Western societal model had decayed during the 1970s. Europe was confronted with Japan's success in mastering the world economic crisis and it was challenged by the U.S. experiment under President Reagan to rescue its world economic position (at that time the experiment appeared viable for many businesses). At this moment, the "demand" of transnational European business and the "supply" of the supranational EC Commission met and provided the precondition for a relaunch with a new politicoeconomic regime.

We then suggest an explanation for the dramatic rise in efforts toward European integration in the 1980s, which is not, however, purely a revitalization but also a *new regime* by comparison to previous national ones in Europe. For Western Europe, the arrangement between the EC Commission as a supranational political entrepreneur and corporations thus combines the idea of liberalization of the European market with new kinds of state services (the two strategic advantages of the EC's rivals, the United States and Japan) in order to prepare for post-hegemonic competition in the world economy. These two elements—a huge as well as homogeneous market and strategic planning—are the obvious advantages of each of the EC's rivals, the United States and Japan

The argument is of a kind that has been termed "supranational institutionalism" by Andrew Moravcsik (1991). He goes on to challenge it as an explanation for the recasting of the EC, and advocates instead an "intergovernmental institutionalism" approach. Moravcsik claims that the Single European Act can be explained by the national interests of the three big member-states, Germany, France, and Britain. In a sort of game theory explanation, he sees these three as having converged to the lowest common denominator of their national preferences. His view stresses that the heads of government and their direct representatives took the lead in the negotiations and produced the breakthrough that is manifested in the SEA.

Moravcsik stresses the role of the three most powerful member states but admits that these governments possessed considerable autonomy from domestic bureaucracies and viewed economic integration as part of a geopolitical grand strategy (ibid., p. 50). In this sense, they share core elements of the perspective of transnational business. The two former world powers, Britain and France, are heavily threatened by further decline in importance, and Germany feels the limits of its spectacular *Wirtschaftswunder* vis-à-vis Japan's new role in the world. Thus Moravcsik's intergovernmental institutionalism argument actually contains considerable reference to the supranational approach stressing shifts in the world economy. The only substantial difference between arguments is whether it was the governments of the big countries that effectively took the lead via the EC council of ministers, or the transnationals via the EC Commission. As Stephen George (1992, p. 12) puts it, we are now converging toward "a common model in which all the elements of external context, internal spillover, supranational actors, domestic politics, and bargaining between sovereign states have their place." Of course, different researchers emphasize different components of the explanatory model, but the main research problem now becomes an empirical one. Our ongoing analysis of the interviews we performed with several key protagonists behind the EC's relaunch in the early 1980s will produce new information relevant to the causal chain on which we put our emphasis.

Technological Weakness and Future Promise of the EC

The shares of North America, Western Europe, and Japan in world product and trade have developed very unevenly since the 1960s. Only Japan was able to increase its share considerably, approximately doubling it. This success is brought into perspective once it is viewed against Japan's quite modest starting levels and the enormous destruction it experienced during the war. Since the beginning of the decline of the long boom of the world economy in the late 1960s, Western Europe especially has lost a surprisingly large relative share.

The real growth rates in industrial products reflect this process of regrouping. The rates for the United States were lowest in the 1970s (on average, 2.8 percent annually for 1970–80, versus 3.1 percent for the EC and 4.8 percent for Japan). In the 1980s, Western Europe fell way behind the United States, especially in the first half of that decade (1.5 percent annually versus 3.2 percent for the United States and 4.0 percent for Japan). As a result of the revitalization, the difference has shrunk since 1986 (1986–88, 3.1 percent annually in the EC, 3.5 percent in the United States, and 4.3 percent in Japan).[8]

Growth of the EC by Merger

The aggregate EC figures mentioned at the beginning mask the weakness of Western Europe. Since the middle of the 1960s, each EC country has lost shares in world product and world industrial production. For example, the Federal Republic of Germany's share of world industrial production fell from 6.4 percent to 5.3 percent in the years between 1963 and 1980. The corresponding figure for France shows a decline from 3.8 percent to 3.3 percent; for Great Britain, from 6.4 percent to 4.0 percent. In contrast, Japan increased its share from 5.1 percent to 9.1 percent, while the U.S. share declined from 35.1 percent to 31.5 percent, although it still remained by far the highest.[9]

The waves of expanding EC membership—1973, 1981, and 1986—resulted in the fact that the EC was able to place itself in front of Japan and at the same time reduce the gap between it and the United States. In 1963, the EC with its then six members had a 15 percent share of world industrial production, and the EC of twelve members increased this—despite national decline—to 20 percent.[10] From this viewpoint, the EC was a somewhat feasible "therapy" against national decline in the world system. But if we consider the area of high technology, the merger of national economic powers proves to be rather unsuccessful.

Information and Communication Technologies (ICT): The Precarious Position of the EC

From the argument we have developed so far, it becomes clear that, up to now, "recasting the European bargain" has hardly been a bid for hegemony, but rather an emergency measure in order to remain a player at the core. The following excerpt from the 1991 EC Commission report investigates in more detail the weaknesses of the EC in competition within the triad of the United States, the EC, and Japan. In the 1980s, the EC lost ground in precisely those branches that pushed forward the new IC technological style—which is based on pervasive information-and-communication technologies and succeeds the Fordist technological style. This is demonstrated by figures compiled for a conference of the EC Commission in 1991 on information-and-communication technologies.

Bearing in mind that the telecommunications sector will be one of the most important branches of industry in the near future, the EC Commission paints a pessimistic picture of the deteriorated competitive situation in Europe, although not without simultaneously mentioning the treatment planned:

> Since the mid-eighties the EC balance of trade in the telecommunications sector has clearly worsened. . . . The main reason is the growing trade deficit with Japan. . . . These figures prove the necessity for the European market integration with increased competition, which will improve the competitiveness and innovation of the European corporations. Modern, efficient digital communications systems are so complicated that a manufacturer must capture 8 percent of the world market in order to cover development costs. But at present the market of any single member state does not exceed 7 percent of the world market. A homogeneous European market with just 25 percent would rank behind the United States (30 percent) and in front of Japan (11 percent) (Commission of the EC 1991, p. 34).

Based on detailed research on the ICT sector, Chris Freeman and Luc Soete reach an alarming conclusion:

> It may be assumed that the benefits of Japanese and U.S. technological leadership in ICT will accrue in the first place to other Japanese and American firms, with whom they have closer technical, financial, organizational and cultural links, even though they may later also diffuse in Europe. In a technology in which component, product, process and system design are all so intimately related and in which new generations succeed each other so quickly, this is an important aspect of technological competition. . . . Both for trade competitiveness and for the efficiency and productivity of all other sectors of the EC economy, there are valid reasons for concern with the relative performance of the EC ICT sector (Freeman and Soete 1991, p. 12).

In a parallel report, Gerstenberger also reaches an unfavorable conclusion about the competitive position of European corporations in the ICT sector:

> A variety of indicators point to the weak competitive position of European suppliers of ICT equipment with respect to production costs and innovative performance. The main challenger is Japanese industry. There are strong indications that Japanese companies are not only quicker with marketing innovations and better in producing new ICT equipment at highest quality standards and low costs, they have also become technological leaders. . . . An inquiry into the reasons for the lack of ICT top players from Europe produced strong evidence for the inhibiting impact of the fragmentation of European ICT markets in the past (Gerstenberger 1991, pp. 9–11).

This evaluation of European weaknesses does not originate from the pen of outsiders.[11] Konrad Seitz (1991), in his well-known book, points out the silent high-technology battle, in which the European high-technology (ICT) industry is threatened by the American-Pacific high-technology duopoly. "Will Europe become a technological colony?" he asks (ibid., p. 337).[12]

More recently, this opinion has found coverage in the media in a not so harmless way, with hysterical and xenophobic undertones: *"Der Chip-Krieg: Japan überrollt den Westen"* (The Chip War: Japan Overruns the West) was the headline in an issue of *Der Spiegel* recently (November, 1992).

New Solutions: "Lean Production" and a "Lean State"

Institutional rigidity plays a role in long-term cyclical social change which we formulate as a succession of societal models. As already mentioned, societal models are conceived of as a link between a technological style and a politicoeconomic regime underpinned by normative theories (Bornschier 1988). In such a framework, institutional rigidity can be explained as over-adaptation to a fading *technological style* or politicoeconomic regime. Such institutional scleroses restrict or delay future choices.

The marked industrial decline of the United States since the end of the 1960s can also be viewed as over-adaptation to the old technological style, the now-fading Fordist production concept of mass production, which crystalized in the United States as early as the 1920s. Even though the style spread across the Atlantic and the Pacific—although not on a large scale until after World War II—it was, to exaggerate somewhat, *America's* style. The incredibly rapid loss of major American industries' leading positions, which has been observed by the MIT Commission on Industrial Productivity (Dertouzos et al. 1989), can be interpreted as a result of such an over-adaptation. One should, however, be cautious of speculations about a general weakness of American high technology; as a study by the consulting firm McKinsey points out, in the areas of biological and genetic technology, U.S. leadership is still intact. Measured in terms of inventions, the United States (with 42 percent of the world share) ranks clearly in front of Europe (with 35 percent) and Japan (with 18 percent). Similarly with the computer industry—hardware and software—U.S. corporations are still undisputedly on top (Freeman and Soete 1991; Gerstenberger 1991).

However, it can be said that the United States has trouble in adopting the Japanese system of industrial engineering and management, that is, "lean production." Lean production as a concept—already applied in Japanese car manufacturing at the beginning of the 1950s by Eiji Toyoda (of Toyota) and Taiichi Ohno—began its successful advance against Fordist mass production because it flexibly combines the advantages of craftsmanship with mass production (Womack et al. 1990).

Because of its pioneering role, Japan—supported by institutional factors of industrial organization and labor relations—apparently finds it easier to develop the new technological style of the "information society" (originally a Japanese term).[13] In Europe, the traditions of craftsmanship have likewise been maintained to a larger extent in industry, which should facilitate the move to the technological future. These are strategic advantages particularly accruing to the Japanese, but also to European industry.

The flanking *politicoeconomic regime* embedded in the paradigm of *Soziale Marktwirtschaft* (which underpins the market with redistributive policies) of the last societal model, the interventionist welfare state, was begun by the two innovators, Sweden and the United States, as early as 1932–33. Roosevelt's New Deal represented a remarkable new start for American traditions; but once the United States took over the role of hegemon after 1945, it came to little. In Europe, on the other hand, the welfare state was continually improved and expanded during the neocorporatist Keynesian postwar era. The social integration and legitimation was exemplary for decades and was also a favorable competitive factor economically (Bornschier 1988; 1989). On the verge of the 1980s, the limits of this politicoeconomic arrangement's ability to release itself from institutional rigidities became apparent. Apart from Great Britain, the European states did not, however, change blindly to supply-side economics, and the social network was not so drastically damaged despite several spectacular political turnarounds.

The "Europe 92" target can also be seen as a sort of cleansing process to remove Europe's neocorporatist crust without abandoning the strategic European advantage of a legitimizing welfare state. While Japan reaps strategic advantage from "lean production" (Womack et al. 1990), similar future EC advantages may stem from a "lean state" project—a cornerstone of the emerging new politicoeconomic regime. This idea will be elaborated below.

One of the vice-presidents of the EC Commission, Filippo Maria Pandolfi (Science/Research), outlined the new industrial policy of the EC in his address on October 17, 1991, in Brussels.[14] According to him, this policy avoids too much and too specific state intervention but creates and maintains supportive public goods.[15] Strategic planning, particularly with regard to technology policy, including risk acceptance and technology management, are elements of the paradigm for a harmonized European industrial policy. Pandolfi further mentioned the creation of trans-European networks in transportation, energy, telematics, education, and training as medium-term tasks. His reference in the address to Martin Bangemann (another vice-president of the Commission) indicates the importance of this policy and its support in the Commission.

Such a "lean state" is in no way a late offspring of "Reaganomics." It strengthens not only the supply side of the economy, but also the demand side, insofar as the diffusion of the new technologies receives specific attention in order to support the increasing group of users and to offer socially created flanking measures to train and retrain workers and users, and to support research. This is also proclaimed in Pandolfi's reorganization of the European Research Promotion policy away from the supply-side measures to the demand side. Furthermore, this lean state is sensitive to social cohesion, unlike Reagan's reconstruction attempt, which reminded many of Victorian-like capitalism. It has already been mentioned that social networks in Europe—despite several growing holes—have in no way been folded up during the last dozen years or so.

New in this bunch of policies is the strengthening of solidarity on a European scale.[16] Core elements of the normative theory of the Community are *cohesion* and *convergence.* This points to an expansion of the welfare state on an EC scale. The new allocations to the cohesion funds during the EC summit meeting in Maastricht (December 1991) speak for the fact that this is not simply lip service. The various structural funds of the EC, which serve social harmonization in the Community, have experienced a considerable increase in allocations. And the cohesion support for the four poorest member states should make these fit for the agreed common currency, improve their infrastructure, and help financially to fulfill the environmental regulations.

Finally, the lean state project indicates a break with the centralist European state tradition, which should not be underrated. A standard language and the elimination of regional cultural variety are neither intended nor discernible. The Commission's slogan is *Unity in Diversity:*

> Despite its accelerating economic and political integration, the Community has been able to preserve the distinctive cultures, languages and traditions of its 12 Member States. As part of the single market, the Community has developed a citizens' Europe . . . (Commission of the EC 1992, p. 2).

In addition, the EC may help to temper conflict within member-states. Belgium is a case in point. Discord between the Flemings and the Walloons, which even threatened to destroy the nation-state, has been alleviated through the EC. Furthermore, unanimity in decision making is not a necessary element. In order to make progress in the project of unification, it is even accepted that individual states do not toe the line. Thus, at the Maastricht summit, Great Britain succeeded in arranging that they do not have to sign the Social Charter of the EC. Similar flexibility may apply to future questions in foreign policy. The neutrality proviso from Ireland—probably like those of Austria, Sweden, Finland, and Switzerland—is a further example of a minimal and flexible new sort of state.

It is certainly correct that considerable elements that characterize the lean state (such as the industrial and technological policy) represent an imitation of the successful Japanese model,[17] which enabled that country to react successfully and flexibly to the changes in the political world economy (Schmiegelow 1986). The strategic advantage of the EC project over Japan could lie in the fact that the lean state of a European kind has no past and therefore no vested interests embedded in organizations and institutional routines that would first have to be restructured.

Concluding Remarks

Single elements of post-Keynesian policies—which together will form part of the emerging future politicoeconomic regime of Western societies—were pioneered in the United States (deregulation) and in Japan (strategic planning and management of core production factors, especially technology, under the auspices of the state). But the EC seems to be quite successful in adopting them and, more important, in innovatively reshaping and extending them, for example, by a more harmonious combination of supply- with demand-side policies and by cushioning social side effects. In this respect, an internal historic factor seems to be important and is likely to pave the way to a future regime that will give a competitive edge to the social innovator. In the case of the EC, the weak but nevertheless emerging future polity is much more likely to recombine cultural and institutional traditions with new challenges in its policies than are the competitors across the Atlantic and the Pacific. The particularity of this lean state is related to the absence of much of a polity in the EC's past.

A closer look at future competitive edges in order to reflect the implications of West European unification for the outcome of hegemonic rivalry in the triad and the future structure of the core would be tempting. But space limits us from doing this here.[18] We shall, however, point to some issues that have to be addressed. Theories of hegemony or world leadership claim invariant cycles of the rise and fall of hegemonic core powers. Such schemes pose some problems in addressing the specific constellation at the verge of the next century, because this particular form of hegemonic instability is different from those in the past. Three elements of a well-balanced hegemony—economic, politicomilitary, and cultural leadership—have fallen apart in the competing triad formed by the United States, Western Europe, and Japan. This novel constellation might well signal a future alternative to the rise and fall of hegemonic core powers.

Notes

1. The economic relations between EFTA and EC were already decisively reinforced after the Ministerial Declaration of Luxembourg in 1984 (see Harrop 1992, p. 19).

2. The exhibition presented in the Community Pavilion is entitled: "From Renaissance Europe to the Renaissance of Europe." One main topic in the Pavilion is "The European Community, a great 20th century discovery." Note that the theme of Seville's 1992 Expo was *The Age of Discoveries*.

3. For a discussion, see Stephen George (1991).

4. Beside sometimes fierce competition among European corporations (from time to time outright "battles" between high-level capitalists, for example, De Benedetti, Agnelli, Berlusconi, and Pirelli against the Belgians, Germans, and French), they have a common interest in preserving the competitive position of their European business sites.

5. Certainly, the EC relaunch not only contained "more market," even if this remained the most effective PR motto for a long time (compare *The Cost of Non-Europe,* the Cecchini Report of 1988 invited by the Commission). Just as important was the role of strategic planning in areas where European states were hardly active before, that is, in technology planning and in management. An outline of the history of the EC industrial policy is given by Jeffrey Harrop (1992, p. 122ff).

6. For an overview of the technological cooperation of the EC see Jeffrey Harrop (1992, pp. 127–31).

7. Translated from the German version of the document. This pertains also to the other quotes below taken from Commission of the EC (1991).

8. The source is Reinhard Rode (1991, p. 239).

9. All figures are from Bornschier (1988, p. 72).

10. Our own calculations, on the basis of figures from Paul Bairoch (Bornschier 1988).

11. Many insider statements could be added. For example, Siemens is the huge German corporation in ICT. Mr. Knorr, member of the board of directors (Vorstandsmitglied) and responsible for the semiconductor business, recently confessed that Siemens cannot produce as efficiently as the Japanese chip competitors. According to him, the cost disadvantage of the Europeans amounts to 18–22 percent. Not lack of capital but rentability, as he points out, is the problem (*Süddeutsche Zeitung,* May 15, 1992, p. 32).

12. For many years, Konrad Seitz was Hans-Dietrich Genscher's planning adviser in the Foreign Office of the Federal Republic of Germany. His duties included European high technology and space policy.

13. *Johoka Shakai,* a term created by the Japanese Youichi Ito in 1966, stimulated by Fritz Machlup's study (1962). The Japanese government proclaimed their "Plan for an Information Society" as early as 1971.

14. This was at the mentioned EC conference on information-and-communication technologies in Brussels (October 1991), which the author attended.

15. For an overview of the industrial and technological policies of the EC, Harrop (1992) is a recommended reading. Harrop also surveys earlier developments back to the Spinelli Report and the Colonna Report.

16. Also new are the planned direct payments to farmers as a form of income.

17. For which the MITI (Ministry of International Trade and Industry) plays a central role. This is a kind of national planning office, with participation from industry, which sets strategic goals for home industry, encourages high performance, and supports flexibility.

18. The original conference paper included a first evaluation of the impact of West European unification on the future structure of the core. We shall deal with hegemonic rivalry and future alternatives to the rise and fall of hegemonic core powers in a separate article.

References

Attali, J. 1990. *Lignes d'horizon.* Paris: Fayard.

Bergsten, F.C. 1987. "Economic Imbalances and World Politics." *Foreign Affairs,* Summer, pp. 31–39.

Bornschier, V. 1988. *Westliche Gesellschaft im Wandel.* Frankfurt and New York: Campus.

———. 1989. "Legitimacy and Comparative Economic Success at the Core of the World System. An Exploratory Study." *European Sociological Review, 5*(3), pp. 215–30.

———. 1990. "Gesellschaftsmodell und seine Karriere. Eine Anwendung auf die Weltgesellschaft." In V. Bornschier et al., eds., *Diskontinuität des sozialen Wandels.* Frankfurt and New York: Campus, pp. 21–54.

Bornschier, V., and C. Suter. 1990. "Lange Wellen im Weltsystem." In Volker Rittberger, ed., *Theorien der Internationalen Beziehungen. Bestandsauf-nahme und Forschungsperspektiven,* Politische Vierteljahresschrift (PVS), special issue no. 21, Opladen: Westdeutscher Verlag, pp. 175–97. Extended English Version: Bornschier, V., and C. Suter. 1992. "Long Waves in the World System." In V. Bornschier and P. Lengyel, eds., *Waves, Formations and Values in the World System.* New Brunswick and London: Transaction Publishers.

Chase-Dunn, C. 1989. *Global Formation. Structures of the World Economy.* Cambridge, MA, and Oxford: Basil Blackwell.

Commission of the EC/Kommission der Europäischen Gemeinschaften. 1991. *Informations-.und Kommunikationstechnologien. Die Rolle Europas.* Generaldirektion XIII: Telekommunikation, Informationsindustrie und Innovation. Luxemburg: Amt für amtliche Veröffentlichungen der Europäischen Gemeinschaften.

Commission of the European Communities. 1992. *Europe on the Move. The European Community in the 1990s.* Booklet distributed at the occasion of the Universal Exposition, Seville, 1992. Brussels: Publications Unit.

Delors, J. 1991. "Wir müssen Grossmacht werden." Interview. *Der Spiegel, 42,* pp. 20–24.

Dertouzos, M.L., R.K. Lester, and R.M. Solow. 1989. *Made in America. Regaining the Productive Edge.* The MIT Commission on Industrial Productivity. Cambridge, MA: MIT Press.

Effinger, M., V. Rittberger, K.D. Wolf, and M. Zürn. 1990. "Internationale Regime und internationale Politik." In Volker Rittberger, ed., *Theorien der Internationalen Beziehungen. Bestandsaufnahme und Forschungsperspektiven.* Politische Vierteljahresschrift (PVS), special issue no. 21, Opladen: Westdeutscher Verlag, pp. 263–85.

Fifth Report of the Commission/Fünfter Bericht der Kommission. 1990. *Fünfter Bericht von der Kommission an den Rat und an das Europäische Parlament über die Durchführung des Weissbuches zur Vollendung des Binnenmarktes.* Brussels.

Freeman, C., and L. Soete. 1991. *Macro-Economic and Sectoral Analysis of Future Employment and Training Perspectives in the New Information Technologies in the European Community. Synthesis Report.* Study for the Commission of the European Communities. Presented at the EC-Conference in Brussels, 17–18 October.

George, S. 1991. *Politics and Policy in the European Community,* 2d ed. Oxford: Oxford University Press.

George, S. 1992. "Intergovernmentalism, Supranationalism and the Future Development of the European Community." Paper presented at the Inaugural Pan-European Conference on International Relations, Heidelberg, Germany, September.

Gerstenberger, W. 1991. *Impact of Information Technologies on Future Employment in the European Community. Study for the Commission of the European Communities.* Presented at the EC-Conference in Brussels, 17–18 October.

Gilpin, R. 1975. *U.S. Power and the Multinational Corporation.* New York: Basic Books.

———. 1987. *The Political Economy of International Relations.* Princeton: Princeton University Press.

Gut, R.E. 1991. "Das internationale Bankgeschäft im Banne von EG 92." *Bulletin. Das Schweizerische Bankmagazin*, April 1991, pp. 7–10.

Harrop, J. 1992. *The Political Economy of Integration in the European Community*, 2d ed. Aldershot: Edward Elgar.

Hurwitz, L., and C. Lequesne, eds. 1991. *The State of the European Community: Policies, Institutions and Debates in the Transition Years.* Boulder, CO, and London: Lynne Rienner Publishers and Longman.

Keohane, R.O. 1984. *After Hegemony. Cooperation and Discord in the World Political Economy.* Princeton: Princeton University Press.

Kindleberger, C. 1973. *The World in Depression.* Berkeley: University of California Press.

Krause, A. 1988. "Many Groups Lobby on Implementation of Market Plan." *Europe,* July/August.

Krasner, S.D., ed. 1983. *International Regimes.* Ithaca, NY, and London: Cornell University Press.

Lane, Frederick C. 1979. *Profits from Power: Readings in Protection Rent and Vice-Controlling Enterprises.* Albany: State University of New York Press.

Leonard, D. 1989. *Das EG-Handbuch.* Mit einem Vorwort von Roy Jenkins. Frankfurt: FAZ Informationsdienste. Original English edition: Oxford: Basil Blackwell.

Lepsius, R.M. 1991. "Nationalstaat oder Nationalitätenstaat als Modell für die Weiterentwicklung der Europäischen Gemeinschaft." In Wildenmann, R., ed., *Staatswerdung Europas? Optionen für eine Europäische Union.* Baden-Baden: Nomos, pp. 19–40.

Moravcsik, A. 1991. "Negotiating the Single European Act: National Interests and Conventional Statecraft in the European Community." *International Organization, 45*(1), pp. 19–56.

Otte, M. 1988. *The United States, Japan, West Germany and Europe in the International Economy 1977–1987: Between Conflict and Coordination.* Idstein: Schulz-Kirchner.

Putnam, R.D., and N. Bayne. 1985. *Weltwirtschaftsgipfel im Wandel.* Bonn: Europa Union Verlag.

Rapkin, D.P., ed. 1990. *World Leadership and Hegemony.* Boulder, CO, and London: Lynne Rienner Publishers.

Rode, R. 1991. "Deutschland: Weltwirtschaftsmacht oder überforderter Euro-Hegemon?" *Leviathan, 19*(2), pp. 229–60.

Sandholtz, W., and J. Zysman. 1989. "1992: Recasting the European Bargain." *World Politics, 42*(1), October, pp. 95–128.

SEA (Single European Act/Einheitliche Europäische Akte) 1987. *Verträge zur Gründung der Europäischen Gemeinschaften (EGKS, EWG, EAG). Einheitliche Europäische Akte. Texte betreffend die Gemeinschaften.* Abbreviated edition. Brussels.

Schenk, W. 1990. "Euro-Protz statt Euro-Sklerose," *Tages-Anzeiger*, 22 May, p. 31.

Schmiegelow, M. 1986. *Japan's Response to Crisis and Change in the World Economy.* Armonk, NY: M.E. Sharpe. (Enlarged German edition: Hamburg: McGraw-Hill, 1989.)

Seitz, K. 1991. *Die japanisch-amerikanische Herausforderung*, 2d ed. München: Bonn Aktuell.

Signorini, C. 1989. "The ECU, a Success Factor for the 1993 Community Market." Address in Madrid, 12 January, p. 6. (Quoted from Sandholtz and Zysman [1989, p. 95]).

van Tulder, R., and G. Junne. 1988. *European Multinationals in Core Industries*. New York: John Wiley & Sons.

Wallace, H. 1991. "The Council and the Commission after the Single European Act." In Hurwitz, L., and C. Lequesne, eds., *The State of the European Community. Policies, Institutions and Debates in the Transition Years*. Boulder, CO, and London: Lynne Rienner Publishers and Longman, pp. 19–32.

Waltz, K.N. 1979. *Theory of International Politics*. New York: McGraw-Hill.

———. 1986. "Reflections on 'Theory of International Politics': A Response to My Critics." In R.O. Keohane, ed., *Neorealism and its Critics*. New York: Praeger, pp. 322–45.

Weissbuch/White Paper. 1985. *Vollendung des Binnenmarktes. Weissbuch der Kommission an den Europäischen Rat*. Luxembourg.

Williamson, O.E. 1990. *Die ökonomischen Institutionen des Kapitalismus*. Tübingen: Mohr (Siebeck). (American edition: 1985.)

Womack, J.P., D.T. Jones, and D. Roos. 1990. *The Machine That Changed the World*. New York: Rawson. (German edition: Frankfurt: Campus, 1991.)

Young, O.R. 1986. "International Regimes. Towards a New Theory of Institutions." *World Politics, 39*(1), pp. 105–22.

MAURIZIO BACH

Technocratic Regime Building

Bureaucratic Integration in the European Community

The current political and social upheavals in Southern and Central Europe present the European Community with one of the greatest challenges in its history. One can only guess at what role the Community will play in the years to come and how this role will develop. Nor is it possible to determine its future "political geography" and institutional order. Things are in a state of flux in Europe as never before.

The political profile of the European Community has been cast in doubt as a result of dramatic developments outside it that have set limits upon its scope for action. This has been exacerbated by constant pressures for expansion and reform from within the Community itself. Nevertheless, there are clear indications that the basic institutional structures of the mechanism for achieving European unity will remain firmly in place.

There are reasons for such optimism. It has indeed proved possible to create an effective system for balancing economic interests and resolving political conflict on a European level. The fact that we have witnessed the creation of a system of order that is without historical precedent transcends national boundaries and is, in my view, a clear sign that the Community will endure. It is legitimated by the international law treaties that founded it, and underpinned by the Single European Act (Beutler et al. 1987).

What follows is based on the assumption that the common economic interests and the politically purposive association of West European states have already given rise to a supranational, quasi-etatist political institutional order with its own legitimacy and sovereignty. The development of this unique institutional order represents a fundamental break with the structures of the European nation-state (Lepsius 1990, p. 254; 1991). This leads us to revise our concept of the state completely. One could even go as far as to say that the process of market-oriented integration makes the distinct features of the social, cultural, and political make-up of the individual states appear to be premodern and therefore irrational relics of isolationist nationalism. The individual states are now forced to act together on a level that transcends their individual differences. They are subjected to extensive political but above all legal and bureaucratic rationalization. Placide Rambaud (1991) has recently demonstrated this by examining the impact of the European Agricultural Policy on the development of the farming community in France. From this point of view, European integration policy should be regarded as a process of institutional differentiation and rationalization quite unlike anything yet seen.

In this essay I shall argue that, essentially, the European Economic Community government's extraordinary capacity to implement decisions is based upon three characteristic features of its institutional order. The first of these is the institutionalization of a self-legitimating legal order, which is to be distinguished from the existing legal orders of the individual member-states and functions independently of them. The second is the development of a corporate order with extensive executive competences and its own administrative staff. The third is the formation of a distinct functional elite.

I do not intend to go into a detailed analysis of the development of European law. I shall mention only as much as is necessary for an understanding of the main focus of this essay, namely, the processes of legal and bureaucratic integration.

Let us turn then to the fundamental constitutional issues. The most important of these, the significance of which cannot been underestimated, is the direct validity of European law within each of the member-states. Community law has primacy over the laws of the individual member-states. European law is thus fundamentally at odds with the laws of the individual states (according to Art. 18 of the EEC.Constitution) (Beutler et al. 1987, p. 173; Capotorti 1988). The supremacy of EEC law is the basis of what Weiler (1981) has described as the "normative supranationalism" of the European Community. This is what distinguishes the Community from all other communities founded by international treaties (Jaenicke 1961; Bindschedler 1961).

Another distinctive feature of the way in which the Community is set up is the division of powers within it. This is at odds with what is normally considered democratic practice. Insofar as there can be said to be a formal differentiation of competences between the legislative and the executive organs in the strict sense, no such division of powers is envisioned for the institutional order of the Community (Ipsen 1987, p. 198). The most important administrative executive functions reside in the European Commission and provide the link with the business of lawmaking itself. The division of powers is regulated in an unconventional manner. There is a clear division between the Commission's authority to make laws and the Council's power to decide upon and ratify them. This gives rise to the rather odd situation in which implementation is connected with a monopoly on the drafting and proposal of legal bills. On the other hand, the Council of Ministers—the supreme decision-making body—has no right to intervene autonomously in the legislative process. The Council and the Commission have an entwined legislative competence. One body that is almost completely excluded from this is the European Parliament, although it now has a solid basis of legitimacy through direct elections. This curious feature of the political decision-making process in the European Community could be described as the realization of the normative primacy of the bureaucracy.

This method of allocating legitimation and assigning competences appears strangely asymmetrical and undemocratic in comparison to the systems of government of the different member-states. But within the legal-constitutional debate, there are those who can produce a plausible justification for it. They tend to favor a distinctly anti-etatist approach (Ipsen 1987). In fact, the disposition and structure of the Community's constitution are in accordance with the move toward political integration that is at the heart of this purposive association (see the preamble to the EEC Constitution). It is this underlying political purpose that is the driving force behind the move toward European integration and an essential part of the system as a whole. For, as Ipsen has repeatedly pointed out (1984, 1987), the European Constitution differs fundamentally from those of the individual member-states. This is the case even as concerns the goals and tasks it sets itself (Art. 2–3 of the EEC Constitution). As Ipsen explains, "It details specific objectives and mandates for action which have to be carried out on an agreed time-scale. Failure to comply with these within the agreed time-scale has specific legal consequences" (Ipsen 1987, p. 201).

Whatever the ins and outs of the strained relationship between the European treaty arrangements and national constitutions, the practical problems of political decision making and implementation are of a different order. From a sociological point of view, the real issue is which institutions have both the authority and the material resources to take decisions, and who has the real power of implementation and control.

There can be no doubt that in the policy-making process of the Community, such authority clearly rests with the Commission. This is particularly the case where dealing with everyday political and administrative problems is concerned (Wallace 1977, p. 52; Beutler et al. 1987, p. 132). What impact does this have on the process of integration in the European Community? What contribution toward integration can we expect of a European government that is concentrated in the staff organizations of the Commission?

Apart from paving the way for the administration and implementation of harmonization policies as dictated by the Constitution, what can the much criticized "European bureaucracy" do to make the member-states come together on a transnational level? In other words, what are the normatively unintended effects that flow from the logic of institution building on a European level?

Previous research on the administrative organization of the European Community might suggest an answer: The high concentration of regulatory power in the Commission makes policy making and problem solving in the European Community an extremely bureaucratic process. Let us look at the reasons for this in more detail.

We know from Max Weber's classic analysis of the bureaucracy (Weber 1921, p. 333) that effective control of the bureaucratic executive by the political leadership is possible only to a limited extent, if at all, and then only under the old parliamentary systems of government that prevailed in the nation-state. As recent empirical studies of government frequently demonstrate, most political initiatives originate in the ministerial bureaucracy (Mayntz and Scharpf 1973; Blankenburg et al. 1974; Mayntz 1978, pp. 43, 61; Windhoff-Héritier 1987). Therefore it is the bureaucracy that has the resources to deal with problems and realize its goals. It has the time and the human resources to deal with these problems. It has developed formal and informal systems of coordination and communication and is in possession of all the necessary information. It has evolved procedural routines and communication infrastructures. These are but a few of the most important characteristics of a complex bureaucratic system. The regulatory potential of political leadership, on the other hand, is generally extremely limited. Frequently, the legitimate leadership is not able to respond adequately to the executive bureaucracy's technical and administrative problems and its need for coordination. This inevitably means that the bureaucracy becomes the real center of decision making (Treiber 1977). Thus real political power and responsibility lie with the bureaucracy.

One result of this is that executive functions become independent. In effect, this means that almost all decisions made in the European Community are taken by highly trained bureaucrats working in the Commission (Weiler 1981, p. 287; Krislov et al. 1985, p. 30; Beutler et al. 1987, p. 131; Berlin 1987, p. 32).

The way the bureaucracy works is so complex that it is very difficult to get an overview. The fact that it has a monopoly on specialized knowledge and classified information and is thus impenetrable to outsiders is one of its outstanding characteristics. A brief glance at some EEC statistics illustrates my point. In 1989, the Council of Ministers made a total of 634 decisions

(Kommission 1990). During the same period, the Commission produced 5,739 legal acts. In addition, it prepared more than 600 proposals and recommendations for the Council. It should also be born in mind that, on average, nearly 90 percent of the recommendations put forward by the Commission were passed by the Council, most, after a vote without any discussion (Krislov et al. 1985, p. 44).

The Commission thus dealt with almost 6,400 decisions with legal impacts in the course of a single year. This means that an average of approximately 25 EEC decisions per working day have to be processed by the individual states' bureaucracies. What these figures show—apart from the extraordinary number of decisions processed by both central organs taken together—is that the Commission outweighs the others in decision-making power. And as we saw before, all the decisions of the Council of Ministers are taken on the Commission's recommendation. The preparation phase and the working out of the details takes place at the level of the Commission. This gives us a clearer picture of the division of powers in the Commission's bureaucracy itself. Of a yearly average of 6,500 regulations produced by the Commission, more than 350 decisions fell to one of the 17 Commissioners. These decisions were arrived at in the course of only 48 meetings—an average of 133 decisions per meeting.

This striking disproportion between the output of norms and the number of political representatives who comprise the body of Commissioners shows just how limited the capacity of those formally in charge to deal with problems must be. The plethora of norms conceals a range of complicated political, administrative, and technical procedural regulations concerning agricultural, commercial, and regional policy, as well as complicated issues regarding the internal market. The difficult task of selecting, processing, coordinating, and implementing the vast array of programs, directives, regulations, and measures that are generated daily in Brussels falls almost exclusively to the Commission bureaucracy (Peters 1992). It is this bureaucracy that ultimately decides on the substance of regulations as well as on modes of procedure. It has considerable organizational resources at its disposal and is thus in a position to determine the degree to which European law is in fact implemented in the individual member-states (Bach 1992a).

It is clear from the EEC Constitution that the Commission was not originally conceived as a public bureaucracy in the traditional sense. It not only has executive functions, but is also entrusted with legislative competences. Nevertheless, the fact that there is a real division of organizational resources, decision making, and regulatory competences within the central legislative organs of the Community clearly indicates that the bureaucracy has more authority than do the representatives of the national governments who meet in the Council of Ministers. It is thus to be expected that the integration policy of the Community is strongly influenced by the specific structures, executive rationales, and of course the self-interest of the bureaucracies engaged in developing integration policy. This impression is reinforced by the fact that most Community regulations are highly technical—for example, regulations for the "packing and labelling of dangerous substances," the "installation of safety belts in motor vehicles," the "use of pesticides," and "guidelines on the purity of emulsifiers, stabilizers, thickening and binding agents for use in the catering industry."

But is the bureaucracy the real driving force behind European integration policy? Does it have as great an influence as we are assuming here? If so, then how is this peculiar form of supranational "bureaucracy" constituted? What makes it capable of achieving integration on a European level? How does it differ from the traditional type of bureaucracy that characterizes the nation-state?

Empirical research on the organizational structure of the European Community has shown that the so-called Eurocracy represents a totally new type of public administration that is without precedent. One of the most significant findings of early neofunctionalist studies of integration (Haas 1964, p. 86) is that the administration of international organizations (for example, the United Nations) does not correspond to Weber's model of the bureaucracy. This is because staff are drawn from many countries, and because the organization has limited competences and is insufficiently rooted in the society in which it is located. These findings have been confirmed by subsequent research (Eckart 1990). The fact that it has legal supremacy in key areas of policy and a high degree of organizational autonomy distinguishes the "Eurocracy" from typical international organizations (Bindschedler 1961).

To sum up the results of my own research in this field (Bach 1992a), the form of organization that prevails in the European Community today is a system of relatively small but highly specialized groups of experts, characterized by a relatively high degree of informality and fluidity. What we are dealing with here is not so much a hierarchical official bureaucracy as an unusual transnational "expertocracy." Some of the hallmarks of the key staff organizations, above all the Commission, illustrate the main features of the system.

We shall give a brief outline of the organizational structure of the Commission: There are currently seventeen commissioners, who work in tandem with a so-called cabinet. The cabinets, with their separate *chefs de cabinet*, meet on a weekly basis. Each cabinet is modeled on the French system of a personal advisory staff and generally is comprised of civil servants of the same nationality as the cabinet's commissioner. The cabinets are in charge of areas that lie between policy making and administration. They have considerable powers, including direct sanction in important issues (Krenzler 1974; Berlin 1987, p. 45). The actual administration is currently organized into twenty-three directorates general and various departments, among them, the general secretariat, the legal department, and translating and interpreting services (Hay 1989; Schmitt von Sydow 1980; Berlin 1987, p. 34). Although there are no formal rules governing this aspect, the proportion of civil servants recruited from the various member-states roughly reflects the level of the contribution from each country. This is analogous to the way in which the commissioners themselves are selected. In 1989, a total of 23,432 civil servants at different grades were employed in all the community institutions. Of these, 15,787 were employed in the Commission, 2,700 as translators and interpreters (Kommission 1990). This is a relatively small number compared to the 22,000 civil servants employed in only the central administration of the Federal Republic of Germany (Rudzio 1991, p. 278).

The Commission is also served by numerous advisory committees and groups of experts who exercise a controlling function and greatly influence the Commission's structure. These consultative committees, which are set up by the Commission, play an ancillary role in the preparation of Commission and Council decisions (Hilf 1982, p. 111; Berlin 1987, p. 427; Schmitt von Sydow 1980, p. 131; Pag 1987, p. 450). Given the highly specialized nature of their responsibilities, the members of these committees are appointed primarily on the basis of their technical and administrative skills. They are drawn from the ministerial governments of the individual member-states as well as from large European interest organizations. It is difficult to get a clear picture of precisely how many of such organizations are involved. Estimates vary from between 400 and 600 with a more or less permanent involvement.

Since the European Community does not have the bureaucracy to implement its decisions, it is dependent upon the governments of the member-states for their implementation. The committees thus provide an important link between the Commission staffs and the different national governments. In fact, the Commission has numerous contacts with experts or civil servants in the member-states. As these experts also generally act as members of the working groups set up by the Council, the fact that they have had contact with each other at an early stage increases the likelihood of any plan being realized (Siedentopf and Ziller 1988).

The terms "co-operative federalism" (Scharpf 1985) and "co-operative bureaucracy" (Wessels 1985) have been used to characterize the way in which the European Community operates. Its system of government is based upon a unique international division of labor among bureaucracies that are legally and organizationally independent. This has led to the formation of a multitude of parallel functional and sectoral administrations, which is unusual in the centralized systems of government that are typical of Western Europe. This results in the formation of networks linking the staffs of the individual member-states' ministerial governments with those of the Commission. The Commission's communication systems can be described as networks because they represent a specifically social type of interaction.

The relations between the bureaucrats are, of course, brought about through institutional contacts. Nevertheless, there is still considerable scope for informal contact. More or less stable groups are established and the more informal relations running through these are thereby institutionalized.

Although the numerous advisory committees have no formal decision-making powers, they often represent staffs of civil servants and experts formed on an ad hoc basis (Grote 1987). It is these that form the organizational networks that bind the supranational European bureaucracy together. They furnish the most important horizontal links between the ministerial departments of the individual states and the directorates of the Commission. The political and administrative efficiency of the Commission, in both the preparatory and implementation phases of its initiatives, is thus inextricably linked with the national bureaucracies (Siedentopf and Ziller 1988, p. 27). For this reason, it can be described as a cross between the various bureaucracies. In any case, as far as the everyday functioning of the bureaucracy is concerned, integration is achieved principally on the government and expert-committee level.

If we take a closer look at these rather curious "instruments of joint management" (Cassese 1987, p. 15), we can learn more about the effects of this process of transnational bureaucratization. One striking feature is the relatively high degree of flexibility in the institutional structures of contact and communication, which nevertheless remain relatively informal. This is in marked contrast to the ideal type of bureaucratic order of the nation-state. The number of staff involved in committee work by far exceeds that of the permanent higher-grade civil servants within the Commission. In 1989 there were approximately 4,700 people employed in the higher echelons of the European civil service (Kommission 1990). It is possible to estimate the number of those seconded to Brussels for a year by multiplying the approximate number of committees (600) by 48—the average number of delegates from the individual states (four) times the number of the member-countries (twelve). This means that there are around 28,800 civil servants who form the core and the "traveling cadre" of the European Community. Counting the higher-grade civil servants of the Commission and the other organs of the Community, there are approximately 35,000 top-rank civil servants and experts in the "Eurocracy." This gives us some idea of the scale of the new European government elite in terms of the manpower involved.

The *Politikverflechtung* between bureaucracies in the European Community is based on the extraordinary mobility of government experts and representatives of large interest groups. The members of the various staffs have to travel to meetings in Brussels. The total number of those who actually travel is probably far greater than the number calculated above. There are on average 150 meetings per week with outside experts in Berlaymont, the Brussels headquarters (Hay 1989, p. 28). It is possible to estimate the number of missions undertaken by multiplying this number by the product of 50 (the number of working weeks in the year), twelve (the number of member-states), and four (the average number of delegates). This gives an annual total of approximately 360,000 civil servants traveling to meetings in Brussels.

Given the extent to which European civil servants are expected to travel, it is not possible to develop highly formalized communication between authorities on a European level. One measure of the relative informality that pervades relations between members of the advisory staffs is that their meetings are seen as forums for informal debate and exchange of information. Even at committee meetings, where there are some rules of procedure, albeit rather informal ones, the participants often come to informal agreements fairly quickly, even when conflicts of interest and differences of opinion are involved (Schmitt von Sydow 1980, p. 64). The procedure for arriving at a consensus is more informal than in other advisory bodies in the Commission. True, what we are dealing with here are opinions that are arrived at in the same way as decisions are taken in the Council (Schmitt von Sydow 1980, p. 66). However, in the vast majority of cases, a compromise decision prejudices the official decision of the Commission. One of the most important functions of these expert staffs lies in their contribution to prenegotiation (Cassese 1987, p. 15). This underlines the importance of informal consensus building for the official decision-making process of the Commission.

Another factor is the network of informal contacts developed by Commission staff. The way in which the various committees and groups of experts communicate with each other has a knock-on effect on the way things are done in the Commission itself, such that it is difficult to control the relations between the individual official experts and the different national bureaucracies. On the other hand, the development of channels of communication across national boundaries in the ministerial departments is also a way of breaking down the hierarchy and order of competences of the individual states' bureaucracies. It is these channels of communication operating on horizontal levels that provide civil servants with privileged access to information on decision-making processes in Brussels. They also often alert them to decisions being taken in other member-states. The ideal type of rational bureaucracy envisioned carefully regulated official communication that would evolve "by the book," according to traditional principles and hierarchy. In modern bureaucracies, the emphasis is very much on the role of the telecommunication (Berlin 1987, p. 302).

The notorious lack of coordination within the Commission is exacerbated by the fact that most of the technical-administrative work of regulation is carried out by specialists who are in the informal networks of the parallel administrations. This leads to the further bureaucratization of the policy-making process and has important ramifications. In effect, it means that in the decision-making process administrative decisions and procedural routines frequently become substitutes for political action.

It is primarily the Commission's bureaucratic enmeshing in policy that lays down the preconditions for the formation of a government elite of Euro-experts in the national governmental departments. Because it forms part of an international network and has supranational powers, this elite breaks through the traditional authority structures of the nation-state. Along with the relatively small staffs of the central institutions of the EEC, a new, transnational governmental elite begins to emerge. At the moment, we can only trace the broad outlines of this organizational form. It is clear, however, that it constitutes a group of leading experts, which effectively routinizes transnational cooperation on a European level.

Let us leave aside the political conference diplomacy at the European summit level and the legally regulated processes of increasing transnational market sociation and turn our attention instead to the internal processes of the formation of institutions. It now becomes apparent that European unity is essentially a creation of the bureaucracy. This is true not only in the obvious sense that the administrative implementation of political goals and programs in the Community represents a categorical, practical prerequisite for integration; but bureaucratic integration, particularly in the everyday practice of "bureaucratic policy," is also achieved through the creation of transnational, horizontal networks and the centripedal fusion of the administrations concerned. Within the framework of the institutional order outlined above, there emerges a relatively independent civil-service elite that plays a key role in the sociopolitical process of change brought about by sociation. As the distinction between legislative and executive competences blurs, the time becomes ripe for the creation of a European purpose association. This in turn would provide additional legitimation. There is thus now an apparent move toward a power structure that is more in keeping with the regulatory demands and tendencies of modern market societies toward globalization (Bell 1973, p. 358). What we are dealing with here is therefore a new type of supranational technocracy (Bach 1992b).

References

Bach, M. 1992a. "Eine leise Revolution durch Verwaltungsverfahren: Bürokratische Integrationsprozesse in der Europäischen Gemeinschaft." *Zeitschrift für Soziologie 1*, pp. 16–30.

———. 1992b. "Vom Zweckverband zum technokratischen Regime: Politische Legitimation und institutionelle Verselbständigung in der Europäischen Gemeinschaft." In H. Kaelble and A. Winkler, eds., *Nation, Nationalismus und Supranationalität*. Stuttgart.

Bell, D. 1973. *The Coming of Post-Industrial Society: A Venture in Social Forecasting*. New York: Basic Books.

Berlin, D. 1987. "Organisation et fonctionnement de la Commission des Communautés européennes." In D. Berlin, S. Pag, and C. Bourtembourg, eds., *The European Administration*. Maastricht: IEAP, pp. 21–442.

Beutler, B., S. Bieber, J. Pipkorn, and J. Streil. 1987. *Die Europäische Gemeinschaft. Rechtsordnung und Politik*, 3. Neubearbeitete Auflage. Baden-Baden: Nomos.

Bindschedler, R.L. 1961. "Internationale Organisation (Grundfragen)." In H.-J. Schlochauer, ed., *Wörterbuch des Völkerrechts*. Berlin, pp. 70–89.

Blankenburg, E., G. Schmid, and H. Treiber. 1974. "Von der reaktiven zur aktiven Politik? Darstellung und Kritik des Policy Science-Ansatzes." In P. Grottian and A. Murswieck, *Handlungsspielräume der Staatsadministration. Beiträge zur politologisch-soziologischen Verwaltungsforschung*. Hamburg: Hoffmann & Campe, pp. 37–51.

Bourtembourg, C. 1987. "La Commission des Communautés européennes: son personnel." In D. Berlin, S. Pag, and C. Bourtembourg, eds., *The European Administration*, Maastricht: IEAP, pp. 497–522.

Capotori, F. 1988. "Legal Problems of Directives, Regulations and Their Implementation." In H. Siedentopf and J. Ziller, eds., *Making European Policies Work*, vol. 1: *Comparative Syntheses*. London: Sage, pp. 151–68.

Cassese, S. 1987. "Divided Powers: European Administration and National Bureaucracies." In D. Berlin, S. Pag, and C. Bourtembourg, eds., *The European Administration*. Maastricht: IEAP, pp. 5–19.

Coombes, D. 1968. *Towards a European Civil Service*. London: PEP.

———. 1970. *Politics and Bureaucracy in the European Community*. A Portrait of the Commission of the EEC undertaken by PEP. London: PEP.

Eckart, A. 1990. *Der Unbeholfene Riese. Hierarchische Koordination in einer organisierten Anarchie: Steuerungs- und Management probleme im Verband der Vereinten Nationen*. Dissertation. Heidelberg. Manuscript.

Grote, J.R. 1987. "Steuerungsprobleme in transnationalen Beratungsgremien: Über soziale Kosten unkoordinierter Regulierung in der EG." *Jahrbuch zur Staats- und Verwaltungswissenschaft*. Baden-Baden: Nomos, pp. 227–54.

Haas, E.B. 1964. *Beyond the Nation-State: Functionalism and International Organization*. Stanford, CA: Stanford University Press.

Hay, R. 1989. *Die EG-Kommission und die Verwaltung der Gemeinschaft*. Luxemburg: Amt für amtliche Veröffentlichungen der EG.

Hilf, M. 1982. *Die Organisationsstruktur der Europäischen Gemeinschaft*. Berlin/Heidelberg/New York: Springer.

Ipsen, H.P. 1984. *Europäisches Gemeinschaftsrecht in Einzelstudien*. Baden-Baden: Nomos.

———. 1987. "Europäische Verfassung—Nationale Verfassung." *Europarecht 22*, pp. 195–213.

Jaenicke, G. 1961. "Supranationale Organisation." In H.-J. Schlochauer, ed., *Wörterbuch des Völkerrechts*. Berlin, pp. 423–58.

Jamar, J., and W. Wolfgang, eds. 1985. *Community Bureaucracy at the Crossroads—L'administration communitaire à l'heure du choix*. Bruges.

Kommission der Europäischen Gemeinschaften, *XXII. 1990. Gesamtbericht über die Tätigkeit der Europäischen Gemeinschaften 1989*. Brüssel/Luxemburg: Amt für amtliche Veröffentlichungen der EG.

Krenzler, H.G. 1974. "Die Rolle der Kabinette der Europäischen Gemeinschaften." *Europarecht 9*, pp. 75–79.

Krislov, S., C.-D. Ehlermann, and J. Weiler. 1985. "The Political Organs and the Decision-Making Process in the United States and the European Community." In M. Cappelletti, M. Seccombe, and J. Weiler, eds., *Integration Through Law. Europe and the American Federal Experience*. vol. 1, part II. Berlin/New York: De Gruyter, pp. 3–109.

Lepsius, M.R. 1990. *Interessen, Ideen, Institutionen*. Opladen: Westdeutscher Verlag.

———. 1991. "Nationalitätenstaat als Modelle für die Weiterentwicklung der Europäischen Gemeinschaft." In R. Wildenmann ed., *Staatswerdung Europas? Optionen für eine europäische Union*. Baden-Baden: Nomos, pp. 19–40.

Mayntz, R. 1978. *Soziologie der öffentlichen Verwaltung*. Heidelberg: Springer.

Mayntz, R., and F.W. Scharpf. 1973. *Planungsorganisation. Die Diskussion um die Reform von Regierung und Verwaltung des Bundes*. München: Piper.

Michelmann, H.J. 1987. "Multinational Staffing and Organizational Functioning in the Commission of the European Communities." *International Organization 32*, pp. 477–96.

Pag, S. 1987. "The Relations Between the Commission and National Bureaucracies." In D. Berlin, S. Pag, and C. Bourtembourg, eds., *The European Administration*. Maastricht: IEAP, pp. 443–96.

Peters, G.B. 1992. "Bureaucratic Politics and the Institutions of the Community." In A.M. Sbragia, ed., *Europolitics. Institutions and Policymaking in the "New" European Community*. Washington: Brookings, pp. 75–122.

Rambaud, P. 1991. "La Communauté européenne et la fin de l'exeption agricole." *Revue française de sociologie XXXII*, pp. 157–77.

Rudzio, W. 1991. *Das politische System der Bundesrepublik Deutschland*, 3rd ed. Opladen: Leske+Buderich.

Scharpf, F.W. 1985. "Die Politikverflechtungsfalle: Europäische Integration und deutscher Föderalismus im Vergleich." *Politische Vierteljahresschrift 26*, pp. 323.

Schmitt von Sydow, H. 1980. *Organe der erweiterten Europäischen Gemeinschaften—Die Kommission*. Baden-Baden: Nomos.

Siedentopf, H., and J. Ziller, eds. 1988. *Making European Policies Work. The Implementation of Community Legislation in the Member States*, vol. 1: *Comparative Syntheses;* vol. 2: *National Reports*. London: Sage.

Treiber, H. 1977. "Programmentwicklung als politischer Proze. Zum Verhältnis von Bürokratie und politischer Führung aus der Sicht der empirischen Verwaltungswissenschaft." *Zeitschrift für Politik 24*, pp. 213–339.

Wallace, H. 1977. "National Bulls in the Community China Shop: The Role of National Governments in Community Policy-Making." In H. Wallace, W. Wallace, and C. Webb, eds., *Policy-Making in the European Communities*. Chichester, pp. 33–68.

Weber, M. 1921. *Gesammelte Politische Schriften*. Tübingen: Mohr.

Weiler, J. 1981. "The Community System: the Dual Character of Supranationalism." *Yearbook of European Law, 1*, pp. 267–306.

Wessels, W. 1985. "Community Bureaucracy in a Changing Environment: Criticism, Trends, Questions." In J. Jamar and W. Wessels, eds., *Community Bureaucracy at the Crossroads—L'administration communautaire à l'heure du choix*. Bruges: IEAP, pp. 8–36.

Windhoff-Héritier, A. 1987. *Policy-Analyse. Eine Einführung*. Frankfurt/New York: Campus.

Part II

The Difficult Transition to Democracy, Market, and Civil Society in Eastern Europe

Jiří Musil

Integration and Disintegration Models

A Comment on the Postcommunist Experience

The short period of euphoria brought by the years 1989 and 1990 to the countries of Eastern Europe has been followed by a feeling of deep worry concerning their future. It is true that the first analyses by impartial though sympathetic observers pointed to the fact that the transformation of these societies would be a difficult and probably long-lasting process (Dahrendorf 1990; Touraine 1990; Offe 1991). Nevertheless, implicit in most of these analyses was the optimistic conviction that the collapse of communism had made conditions good for the gradual formation of civic societies and for their integration with Western Europe. In this respect, the analysts were of the same opinion as the active participants in the revolutions. It seems that they somehow forgot the specific economic and social heritage of East European and, to a lesser extent, Central European countries.

These early analysts naturally concentrated on the opening of the doors to democracy that accompanied the collapse of the Soviet-bloc regimes. Less thought was given to the fact that this collapse would let loose unpredicted tensions and old problems in the region. For example, it was somehow forgotten that some parts of East-Central Europe had undergone an unprecedentedly rapid process of modernization in the last 45 years, and that the distorted form of this process had led to many disequilibria. Industrialization, which had been achieved according to the Soviet model with great speed, rapid urbanization, extensive migration, and the disintegration of traditional rural communities, caused many tensions, and these were kept under control only by the use of power by the authoritarian modernizers. In addition to the problems caused by rapid modernization, there emerged unexpected tensions and conflicts that were rooted far in the precommunist past, between ethnic groups, historic regions, and different cultures. The reemergence of these ethnic conflicts and nationalist movements was a surprise to many intellectuals and dissident politicians who had lived in a consensual culture that drew meaning from the fight against a common enemy; this was often the case in Czechoslovakia.

An Endangered Scenario

The program of civic society, as expressed by the actors of the 1989 democratic revolutions, included not only the separation of society from the state and the formation of a rich network of independent social and cultural organizations, but also the conviction that the basic element of the new democracies should be the *free citizen*, not the member of a nation or of a social class. Moral and political universalism accompanied by individual responsibility was to become a barrier against national, class, and other particularities. In opposition to collectively organized socialist internationalism or to nationalistic particularities, emphasis was laid on an autonomous and ethnically anchored universalism rooted in the rationalism and individualism of the Enlightenment.

The motto "Back to Europe" did not, however, express only the effort to renew links with the spiritual traditions of Old Europe, as some authors affirmed (Habermas 1990; Furet 1990); to a great extent it also expressed the wish to become a part of an economically as well as politically integrated Europe that at the same time was freeing itself from nationalism. From the Western perspective, the mirror image of this Central European effort toward integration is the effort to suppress and control postcommunist neonationalism, in particular by demanding the preservation of the multinational states that were established after World War I in Eastern and Central Europe, the continuation of economic cooperation between some members of COMECON such as Czechoslovakia, Hungary, and Poland (Soros 1991), and respect for minorities' rights in this complicated and traditionally crisis-prone area. The ability to live in peace and cooperation within the existing multinational federation, as well as to maintain human rights, was for some time considered a test for admission into many European organizations. In the background, of course, was the fear of destabilization in Eastern and Central Europe, which would require unwanted Western engagement at a time when all available energy should be concentrated on the process of integration of the twelve members of the European Community.

The optimistic scenario of the development of postcommunist societies has been realized only in part; at the same time, the whole of Europe is threatened by the simultaneity of integration and disintegration processes. Let us first compare the situation in the so-called Other Europe with that of Western Europe.

Integration Processes and Theories

Though some objections to the Maastricht agreement have recently appeared within the EEC, the tendency to integrate has thus far prevailed over that to disintegrate. The reemergence of peripheral nationalism in its politically salient forms—in Northern Ireland, the Basque provinces, Catalonia, Scotland and Wales, and Wallonia and Flanders—may perhaps change the internal organization of some member-states. However, it is highly unlikely that these instances will significantly disturb the long-term trend toward European integration. Neither the decline of Italian national conscience—the *"nationale Entsolidarisierung"* as Gustav Seibt put it—nor the weakening of German national conscience as a consequence of the unification of Germany and the outbursts of xenophobia in some German cities will become serious obstacles to European integration.

Developments in Central and Eastern Europe, on the contrary, have more dangerous features. The simple reality that in 1993 there are twenty-two sovereign states in Eastern Europe, instead of the original nine, is symptomatic of this danger.

In some countries, such as Czechoslovakia, disintegration of the state occurred amid the transformation of the entire economic and political system. The disintegration of a state can slow down or even stop economic and political transition, postpone membership in the EEC, or engender other complications in external relations.

Having thus been trapped by history once again—how many times has it already happened?—the countries of Central and Eastern Europe should accept the challenges to review critically the models of integration that form the background of our reflections on the future of Europe and to analyze the causes of the disintegration process.

There are two main approaches to the theory of integration: the older one, which can be labeled as functionally transactional, and the newer, community-based one. The intellectual sources of the functionally transactional integration model of national states into so-called higher forms of international community are numerous and varied, and go deep into the past. They can be found in the liberal economic theory of the expanding market and division of labor, in some generalizations of the historical school of economics, in the sociology of Spencer, Durkheim, and Tönnies as well as in Ratzel's anthropogeography, in human ecology, especially Hawley's interpretation, and in the work of several regional and political geographers concerned with development of sociospatial systems. Here I can try only to outline the principal features of this model, an amalgam of these sources. This model has become an argument for practical integration policies. If, in Durkheim's words, such a model expresses the "organization of the advanced societies," then support of its trends can speed up the development of the system, which is the necessary consequence of the logic of modern societies' organization. This rather deterministic standpoint is usually accompanied by an ethical or normative argument that stresses the advantages of integrating national states into supranational units.

More generally, integration processes are a necessary part of the development of advanced industrial societies and of modernization, and they could not take place without modern industrial states and urbanization, which are characterized by the concentration of economic and political power and by spatial territorial hierarchy. The improvement of transportation and communication is a vital part of and a condition for integration. Moreover, integration depends on the increasing compatibility of legal systems, on a growing efficiency and interpenetration of administrations, and on a certain amount of cultural standardization. A certain amount of social similarity—for instance, in standards of living, social services, and labor codes—within the individual countries is another precondition of the success of integration processes. Within this model, some degree of social and cultural similarity is generally considered necessary for integration. However, Czechoslovak experience proved that similarity or even identity of sociostructural features is not sufficient to preserve a unitarian or federal state. Czechoslovakia split at the very moment when its constituent parts were, structurally speaking, more similar to each other than ever. The Czechoslovak lesson should be remembered in the context of West European integration processes; preservation of a federal state depends not only on structural similarities but to a large extent on feelings of common identity and mutual solidarity.

The integration model itself can be described as a complex of interlinked processes, which primarily include:

- the formation of constantly expanding market territories, in conjunction with a shift from local to urban, national, and international markets;
- the deepening of the territorial division of labor and a growing specialization and concentration of economic activities;
- the establishment of complementarity and interdependence of cities, regions, and states on the bases of difference and symbiotic competition;
- the growth of exchange of goods, capital, and information among the individual countries;
- direct interaction and competition among regions, large cities, and metropolitan areas in the various countries, and specialization within them;
- a growing mobility of labor among regions and states, and an increasing number of mutual cultural, social, and scientific contacts;
- a growing participation in supranational activities and international organizations.

This functionally transactional model of integration rests on what Ernest Gellner (1992) describes as the narrower or Weberian rationality. This rationality was a precondition for the development of science and technology and of highly productive economies.

The community-based model of integration, on the other hand, points to the need for another type of rationality, which Gellner connects with Durkheim: "Rationality, in a generic sense, can be equated with the submission to socially shared, communally distinctive and compulsively internalized concepts" (ibid.). In this model, emphasis is laid on communication, cohesion, and cooperation.

International integration, according to this second model, is a process by which, in addition to loyalty to locality, region, and state, there gradually emerges loyalty to the supranational community. The decisive moment is that of the creation of community: People living in a newly developing and integrating political unit begin to share "mutual ties of one kind or another which give the group a feeling of identity and self-awareness" (Jacob and Teune 1964). This model emphasizes the need for a consensus in European culture based on common values and ideas, common interests, and common dangers.

The second model provides an answer to the central flaw of the first, the expression of Zweck-Rationalität: namely, that it is difficult to imagine that an integrated Europe can be created in the form of a huge and well-managed international corporation. The new Europe must also be a community based on clearly formulated goals, shared values, solidarity, and participation. Without consciousness of European citizenship, there will be no united Europe. An instrumental economic, organizational rationality, if not accompanied by a value rationality, can lead to new forms of domination. More and more frequently, voices are heard—not only from within the smaller European countries but also from within France and Germany, the two main locomotors of European integration—warning against new forms of hegemony by these two protagonists of integration.

In spite of these problems, and in spite of the conceptual differences regarding the most desirable form of European unity, the long-term trend is evident. Step by step, Western Europe is becoming more integrated. Meanwhile, a mere glimpse shows that Central and Eastern Europe are developing along entirely different lines. Not only did regional trade diminish sharply with the disintegration of the counterpart of the EEC, COMECON, but rapid fragmentation is taking place within existing East and Central European federations. Destructive regionalism has begun to appear even in such unitarian states as Poland.

Fragmentation and Disintegration Processes

Numerous studies on postcommunist societies explain the fragmentation processes as consequences of nationalism. Nationalism is understood as a kind of latent destructive vice, as something given that had not previously had the opportunity to manifest itself. It seems to me that it is much more important to pose this question in reverse form: *What has caused the outbreak of nationalism, regionalism, and other fragmentation processes in these societies?*

Several hypotheses attempt to explain postcommunist nationalism:

1. Nationalism is a reaction to the forced integration and centralism practiced in the name of socialist internationalism.

2. The events of 1989 were "rectifying revolutions," the main goal of which was to return the former socialist countries to the natural political development of the other European nations. This "rectification" includes the idea that *only now* can the Wilsonian principle of the self-determination of nations be fully applied: What Georgia, Ukraine, or Armenia, for example, were not able to achieve after 1917, or what the Baltic republics had taken from them in 1940, they will achieve now.

3. The third interpretation applies to cases such as that of Slovakia: The stronger partner in a federation stimulated or even created the new identity of the weaker partner—for instance, by developing education and industrialization—and this junior partner, which was for long decades a member of a unitarian or federal state, now claims full independence.

4. The phenomena of an ideological vacuum and anomie in postcommunist societies are emphasized. The space left empty after the collapse of Marxist ideology is quickly being filled with populist nationalism, which for a large stratum of some East European countries is more attractive than liberal democracy, and reflects the renewal of national traditions.

5. M. Hechter's (1975) concept of the internal dependence of the weaker part of a nonunitary state on the stronger one is combined with the idea of mobilizing elites (McKay 1982). On the basis of existing or assumed inequalities, there emerge new political elites that use this argument and with it mobilize the masses.

6. This hypothesis is based on the opinion that postcommunist neonationalism is the consequence of the latent feeling of Central and East European countries' inability—but often also of their unwillingness—to accept Western political and economic models; here, the recognition that East European societies do not have the internal social and political preconditions for developing a robust market economy and liberal democracy is

easily transmutable into both explicit nationalistic opposition to joining the universalist European Societas Civilis and the cultivation of introverted ideologies that stress social and cultural specificities as well as the protection of national economies. Such nationalist attitudes may be coupled with other standpoints or political philosophies such as populism, socialism, and capitalism.

The sixth hypothesis is important. It shows the possible dangers of a certain repetition of nineteenth- and early twentieth-century European development, when the difficulties of applying the liberal West European model in Central and Eastern Europe resulted in a questioning of the positive values of this model. The spirit of Johann Gottlieb Fichte's national socialism or, in a better example, of national capitalism as preached by Friedrich List, has begun to hover over Europe once again (Szporluk 1988, Berend 1986). As at that time, postcommunist Central and Eastern Europe today are exposed to the challenge of the more dynamic and efficient economy, technology, and organization of Western Europe. This occurs against the backdrop of a situation in which the states of this region must, after the collapse of their old political structures, redefine their *raison d'état,* often beginning from a definition of their fundamental identity, and in which many of them are completing the postponed process of national emancipation at the same time that they are trying to privatize their economies. In a certain sense, the present differences between both parts of Europe are bigger than they were in the nineteenth century. It is incredible how severely we underestimate the differences in social development and the cleavages that have arisen between the Eastern/Central and Western societies of Europe during the last half century.

The difference in stages of social evolution between the "two Europes" is so great that only the utmost efforts on both sides can help to overcome it. That we are standing at a crossroads seems evident: If the choices made are unfavorable, postcommunist Europe could again slide down to the position of what Ivan T. Berend (1986) has called the "crisis zone of Europe"—relatively closed countries not much involved in the international division of labor; countries whose living standard would be lower for a long time and that would lack functioning bureaucracies, a modern middle class, and capable ruling elites; countries that would have many dissatisfied and ambitious intellectuals and a passive working class. Even if they escaped collapsing into such an extreme kind of "incomplete society," the countries of Central and Eastern Europe would remain unbalanced.

To achieve the favorable alternative, many difficult conditions must be achieved, including the emergence of an unfragmented and relatively stable ruling elite that would be able to formulate goals and values for the new states, and economic reconstruction leading to a market economy and at the same time the creation of social institutions enabling reform. Social consensus must be safeguarded or, at least, great social conflicts must be minimized; classical parliamentary democracy should be combined with corporatistic negotiation mechanisms; the process of national emancipations must be carried out without bloodshed and followed immediately by the formation of links with supranational formations. Finally, the optimistic scenario cannot be realized without foreign material and spiritual assistance.

Let us however return to our main issue: the relationship of the integration and disintegration processes. A simple question should be asked: Is the dismemberment of existing states a disintegration of society under all circumstances? When I was preparing this paper, I reread Thomas Garrigue Masaryk's *New Europe* (1920). Masaryk actively worked for the dismemberment of the Austro-Hungarian Empire and fought for the creation of new small states based on national self-determination. At the same time, however, he wanted to create a new united Europe as quickly as possible. Is not the present situation to a certain extent similar? Are we not observing in Central and Eastern Europe a process of *necessary restructuring*, whose first phase is the disintegration of old political units only after which the integration of the newly emerging national states into an integrating Europe will follow? Are we not witnessing here a combination of economic and organizational rationality with the need for the national and supranational identities expressing the modern value rationality? Is it not a societal process of a complementary nature when almost simultaneously the old, outlived, and often rejected state structures are dissolving while new ones come into being and integrate again? The key question is *how* this restructuring is carried out, and whether the restructuring will get stuck in the fragmentation phase. If Eastern Europe succeeds in making the transition from the disintegration to the integration phase, Masaryk's visionary prediction written at the end of World War I would come true: "The independence of small nations is not opposed to the tendency of the development which strengthens the increasingly closer ties between states and nations; it is true that individuals and nations have a need to unite with others and history heads for the organization of all mankind. . . . A real federation of nations will emerge only when the nations are free and unite of their own will. This is the direction of Europe's future."

References

Berend, I.T. 1986. *The Crisis Zone of Europe*. Cambridge: Cambridge University Press.
Dahrendorf, R. 1990. *Reflections of the Revolution in Europe*. London: Chatto and Windus.

Furet, F. 1990. Lecture given at the Institute of Sociology, Czechoslovak Academy of Sciences, Prague.

Gellner, E. 1992. *Reason and Culture*. Oxford: Blackwell.

Habermas, J. 1990. *Die nachholende Revolution*. Frankfurt: Suhrkamp.

Hawley, A.H. 1986. *Human Ecology. A Theoretical Essay*. Chicago and London: University of Chicago Press.

Hechter, M. 1975. *Internal Colonialism: The Celtic Fringe in British National Development*. London: Routledge.

Jacob, P.E., and H. Teune. 1964. "The Integrative Process; Guidelines for the Analysis of the Bases of Political Community." In P.A. Jacob and J.R. Toscano, eds., *The Integration of Political Communities*. Philadelphia: Lippincott.

McKay, J. 1982. "An Exploratory Synthesis of Primordial and Mobilizationist Approaches to Ethnic Phenomena." *Ethnic and Racial Studies,* no. 5, pp. 395–420.

Masaryk, T.G. 1920. *Nová Evropa. Stanovisko slovanské*. Prague: G. Dubský.

Offe, C. 1991. *Capitalism by Democratic Design. Democratic Theory Facing the Triple Transition in East Central Europe*. Buenos Aires: IPSA Congress, July.

Rupnik, J. 1989. *The Other Europe*. London: Weidenfeld and Nicolson.

Seibt, G. 1992. "Europa Idee ohne Gestalt." *Frankfurter Allgemeine Zeitung*, July.

Soros, G. 1991. *Směnka na demokracii* [Underwriting Democracy]. Prague: Prostor.

Szporluk, R. 1988. *Communism and Nationalism: Karl Marx versus Friedrich List.* Oxford: Oxford University Press.

Touraine, A. 1990. "Zrod postkomunistický ch spoločností." *Sociólogia*, vol. 23, no. 4, pp. 301–18.

WLODZIMIERZ WESOLOWSKI

Postcommunist Transition to Democracy

Conflicting Principles of Political Action and Change

As time passes, it is becoming clearer that the transition from communism to democracy and market economy in East-Central Europe (Poland, Hungary, the Czech Republic, and Slovakia) is shaped by many local factors: traditions, both old and new; the different degrees of cultural proximity to Western societies; the quality of leaders and political activists; the expectations and behavioral patterns of the masses; and the consequences, unintended as well as intended, of the first protests.

When the countries of the former Soviet Union and the former Yugoslavia are included in comparisons, the range of differences increases. We see that at least two contrasting models of political systems may emerge in the postcommunist countries.

The first is a system of bureaucratic authoritarianism combined with nationalist ideology that exploits both old communist structures and nationalist emotions to build the new regime. Such systems retain some features of a command economy. Countries that are moving in this direction include Ukraine, Russia, Serbia, and Romania.

Second, and typologically at the opposite extreme, are countries becoming liberal-democratic states. Examples are Hungary, Bohemia, and Poland. Their constitutional state organs function acceptably though not in an exemplary way. The political rights of citizens are secured. The transformation to private ownership and market-regulated economies seems assured in these countries.

Within a democratic type we see variations. Sociohistorical context complicates the typological profile. In Poland, for example, there is a special place for organized workers in the first stage, and possibly in the subsequent stages, of the transformation.

There are also some particularities of mass psychology (attitudinal properties) that will probably play a role in shaping specific features of each democracy within the region. I will refer to some of them while analyzing the Polish case. Emphasizing the present "Polish features" does not preclude, however, that some similar patterns will emerge in other countries of the region. In fact, I am inclined to see some converging trends in the future developments in Hungary, Poland, and the Czech Republic. These converging features may be linked to my typology of "social ties" or "social relationships." What is of *greatest* interest to me is a particular role of a *communitarian* type of the relationship.

Let me suggest three master concepts: *associative ties*, *communal ties*, and *communitarian ties*. These concepts have not, before now, been used to analyze the transformational processes in the former Soviet bloc. But they are not completely alien to sociologists. They derive from the famous *Gemeinschaft/Gesellschaft* dichotomy introduced by Ferdinand Toennies (1974) and from the Weberian concepts of *associative* and *communal* relations (Weber 1968).

The first two master concepts, *associative* and *communal ties,* are in a Weberian sense "pure" *ideal-typical* constructs. They overemphasize certain sets of characteristics that in reality are rarely met in a complete constellation with a high intensity of each characteristic.

In contrast, the third master concept, *communitarian ties,* is of a mixed character, and there may be many subvariants of it. In pointing to the possible variants, I am again following Weber's methodological belief, that mixed types of social arrangements are closer to reality. They may also be more likely than "pure types" to survive and function successfully. (This does not mean that "pure types" cannot exist at all.)

Groups held together by *associative ties* show certain characteristics: They are freely joined and freely left. They usually rely on sociopolitical discourse to reach conclusions. They pursue interests and goals laid down by their members. They show a propensity for internal loyalty based on rational calculations, yet when they negotiate with other groups, they treat them as equally valid social units.

These associative characteristics create a framework for resolving conflicts between groups and are typical of stable Western democracies. At the most abstract level, they can be seen as generic features of civil society and a democratic state. Society organized in the state is a "union of unions," to use here the phrase of John Rawls (1971). If associative groups use established procedures of the democratic political game, they may have an integrative influence on the whole societal system.

Communal ties are of a different character. An individual is born to them, or at least is considered by fellow members to have been born to them. Individuals are integrated into the group by a set of symbols, values, and beliefs that produce a high degree of loyalty and devotion to the group. At the same time, communal groups display a tendency toward separateness and closure. For all these reasons, they are much more prone to generate intergroup conflicts than are associative groups. In extreme cases, other groups appear not only to be alien but also fundamentally misguided in their values; they may see other groups as a threat. The communal group's high degree of internal cohesiveness is coupled with a high potential for divisiveness within the society as a whole. Ethnic or national groups as well as religious groups belong to this type of group, which I will also refer to as "spiritual communities." In forming this concept of "spiritual community" I am inspired by Benedict Anderson's *Imagined Communities* (1983).

The third type, which I am calling here *communitarian ties*, combines characteristics of associative and of communal bonds. Freedom of access to the group is coupled with acceptance of some core values. Communitarian groups act to increase cooperation, both within the group and among groups. The procedures for resolving conflicts combine two elements: First, they refer to some core "human value"—for example to the principle of Christian brotherhood. Second, they involve pragmatic principles that have developed over a long time. In my concept of communitarian ties, I am drawing on the recent debate between "liberals and communitarians" (Mulhall and Swift 1992).

There are two types of communitarian bonds with different intellectual roots and practical guidelines, though their social results can be quite similar. The first respects tradition and is guided by a belief in one's duties toward one's fellow human beings and a larger community of "like" or "similar" people. Christian social doctrines (Protestant and Catholic) have usually been seen as promoting a communitarian social attitude. The Protestant version stresses the role of smaller communities with faithful and egalitarian relationships inside the community, while the Catholic version stresses spiritual bonds of universal Ecclesia and the hierarchy within it.

The second subtype of communitarian thought and practice has its intellectual roots in social-democratic principles and practices. Some versions of liberalism are also close to it. This school of thought is united around the belief that society is, or should be, bound together by the principles of cooperation, mutual aid, and the organized provision of basic goods for every member of the society. Social relations are both associative, in providing welfare, and communal, in producing social cohesion through affiliation to certain core values, such as solidarity, liberty, and democracy. Society as a whole is seen as a community of the highest order. Consequently, there is an approval of the state as an agent acting on behalf of the society.

A society organized according to any of these three types of social bond will experience both integrative and disintegrative tendencies. The three types may be seen as releasing definite social forces that now operate within postcommunist societies. Therefore, while my analysis will be concrete and historical, I will try to raise it to a theoretical level at which these three types of bonds are conceived of as dynamic agents of change.

From Communal Ethos to Individualistic Creed?

In Poland, Solidarity as a sociopolitical movement bore some resemblance to Western social movements (Dalton and Kuechler 1990), but the differences were greater. While Western movements since the 1960s have been single-issue movements, Solidarity was a general movement opposing communism. Its critique of the old system was holistic, and its principles and program sought to organize society in a completely new way. The so-called Solidarity ethos focused on certain core values in its social thinking. These included national independence, human dignity, societal solidarity, and fair industrial relations.

Solidarity resembled West European social movements in its reliance on direct actions like demonstrations and on direct democratic procedures, and in its distrust of fixed internal structures. It was determined to avoid distinctions between the leaders and the led and assumed that everyone viewed the situation in the same way and had the same goals. Personal contacts mattered a lot. At the factory level, workers practiced direct democracy in making decisions. At the regional and the national levels, leaders were treated simply as experts or organizers to whom the body of the movement temporarily delegated some functions in pursuit of the common goal. Not even Lech Walesa, though he was seen by many as a charismatic leader, was an exception. He was just one of us, and nobody was prepared to give him any special powers or prerogatives. All these were strong communal features (Kowalski 1990).

Over all these features reigned the very concept of Solidarity itself. This idea drew on elements of Polish culture, both popular and intellectual. This included Christian theology, as well as the philosophy of Polish Romanticism, a movement that was as much literary as political and which has been transmitted to this day through the literature taught in schools. Solidarity also had roots in the living social memories of the Polish people's heroic and communal opposition to Germanization and Russification over the past 150 years.

Solidarity, as it emerged in 1980–81, was therefore a product of Polish culture. It placed a strong emphasis on sacrifice and devotion to human values. It also considered the idea of self-government to be important. The Solidarity program, adopted at the 1981 congress, proposed an organization of society based on networks of self-governments.

After communism collapsed, it became clear that the Solidarity ethos did not provide a set of workable principles for the future organization of the society. Entering the victorious stage of the anticommunist revolution—in other words becoming the ruling movement—demanded a historical switch in the perception of goals and principles of societal organization and integration. Market economy, private property, and parliamentary (indirect) democracy had to be brought into being. For those purposes, the Solidarity ethos, and Solidarity's internal organization and methods of acting, were inappropriate, and even counterproductive.

All of the consequences of this historical switch have not yet been fully recognized. Let me discuss some consequences that have been already mentioned by other commentators, and suggest some others that have not. Between 1981, when martial law was imposed, and 1989, the year of Solidarity's resurgence and ultimate victory, there were eight years to reflect on principles, strategies, and structures. At the intellectual level, this involved facing the fact that the future democratic society would have to be organized on different principles than those of self-government; on formal democratic rather than direct communal ties. It had to be faced that direct action would not be useful in constructing a viable democratic system, that the role of trade unions had to be limited, and so on. Intellectual circles came to realize that Solidarity itself was in a way the swan song of Polish Romanticism (Janion 1991).

Popular opinion has been changing slowly and has diversified. Since Solidarity came to power, there has been an accelerating diversification of strategies; of what is to be done and how it is to be done; of the roles of the leaders and the led in the whole process of transformation; and of the roles of the trade union Solidarity and the political movement Solidarity. However, the popular type of thinking embedded in the imagery of national liberation and in the Christian faith has not disappeared. Assessing their strengths is the most difficult though the most important aspect of sociological analysis today.

Since 1989, the program to reform the economy and to build a democratic state has been at the front of people's minds. Society has perceived the situation in both areas as unsatisfactory. In economics, the decline in the standard of living has continued unchecked. Privatization has been very slow. Everywhere there have been signs that public-sector industry is falling apart. The policies adopted by the government for economic transformation have inadvertently led to the deactivation, rather than the mobilization, of the people.

Viewed overall, society in the last three years seemed to oscillate between apathy and rebellion. In factories remaining under public ownership, in hospitals and in schools, some groups of people were withdrawing from public life completely, while others were ready to organize militant strikes. In July 1992, the accumulated dissatisfaction produced a big wave of strikes. They mounted again in the winter of 1992 and the late spring of 1993.

On the one hand, the rebellious workers refused to accept that they should have to pay a high price for the glorious victory over the Communists. They still see the victory of Solidarity as solely of their own making, not as a gift of geopolitics or the international collapse of communism. On the other hand, those who are apathetic possibly see no viable alternative to the path that has been chosen, the path leading to a society based on individual endeavor, risk, and political bargaining—a society that was not envisaged in the Solidarity ethos.

Underpinning this situation is a growing split between the leaders and the rest of society. The leaders are determined to install a completely new set of regulatory principles for societal organization: individualism, as a source of success; contracts, as the regulative principle between individual duties and obligations; liberty, to take risks that could result in failure; and the mediation of conflicts through bargaining outside of governmental structures. These are all elements of the liberal creed. Typologically, associative relationships are pertinent to a liberal society.

In the economic sphere, the successive Solidarity governments have all carried out neoliberal, laissez-faire programs. Many results of those programs have dissatisfied workers and employees and have led them to question the direction that reforms are taking. Over the whole year of 1992, the results of public opinion polls showed that 60 percent or more respondents held the opinion that "things are going in a wrong direction" (Demoskop 1993).

In politics, to a greater degree than in economics, the liberal program of the leaders has been much more in accord with popular expectations. This is true, for example, regarding individual freedom, political rights of free speech, freedom of association, and freedom of the press. But public opinion, though unorganized, has shown clearly its disapproval of the political conduct of the governing elite. The quarrels among the leaders of the emerging parties, which have contributed to an inefficient party and government system, have been especially important in creating the negative image of government and of politics in general. When a sample of the population was asked what kinds of conflict exist at present in Polish society, the answers most often pointed to conflicts within the structure of power: among the political parties and among the state organs (the president, the parliament, the cabinet) (CBOS 1992). Sociological research gives evidence of the return of the popular division into "them" and "us" in people's perceptions of social cleavages (Adamski 1993; Ciacek and Nowak 1993).

The lack of trust in the political institutions and the leaders is coupled with a distancing of the people from economic concepts, from government actions, and from the official political scene. This, in consequence, leads people to completely neglect their participation as citizens in the established democratic processes and institutions. Thus the potential *transformative power* is weakened and stays dormant in those sections of the population that otherwise could be activated (Wesolowski 1993).

The failure of the neoliberal program to effect a speedy and effective transformation of the economy has revitalized communal feelings and communal strategies. Those unable to participate in individualist strategies for arranging their own lives are returning to a modified version of the early Solidarity assumptions and modes of action. During strikes, people voiced dissatisfaction with the methods of privatization that exclude them from negotiations and planning. They still urge the government to represent them and not to abandon them to impersonal market forces. Two national trade-union federations evidently favor communal attitudes. The first is a federation grouping the former Communist branch unions. The second is a radical wing of the former Solidarity, called Solidarity '80, which split with the core trade-union organization because it perceived Solidarity's mainstream as too moderate in its fight against communism and too submissive to the liberal policies of the government.

The core of the Solidarity trade-union organization is looking for a rather moderate position. There is a possibility that it will opt for arrangements with features of the communitarian type of relationships. This will require a rather difficult though not impossible trade-union policy: opposing the rebellious workers and the neoliberal government equally.

From the rebellious factories and mines there emerges an interesting picture of how the militant workers believe conflicts should be resolved and society should be governed. Some groups of uncompromising workers urge Walesa, as president, to bypass the laws and resolve industrial conflicts directly. This would mean that the political process would be extended beyond the field of formal democratic institutions into that of direct negotiations among the president, the government, and workers. From their "class" standpoint, these rebellious workers see politics as something that happens between the rulers and the ruled. Democratic institutions are outside this relationship.

On the whole, the recurring wave of strikes revealed three important elements in the outlook of the militant Polish workers. First, they deliberately aimed to gain *direct political influence* in order to satisfy their economic interests. They wanted to circumvent the leaders of the official Solidarity trade unions, and to compel the government to change the laws covering industrial regulations.

Second, they were half-consciously *re-creating* a sociopolitical identity that is specific to workers and had last been seen in 1980–81. They wanted to resurrect a political movement in defense of "the common people." They saw themselves as the avant garde of the people, driven to oppose the incompetent and insensitive governmental elite. They appealed to the vision of a working class with a common interest and a collective sense of identity.

Third, they were *reactivating* workers' communal ties through strikes as direct communal action. In the factory, a strike creates a feeling of fellowship, of intimacy and of strong social cohesion. Workers across the country, including those who do not strike as well as those who do, tend to be hostile to all attempts to individualize their economic position, whether those attempts are by management or by impersonal economic processes. They oppose processes of selecting those who will stay on the job and who will have to go. They display *anti-individualism* and preach solidarity.

These features attest to an attempt at revoking the communal ties that were so pronounced in the Solidarity ethos and practice of 1980–81. These features also indicate a lasting adherence of the militant workers to the communal type of social imagery.

However, there are also some signs of an emerging communitarian type of social imagery and practice. These practices could help the "moderate communal" and the "moderate associative" types of societal bonds to evolve, and—in the long run—they could help to crystallize mature communitarian social relationships. The symptoms of this new orientation are seen in factories in which the employee committees have prepared thoughtful, detailed plans for marketization and privatization, securing in these same plans the material interests of workers and their rights to participate in management. The new trend is also seen at the top level of the Solidarity trade-union organization. Recently, the long awaited Social and Industrial Pact has been signed between the trade unions and the government. The leadership of the Solidarity trade union played a pivotal role in preparing several parts of that pact, though the postcommunist trade unions and the deviant Solidarity '80 signed it too. The participation of workers in all aspects of the transformative processes is written into the pact (Kowalik 1992a; 1992b).

The communitarian attitude produces both a readiness to defend tangible group interests and a will to deliver social support to citizens faced with an economic or political threat. Communitarian values may be seen as embodied in the pact because they appeal to the concept of the common good of the national community organized in a liberal state.

Trade unions have emerged in the liberal democratic society as the most important incarnation of civic association in the sphere of economic life. In the course of capitalist development, the sphere of socioeconomic bargaining has acquired some permanent features and stabilizing functions. These features have not fully developed in Poland yet. They are in a nascent and formative stage. Together with the larger socioeconomic environment, the associative-group mediation process may be characterized as follows:

(a) Group interests are clearly articulated and well defined. They are group-centered and "selfish." They are pragmatically calculated as "achievable" within the given system and by that token they are intrasystemic.
(b) Parameters of the whole economic system are settled and constitute a comprehensible framework for action for each interest group that is involved in the intergroup mediation.
(c) The gains and the losses of each group—partners to social bargaining and mediation—depend on the accumulated potential of each group (such as financial resources, organizational strength, and actualized bargaining skills); factors that are external to this complex play a secondary role.

Not all of these features have yet formed. Instead, and at the very time they were expected to be taking shape, powerful counteracting factors are in operation: a strong feeling of national cohesion; the perception of other nations' economic interests as a threat; the egalitarian sentiment of a "common fate" of all "working people"; the popular thought that the whole community is responsible for the individuals and groups that suffer unearned discrimination from the systemic changes (permanent unemployment, low pensions, insufficient resources to protect the family). These attitudes are deeply rooted in popular psychology and belong to the "communal" type of social imagery. They are upheld by some ongoing social practices (many strikes have been organized as "solidarity strikes" to support fellow workers from other industries or to protect the interests of the unemployed or pensioners). Hence, the strategic question to be answered today by intellectuals, politicians, and experts is whether to combat uncompromisingly the communal sentiments of the Polish people and forcibly develop a pure type of associative relations, or to apply a strategy that will be conducive to the formation of the communitarian type of relationships.

Political Fragmentation and Three Types of Parties

Polish economy and society have almost inevitably entered the stage of "no-system" or "systemic indistinctiveness" (Kolodko 1992)—that is, a co-existence of conflicting institutional arrangements, unclear social attitudes, and vague guidelines for action. Society is comprised of an only partially understandable conglomerate of groups. After three years of market reforms and delayed institutional changes (privatization processes), the economic interest structure is neither new nor old. People have difficulty calculating their interests in the long run (Kozek 1991, p. 186). The impulses from the structure of interests to the political scene tend to reflect the old perceptions of interests rather than the new ones, or else they are linked to the pressing, existential needs of those segments of population that are most threatened by the process of transition. In parallel, Polish political parties that emerged after 1989 exist at the level of leadership but not at the grass roots. Therefore the political scene does not as yet resemble the "civil society" model. In the economic life of the society, no single principle of the structurization of interests has yet been able to dominate others. In political life, no single definite vision of a "good polity" has emerged to dominate popular thinking and provide guidelines for politicians. The inadequacy of the Solidarity ethos for the construction of liberal parliamentary democracy has given way to the great diversification of political concepts.

Just before the election in 1990–91, more than a hundred would-be parties appeared on the Polish political scene. Since that election, the Polish parliament has been made up of twenty-nine factions (Gebethner and Raciborski 1992). Only some of them have links—rather weak links, at that—with larger sections of the population. Most parties lack real local branches. These political parties are not real parties because they serve neither as an articulating channel nor as an organizational link between society at large and governmental bodies. They lack well-articulated, specific political and economic programs.

Unlike in Western societies, Poland's fragmented party system cannot be mapped on a simple left-to-right political axis, as individual parties often combine elements from widely different parts of the spectrum. The many competing ideological divisions in Polish politics also prevent the party system from coalescing into comprehensible larger units.

There are five main ideological divisions cutting across the Polish party system: *national* and *universal*; *confessional* and *secular*; *authoritarian* and *democratic*; *laissez-faire and interventionist*; and the *communist-purging* and *communist-forgiving* division. By interventionist, I mean both those advocating an active government role in the economy and those supporting "safety-net" programs. The fifth division is peculiar to former communist societies. It is between those demanding the purging of former communists from many or all areas of public life and those who wish, in the phrase of Tadeusz Mazowiecki, to "draw a thick line under the past."

On the national/universal dimension, parties are characterized by their approach to the nation's interests and icons. At one extreme, we find parties warning that the national culture and interest are in danger from international capital, from Germans, from Russians, and from non-Poles (by which they tend to mean Jews). Meanwhile, at the other extreme are parties that favor integrating Poland into Europe (and that of course includes Germany), that favor the strengthening of cultural ties with Western Europe, and that favor attracting foreign capital to rescue the economy.

Nearly every main division is somehow muted by subdivisions. For example, on the nationalist side, there will be those who simply urge caution in negotiating economic treaties with the EC and want trade links with other countries on the best possible terms, while others believe that Poland must defend herself from internal and external plots and advocate keeping the Polish people in a permanent state of readiness against alleged enemies, even to the extent of creating paramilitary organizations.

One can find similar subdivisions within each main division. Possibly the most important are the subdivisions along the confessional/secular divide. It is widely accepted that in Poland there is a growing conflict between secular politicians and some politicians closely linked to the Roman Catholic Church hierarchy who push for antiabortion laws and for religion to be taught in schools in a way that would discriminate against children from nonbelieving families. However, there are many Roman Catholics, from prominent intellectuals to the rank and file, who oppose making Poland a confessional state. They are silent on abortion, but on other issues they show more modern, if not liberal, positions. They are not traditional conservatives, but rather progressive thinkers and activists trying to bring the Catholic Church closer to Western thinking about its role and about the proper relationship of Catholics with the rest of society. They are in open conflict with conservative Catholic politicians who insist on the need to place public life under the control of so-called Christian values, or who combine a conservative obedience to hierarchy with a nationalist hatred of "alien people" allegedly threatening Polish culture and the Catholic faith.

There are also subdivisions along the laissez-faire/interventionist dimension. Among the laissez-faireists are those who believe that capitalism will emerge "by itself" and who propose a complete freeing of the nascent forces of capitalism and market from any control, as well as those who accept the need for a governmental guiding hand in the transition to capitalism and a market economy. Meanwhile, interventionists themselves are divided between those who want society to maintain a safety net for the disadvantaged, and those who want to postpone it until better days.

Quite important, there is a low degree of convergence among the main divisions. Let me give some examples. It is less common than is often thought that a politician who is quite nationalistic will be strongly confessional and strongly authoritarian too. Someone who fights for workers' interests will not necessarily oppose reforms to introduce capitalism; he could strongly favor privatization. A politician who wants to give the president more power and even create a more authoritarian state could be agnostic or oppose nationalism.

Subdivisions bring configurations that give the Polish political scene the quality of a mosaic with blurred contours and misplaced parts. This mosaic makes the formation of a coalition government difficult and firmly contributes to the chaotic state of Polish politics at the top. It seems that political divisions are much stronger between politicians themselves than they are among ordinary people. This is my psychological hypothesis. The virtual disconnection of the parliamentary parties from society at large keeps the interaction between the leaders and the led weak. It is true that leaders partly reflect the confessionalism, nationalism, and anti-Semitism that exist within the population; but mostly they instigate prejudices and infuse stereotypes. They find responses among marginalized people. Normal people are busy dealing with their everyday lives and problems; they do not trust politicians. Hence, the alienation of the leaders from the masses, while not on the whole a positive feature of the political system, may prevent leaders from inflaming the emotions of the people. However, the steady deterioration of the economic situation of large groups may change this situation and make people more susceptible to nationalistic, populist, and confessional appeals.

It is a negative aspect of Poland's present political situation that parties are weak in interacting with the various strata of the population, framing alternatives, and producing viable economic programs. This is true even of those parties for whom the important line of cleavage is that of laissez-faire and interventionist.

It seems clear that the political-ideological divisions are of two types. The national/universal and confessional/secular groupings belong to a category that produces parties unified by symbols and values rather than by interests. If a party puts religious belief or a nationalist ideology at the front of its program and action, it is a party of spiritual community: it promotes *communal ties* and attitudes. At the center of its ideology are values that cannot be renounced under the pressure of economic interests or particular circumstances: values are not a subject of negotiation. A convinced patriot will never renounce his nationalist symbols and will not use national values as bargaining chips. The same is true about a Catholic and his or her religious beliefs.

The laissez-faire/interventionist division produces parties of a completely different type. They are more prone to trade and to bargain and to accommodate the interests of the different strata of the population. Their ideology does not consider membership in a social group to be exclusive, fixed for life either by birth or through a ritual. Whereas I call the first group of parties *spiritual parties*, or *communal parties*, I am inclined to call the second group *parties of a civil society*. They are typical of modern democracy and associative ties.

To give a few examples: The Liberal-Democratic Congress is an "integrist" liberal party, promoting a neoliberal economic program and a state of secular character. It clearly belongs to the civil society type of parties. Similarly, the Social Democratic Party (postcommunist) concentrates its pronouncements almost solely on economic issues (social and industrial policy). Thus, these two parties form units on the "civil-society" axis. On the "left" side of this axis there is also the party "Labor Union," which had roots in the Solidarity movement. On the "right" side, together with the liberals, may be located the Conservative Party (in a moderate way, it adheres to national and Christian values).

To nationalist parties belong the Confederation of Independent Poland and the "Movement of the Third Republic," which see both the liberals and the social democrats as traitors of the economic interest of the nation and as a great danger to the national identity of Poles. They fight against the alleged domination of communists in the economy and against the "cosmopolitan" attitudes of liberals. The Christian-National Union is promoting the active role of the Catholic Church in public life and securing the reflection of Christian values in state law. It is in open conflict with postcommunists, though it cooperates with liberals (entering with them into the governmental coalition). On the whole, every "spiritual-community" party tends to construct the axis which at its antagonistic pole portrays postcommunists as a post-totalitarian party with a cosmopolitan and atheistic orientation. Some strongly nationalistic Catholic groups, such as the radical fraction of the Christian-National Union or Catholic Action, see both the liberals and all "socialists" as located at the opposite extreme of the ideological axis.

In 1991–92, nine parties were active in forming governmental coalitions. Although only four governmental coalitions have been formed, a great variety of others have been seriously considered, some of an extremely peculiar composition. Only the postcommunist Social Democratic party was consistently excluded from all calculations.

There is a lot of speculation about whether there is a chance in the next election for the emergence of a Western-style, four- or five-party system. Will this bring the Polish party system closer into line with that of Western Europe?

It seems to me that an important question one can pose about the future Polish party structure is which type of party will dominate the formative processes of the coming years. Will the crystallization of larger parties be dominated by the national/universalistic division, by the confessional/secular one, or by laissez-faire/interventionist grouping? Which axis, if any, will achieve dominance over all other possible diversifications of political orientations? There are, evidently, other questions linked to this one. Will the civil-society parties or the spiritual-community parties get the upper hand? And the most important question: What are the chances for a communitarian type of party?

Liberals and Communitarians

A prominent Catholic intellectual, Stefan Wilkanowicz (1991), warned that Polish political culture is moving in a dangerous direction. The complex that he called *Christian-national-solidaristic*, which had been so prominent in the Solidarity movement, was waning, and the more individualistic *utilitarian-Darwinist* complex was waxing. He openly denounced the Darwinist component as glorifying ruthless competition and the survival of the fittest. Being Catholic, he believed that the rise of the utilitarian-Darwinist complex held many dangers for society's future cohesion and moral standards.

In the light of recurring strikes, the strength of this individualistic complex, at least among the masses, looks doubtful. On the other hand, it seems impossible to go back to the Christian-national-solidaristic complex as it existed in the early 1980s. This dilemma demands that both analysts and politicians reconsider the various possible roads to a future democratic order.

Poland has a serious lack of a strong network of intermediate groups that would link society and state organs in a democratic way. There is a deficit of those associative ties typical of Western civil societies. But above all there is a deficit of doctrines that would legitimize state actions. The slow pace of economic reforms and chaotic politics has created a political vacuum that produces rebels or skeptics and cannot produce committed supporters and devoted activists.

It seems that the economic and political doctrine of orthodox liberalism is not adequate to produce legitimacy for the new, emerging system. I would venture a hypothesis that, in the coming years, it will be doctrines with strong communitarian aspects that will show a greater potential for producing legitimating beliefs among people.

Allow me to refer to the debate currently going on between liberals and communitarians in England and the United States initiated by the works of John Rawls (1971) and critically followed by those of Michael Sandel (1982), Michael Walzer (1983), Charles Taylor (1990), and others. Critics say that orthodox liberals locate the state's legitimacy in its securing and promoting of individual freedoms. The fundamental freedom is the individual's right to choose and pursue his own idea of "the good life." But for individuals to have this freedom, they not only need to be free to choose their own concept of the "good life"; they also need the resources to pursue it.

The communitarian critique points out not only that there are shared ideas of "the good life" woven into social life, but also that access to specific goods in a given culture is unequal among different people. This controversy is evidently linked to the concept of a shared tradition on the one hand, and to the contemporary role of the state on the other. Liberals argue that the state should remain neutral with respect to individual ideals and their pursuit. Communitarians, on the other hand, say that both voluntary associations and state agencies are obliged to help people to find the resources for achieving a decent life and social citizenship. Using my own terminology, social ties should be predominantly of an associative nature or a combined associative-communal nature.

A theoretical discussion helps to analyze the quite practical sociopolitical problem in Poland. It seems that the legitimacy of the state in the coming years can better be secured by theoretical and practical references to communitarian principles than to those of orthodox liberalism. People themselves, without the help of state policies, will not be able to pursue their own life plans. On top of liberty, they need employment, decent housing, just industrial relations, education for their children, health care, and social support. A liberal economic and political order does not provide the mechanisms to translate political freedom into the socioeconomic means for each family to pursue its own definition of the good life. As Walzer (1990) put it, some corrective function of the state must exist in a liberal state. If a liberal state secures this mechanism, Walzer argues, it becomes a true liberal, or supraliberal, state, because by doing this it corrects the inadequacies of the orthodox liberal arrangements.

The contemporary communitarian version of social thought has some affinity to socialist ideas (Miller 1989; Israel 1992). But more important, it has also been strongly articulated, and in an elaborated form, within the Roman Catholic doctrine of the social market economy and of the social functions of the responsible state (John Paul II 1986; 1991). The affinity at the theoretical level between the social teaching of the Catholic Church and the social democratic type of communitarian doctrine could lead communitarians and Roman Catholics into an intellectual alliance. But it will also be possible to exert pressure to put these communitarian principles into practice. Such a development could find support from genuine contributions to social philosophy by some Polish thinkers (Mazowiecki 1990; Strzelecki 1974).

In the light of both older and more recent Polish traditions of communalism in Poland, moving toward one or another *communitarian* philosophy and sociopolitical practice may provide a more easily achieved accommodation of workers and employees to the capitalist economy. A communitarian arrangement may also provide a more certain road to the legitimation of the new democratic order.

One can say that there exists in Poland a need for a strong and well-articulated party that would claim to represent the spiritual community of Roman Catholics and yet not necessarily be a party primarily of a conservative confessional orientation, but rather a party of social orientation for which both individual freedom and the social protection of the needy are prominent features. Such a party actually exists and has already played a key role in the formation of two governmental coalitions. This is the Democratic Union—more precisely, the dominant faction within it. However, it is slow and reluctant to articulate its fundamental premises.

In many smaller Christian parties, there is also a growing insistence on the introduction of practical social programs to be implemented by local communities. On the whole, there is growing support for the operation of free market forces among the circles of progressive Catholics, however modified this support is by the principle of a social sense of justice and the demand for employment and for dignity in any kind of work. The inspirations of Vatican II have been definitely communitarian.

In contemporary Poland, there is also an opening for a party that will invoke, first, secular traditions, and, second, social memories of the associative actions of workers, doctors, and teachers, to form a modern social democratic program. This I would call the revival of the communitarian approach that was woven into the Polish legacy by the so-called organic work of the Polish intelligentsia in the nineteenth century and by the Polish socialist movement at the beginning of this century. The socialist doctrine in its social democratic version is communitarian.

There exist small parties that try to link their contemporary programs to the legacy of the prewar socialist party (Polish Socialist Party) or to the employee-interest–oriented tendencies within the Solidarity movement (Labor Union). Both are weak, and the long shadow of the practices of "real socialism" yet diminishes their potential appeal to workers. Because of its past, the postcommunist party (Social Democratic Party) has yet to prove that it no longer proscribes itself from accepting associative relationships and becoming "communitarian."

The functioning of communitarian parties in the emerging political system may be amenable to social cohesion and responsibility in many spheres of life. Because of Polish history and living traditions, they may give meaning to people's involvement in democracy and activate people to civic actions. Moreover, they may contribute to the development of beliefs that bestow a civil type of legitimacy on the state.

Certainly, under unstable conditions, no type of social tie is immune to hidden or overt clashes of societal forces, to spontaneous, half-deliberate, or consciously formed processes. Which type of ties will finally become stronger in Poland and dominate the future social order remains to be seen.

References

Adamski, Wladyslaw, ed. 1993. *Societal Conflict and Systemic Change. The Case of Poland 1980–1992.* Warsaw: IFiS.

Anderson, Benedict. 1983. *Imagined Communities.* London: Verso.

CBOS (Centrum Badan Opinii Spolecznej). 1992. *Serwis Informacyjny* (Center of Social Opinion Research. Informational Service), no.10.

Ciacek, Pawel, and Krzysztof Nowak. 1993. "Spoleczenstwo po szoku" (Society after a Shock). In *Gazeta Wyborcza,* April 27.

Dalton, Russell J., and Manfred Kuechler, eds. 1990. *Challenging the Political Order: New Social and Political Movements in Western Democracies.* Cambridge: Polity Press.

Demoskop—Przeglad. 1993. *Badania opinii publicznej* (Public Opinion Research), no.1 (16), January.

Gebethner, Stanislaw, and J. Raciborski, eds. 1992. *Wybory '91 a polska scena polityczna* (Elections '91 and the Polish Political Scene). Warsaw: Wydawnictwo Fundacji Inicjatyw Spolecznych "Polska w Europie."

Israel, Joachim. 1992. "Sweden: Rise and Decline of a Welfare State." In *International Review of Sociology, Monographic Section: Advanced Societies at the Threshold of the Third Millennium: Status and Perspectives.* Rome: Borla, pp. 95–140.

Janion, Maria. 1991. "Koniec epoki?" (The End of the Epoch?). In *Zycie Warszawy,* December 7–8.

Janion, Maria. 1991. *Projekt krytyki fantazmatycznej* (The Project of an Phantasmatic Critique). Warsaw: PEN.

John Paul II. 1986. *Laborem Exerceus.* Lublin: Wydawnictwo Katolickiego Uniwersytetu Lubelskiego (Lublin Catholic University Press).

John Paul II. 1991. *Centismus Annus.* Wroclaw: Wydawnictwo Wroclawskiej Ksiegarni Archidiecezjalnej (Wroclaw Archdiocese Bookstore Press).

Kolodko, Grzegorz W. 1992. *Transformacja polskiej gospodarki: sukces czy porazka?* (Transformation of the Polish Economy: Success or Failure?). Warsaw: Polska Oficyna Wydawnicza BGW (BGW Polish Publishing House).

Kowalik, Tadeusz. 1992a. "W strone umowy spolecznej" (Toward Social Agreement). In *Przeglad Spoleczny*, no. 1, April.

Kowalik, Tadeusz. 1992b. "Pakt o przesiebiorstwie" (Pact on Enterprise). In *Przeglad Spoleczny*, no. 7, November.

Kowalski, Sergiusz. 1990. *Krytyka solidarnosciowego rozumu* (A Critique of the Solidarity Reason). Warsaw: PEN.

Kozek, Wieslawa. 1991. "Wizja ladu gospodarczego i sposoby jego osiagania w wybranych typach srodowisk pracy" (Visions of the Social Order and the Means of Achieving It in Selected Work Milieus). In *Spoleczenstwo wobec wyzwan gospodarki rynkowej* (Society in the Face of Challenges of the Market Economy), edited by Wieslawa Kozek and Witold Morawski. Warsaw: University of Warsaw, Institute of Sociology, p. 186.

Mazowiecki, Tadeusz. 1990. "Spotkania Chrzescijanstwa z ideami socjalisty-cznymi i kontrowersje miedzy nimi." (Encounters of Christianity with the Socialist Ideas and the Controversies Between Them). In *Losy idei socjalistycznych i wyzwania wspolczesnosci* (The Fate of Socialist Ideas and the Challenges of the Modern Times), edited by Wlodzimierz Wesolowski. Warsaw: Polish Association of the Club of Rome.

Miller, David. 1989. "In What Sense Must Socialism Be Communitarian?" *Social Philosophy and Policy*, vol. 6, no. 2, pp. 51–73.

Mulhall, Stephen, and Adam Swift. 1992. *Liberals and Communitarians.* Oxford: Blackwell.

Rawls, John. 1971. *A Theory of Justice.* Cambridge, MA: Harvard University Press.

Rychard, Andrzej. 1993. *Reforms, Adaptation and Breakthrough. The Sources of and Limits to the Institutional Changes in Poland.* Warsaw: IFiS.

Sandel, Michael. 1982. *Liberalism and the Limits of Justice.* Cambridge: Cambridge University Press.

Strzelecki, Jan. 1974. *Kontynuacje (2)* (Continuations 2). Warsaw: Panstwowy Instytut Wydawniczy.

Taylor, Charles. 1985. "Alternative Futures: Legitimacy, Identity and Alienation in Late Twentieth Century Canada." In *Constitutionalism, Citizenship and Society in Canada*, edited by Alain Cairns and C.Williams. Toronto: University of Toronto Press.

Taylor, Charles. 1990. *Sources of the Self.* Cambridge: Cambridge University Press.

Toennies, Ferdinand. 1974. *Community and Association (Gemeinschaft und Gesellschaft).* London: Routledge and Kegan Paul.

Walzer, Michael. 1983. *Spheres of Justice.* New York: Basic Books.

Walzer, Michael. 1990. "The Communitarian Critique of Liberalism." *Political Theory*, vol. 18, no.1, pp. 6–23.

Weber, Max. 1968. *Economy and Society. An Outline of Interpretive Sociology.* Berkeley and Los Angeles, CA: University of California Press.

Wesolowski, Wlodzimierz. 1992. "Poland's Transition to Democracy: How Much Pluralism?" In *Towards Greater Europe? A Continent Without an Iron Curtain*, edited by Colin Crouch and David Marquand. Oxford: Blackwell.

Wesolowski, Wlodzimierz. 1993. "The Role of Political Elites in the Transition from Communism to Democracy: The Case of Poland." In *Sisyphus—Sociological Studies,* vol. 2 (VIII), pp. 77–100.

Wilkanowicz, Stefan. 1991. "O nowy ksztalt wartosci" (For a New Shape of Values). *Znak*, no. 438, November.

IVAN BERNIK

Politics and Society in Postsocialism

The seemingly endless discussions about the structure of socialist societies and their developmental perspectives, at least as far as European socialist societies were concerned, were abruptly stopped not by the social sciences themselves, but by the radical transformations of these societies. Thus the social sciences have had to adapt to the new situation by redirecting their attention to the emergence of postsocialist societies. It seems that in many cases they have almost been too eager to take into account new research problems and to forget the old ones; many of the analyses of the emerging postsocialist societies pay no attention to the "outdated" discussions of the developmental perspectives of socialist societies. This amnesia suggests that both the analytical tools applied in analyses of socialist societies and the results of these analyses have no immediate relevance for understanding the emergence of the postsocialist societies. The social sciences that are studying the emerging postsocialist societies obviously face the same general problem as do the societies themselves—they have to begin, in many respects, from scratch.

This essay tries to question some aspects of the above-mentioned assumptions. It will try to show that the accumulated knowledge about socialist societies represents a stimulative starting point for the analysis of the emergent postsocialist societies. This approach by no means implies that there exists a continuity between both types of society; my claim is that by focusing on the substratum on which the new societies grow, both continuities and discontinuities can be highlighted. That is why, in the first part of the essay, some basic characteristics of socialist societies and the prevailing assumptions regarding their developmental potentials will be summarized. Subsequently, we shall focus on the emerging systemic properties of postsocialist societies. Special attention will be paid to the question of how these properties are linked to the structural contradictions in socialist societies. This rather abstract analysis will be followed by a "portrayal" of the main social actors in the radical transformation of socialist societies. In this context, it will be indicated that the role of the protagonists of the transformation of authoritarian regimes to democratic ones has not been exempt from deep changes. On the basis of the analyses of structural changes and changes in the roles of protagonists of these changes, it will be argued that postsocialist societies face an enigmatic future.

The Decline of Socialism: The Resurgence of Civil Society?

Analyses of socialist societal systems agreed, despite differences of analytical approaches and differences among individual socialist societies, on at least one important point: The functioning of socialist systems was characterized by the domination of politics over other spheres of society, especially over the economy. In its simplified form, this idea gradually acquired the status of truism, devoid of any innovative analytical relevance. Nevertheless, recent elaborations of this idea in the framework of social systems theory have indicated that "the domination of politics" should be understood as an indicator of the low level of functional differentiation in socialist societies (Pollack 1990; Bernik 1990). The stewardship of politics over "society," that is, over other societal subsystems, implied a low functional specialization for politics and unclear systemic borders between politics and the other societal spheres. Every social activity, from economy to art, was perceived as a matter of political concern. It also meant that every social activity—publishing a book of poems, for example—had a political connotation. To exaggerate—there was no poetry (or science or law or economy) in socialist societies in the strict sense of the word, but there was also no politics as a specialized and self-limited activity.

From this analytical standpoint, both the developmental advantages and disadvantages of "the domination of politics over society" can be highlighted. In the initial phases of "socialist development" the high systemic integration enabled politics to play the role of mobilizer of societies' developmental potentials. Its role was most notably exemplified by the politically accelerated process of industrialization (Lane 1976, p. 53). The modernizing function of politics was especially obvious in economically less developed socialist societies. But even in these societies, the high systemic integration of society, associated with the centrality of politics, gradually showed its dysfunctions. The high systemic integration of socialist societies prevented the formation of relatively autonomous functional societal subsystems (such as economy, science, and law), thus reducing the society's developmental capacities and options. The most obvious indicator of this dysfunction was the slowdown of economic growth and finally the stagnation of all socialist economies in the 1980s. At the same time, the political subsystem, as a caretaker of the "society," was increasingly overburdened. The attempts to relieve the burdens by means of various reforms "from above," initiated in some socialist countries, proved to be devoid of any significant effects.

In contrast to this analytical perspective, in the late 1980s there prevailed among social scientists the idea that the development of socialist societies could be explained by a contradictory relationship between politics (that is, the socialist state) and society. By this perspective, the once-omnipotent socialist state faced an increasingly dynamic and powerful society. The most important sign of this increasing dynamism was the growth of the "second society" (Hankiss 1988). This concept indicated the emergence of those parts of society that were relatively independent of political control. The emergence of a "second society" was not limited only to the economic sphere (the gray and black economies); it emerged also in the sphere of politics (in various forms of political dissent) and culture (as underground culture, samizdat, and so forth). Many social scientists held that the growth of the "second society" signaled a decisive failure of the socialist state's attempts to organize the whole society as "a big office and a big factory." They also predicted future developments: The state would, under the pressure of "society," sooner or later retreat to its "natural borders." This would enable all spheres of society to reorganize themselves and to develop their intrinsic potentials fully.

These ideas were most elaborately expressed in the so-called theory of civil society, which characterized socialist societies as a zero-sum game between the civil society and the totalitarian state; the broader the prerogatives of the state, the more limited the faculties of the civil society. The stability of socialist regimes was to a high degree due to the debasing of civil society. That was why the troublesome "slow growth of civil society under repression" (Nowak 1991, p. 61) in at least some socialist societies during the 1980s, which was epitomized especially by the growing political and cultural nonconformism, was seen as a decisive sign of the imminent collapse of the old regime.

Thus the concept of civil society, though vaguely defined and often related to nonconformist intellectual activities only, became for proponents of the civil-society project an almost magical tool in explaining the collapse of the old order and the emergence of a new society. From their point of view, at least in the most developed socialist societies, there were more and more structural preconditions for deep changes—the socialist state was becoming increasingly ineffective in its attempts to control the society, whereas the once moribund society was getting ready to regain its "stolen" prerogatives. It was only a question of time before these structural preconditions would find expression in open conflict between the representatives of the old order and the bearers of the new one. The result of this conflict would not just be a change of the power elite but a radical transformation of the structure of society, which would enable it to develop all its intrinsic forces. Civil-society theorists believed that this transformation should also have a paradigmatic value for Western societies, whose autonomy and the self-organizing capabilities also needed revival.

The New Society: "Political Capitalism" or "Democratic Socialism"?

In this section, I shall try to examine briefly the extent to which the above claims were validated by the transformation processes in Eastern Europe. More precisely, I shall try to show that the collapse of socialist society did lead to radical changes, but the nature of these changes differs in many respects from the expectations of the civil-society theorists' predictions.

Despite the fact that the pace and even the extent of transformation processes in the individual former socialist societies differ substantially, some common features of these processes can be identified. The most obvious is the emphasis that was given to changes in only one societal sphere—the political sphere—which made it appear that the collapse of socialist regimes could be interpreted simply as a "transition to democracy," comparable to similar transitions in other parts of the world (Huntington 1991–92). Though the emergence of postsocialist societies cannot be reduced to the process of political democratization only, this process nevertheless has wide implications for the functioning of the whole societal system.

The formation of a democratic infrastructure (political parties, free elections, parliamentary procedures, and so forth) implies a radical break with the previous political system. In contrast to the old system, which was characterized by the repression or at least the "unification" of different political interests, the new one can process a multitude of opposing interests. In other words, its internal complexity is much higher than that of the old political system, a feature that is complemented by mechanisms (such as highly formalized procedures for decision making) that make its self-organization, that is, the reduction of its high complexity, possible. Thus a multitude of differences in a democratic political system are continually processed to the difference between government and opposition (Luhmann 1990, p. 23). The mechanisms of complexity reduction make communication in a democratic political system highly "artificial"; the system deals increasingly with its self-generated problems and not with the problems of the "society."

The democratization of political systems in former socialist societies, irrespective of the imperfections of this process in individual cases, has at least two far-reaching implications for the functioning of the whole society. The growing "artificiality" of political communication, stimulated by the confinement of politics to political parties, political groupings, and parliament, indicates that the political system is gaining a relatively high operative autonomy from other societal spheres. In other words, democratization implies the functional specialization of politics. In the language of civil-society theorists, it therefore means a clear delimitation of the state from "society." The growing operative autonomy of the political subsystem does not mean a separation of politics from "society," but a radical change in the relationship between the political subsystem and its societal environment. On the part of the political subsystem, this change is determined by the fact that its complexity is related to its growing ability for self-reflection (Luhmann 1983; Willke 1989). To a much higher degree than authoritarian political systems, it is able to recognize the difference between itself and other parts of society. Moreover, it is also able to learn from its experiences. That is why democratic political systems are structurally predisposed for a much more reserved approach to the regulation of other societal spheres than authoritarian ones are.

There is no doubt that democratization means exactly what the proponents of the civil-society theory envisioned. It has liberated "the society" from the omnipotent state, or at least from the state with omnipotent regulative ambitions. According to them, the liberated society should start to flourish. Its expected revival can be conceived in sociological terms as a complex of processes of functional specialization of the individual societal spheres, complementing the process of the functional specialization of politics. In these processes, relatively autonomous and self-regulated social subsystems are formed. In other words, the democratization of politics not only enables but actually requests the formation of a market economy, the autonomy of a legal subsystem, self-governed science and art, an autonomous mass media, and so on.

In contrast to the optimistic expectations, however, there are virtually no signs of an extensive revival of "society" in the former socialist societies. Moreover, some sociologists claim that these societies are actually experiencing "a state of anomy" (Kolarska-Bobinska 1990, p. 281). From our point of view, this dramatic statement indicates that the changes in other societal spheres—that is, their functional specialization—are lagging behind the changes in the political subsystem. It seems that "the society" was powerful enough to free itself from the authoritarian state, but it is obviously not powerful enough to make use of the new possibilities created by political democratization. Moreover, it seems that individual societal spheres view the establishment of their autonomy and a reliance on self-regulation as too heavy a burden. To alleviate this burden, they are looking for more support from politics; the political sphere should initiate and regulate changes in the individual societal subsystems. Thus the political subsystem should once again play the role of the central modernizing force in society. However, as already shown, a democratic political system has quite limited resources at its disposal to respond to these challenges; it can rely on redistribution of money, on introducing new legal regulations, and on political power (Luhmann 1983), but this alone cannot create a market economy, an effective educational system, self-regulated science, and so forth.

Contrary to many expectations, the emergence of postsocialist societies has so far not led to an active society, but rather to the paralysis of society. The fact that political changes are not matched by changes in other societal subsystems can even endanger the newborn democracies' chances for survival. This claim can best be exemplified by the much-discussed relationship between politics and economy in postsocialist societies. It has already been indicated above that, according to prevailing expectations, the lifting of the political stewardship over the economy should lead to the rapid revival of key economic institutions, such as property rights and market(s), and thus to a gradual improvement in the economy's performance. The actual course of change has shown that the relationships between economy and politics in emerging postsocialist societies are much more complex and, in many respects, contradictory. According to C. Offe (1991), the interdependencies between postsocialist politics and the economy are characterized by "the dilemma of simultaneousness." This concept actually indicates the absence of simultaneity; the transition from an authoritarian to a democratic political order has not been complemented by a transition from a state-run economy to a market economy. The "second economy," which was earlier seen as an embryo of market economy, has proved to be ineffective in generating structural transformations of the economy. In the absence of its own transformative potentials, the transformation of the economy is stimulated mostly by political means. The basis of the new dependence of the economy on politics is strongly related to the fact that the formation of a relatively self-regulated economy is one of the preconditions for the completion of the transition to democracy.

The new dependence of economy on politics is aptly termed by some analysts as "political capitalism" (Staniszkis 1991, p. 329; Offe 1991, p. 284). The term suggests that the political attempts to synchronize political and economic processes of change can lead to contradictory effects. On the one hand, as already indicated, the political system is "interested" in the marketization of economy; but on the other hand, it tries to prevent all those economic changes that can endanger the legitimacy of the new political order. As such effects as a decline in the standard of living, unemployment, and growing income and wealth inequalities prevail in the short run, the political system can try to impose a more direct control over economic processes. In such a case, the attempt to introduce capitalism by political means will end in a new kind of merger between politics and economy.

According to some authors, signs already exist to indicate that the attempts to synchronize political and economic changes by political means have ended in a mutual blocking of both. L. Nowak (1991, p. 70) argues that all the transformations of former socialist societies have so far led only to the establishment of "democratic socialism." According to him, democratization of the political system has brought no important consequences, because the control not only over productive assets, but also over the means of persuasion and mass communication, remain "in the hands of the political minority, viz. in the hands of the state" (ibid., p. 70). By this perspective, the dilemma of simultaneity has turned into a trap of simultaneity. A political system overburdened by enormous regulative prerogatives cannot be democratic in the sense outlined above; and an economy run by the state cannot guarantee the optimal mobilization of economic resources.

Both the concept of "political capitalism" and the rather paradoxical concept of "democratic socialism" suggest that the emerging postsocialist societies are faced with a multitude of developmental options. On the basis of the above analysis, it would not be difficult to enumerate the most important ones, but any attempt to single out the most probable ones would go far beyond the scope of this paper.

The Actors of Transformation: The Winners and the Losers

An answer to the question of who the protagonists of historical events were in European socialist countries now seems almost commonplace. Despite great differences in the pace and scope of changes in individual countries, a general answer applies to them all. The main catalysts, if not the direct protagonists of the major transformation, were intellectuals. With their activities, they created free space in which broad masses of people could also participate in political events of immense importance.

A closer look at this answer reveals that its wide acceptance among social scientists is due at least in part to the vagueness of the concept of "intellectuals." Even if intellectuals are defined as individuals who are engaged in the creation, elaboration, and dissemination of theoretical knowledge, ideas, and symbols (Geiger 1949, p. 12), they comprise a broad social category that is internally differentiated in many respects. It would be empirically untenable to argue that the whole stratum of intellectuals was opposing the socialist regime; both loyal supporters and opponents of the old regime were recruited from this stratum. That is why the question of which groups of intellectuals dared to voice their dissent cannot be avoided. A solid analytical basis for this answer was already given in the 1970s by two Hungarian social scientists writing under the pseudonym M. Rakovski (1988). They argued that in this stratum in socialist countries was a small group of intellectuals who tried and, despite the strict control of political authorities over intellectual activities, to a large extent managed to create and reproduce their own ideology and culture. Though they possessed no power that might amplify their dissenting voices, this group of intellectuals was closely watched and sanctioned by political authorities. That is why the authors called the members of this group "marginalized nonconformist intellectuals" (Rakovski 1988, p. 77).

Though a relatively small group, these nonconformist intellectuals had a few common denominators. They were engaged in a variety of intellectual activities, the majority of them related to the different spheres of cultural creativity, such as art, science, and journalism. Because of their internal differentiation, they could not be defined in structural terms, but mostly by their "mentality"; that is, to this grouping of marginalized nonconformist intellectuals belonged those individuals who "made their position very clear in word and deed, rejecting the policy of the party establishment" (Šiklova 1990, p. 349).

Of course, these intellectuals' political nonconformism was not established by the mere rejection of "the policy of the party establishment," but also by the negative sanctioning of this rejection by the party establishment. Negative sanctioning was a sign that political nonconformism was perceived by socialist regimes as a serious threat to their stability. Nevertheless, political nonconformism was treated differently in different socialist societies. These differences became particularly obvious when the socialist regimes had become increasingly unable to fulfill the expectations of the masses, during the time of their decreasing legitimacy. On the one hand were the regimes such as those in Bulgaria, Rumania, and Albania that stepped up the repression of political nonconformism to nip it in the bud. On the other hand were regimes such as those in Hungary, Poland, and Slovenia that attempted to establish certain forms of dialogue with nonconformist intellectuals and even to implement some of their ideas. The different response of the political elite to political nonconformism greatly influenced the initial phases of the transition toward democracy. In the former cases, where almost all dissenting activities were suppressed, the accumulated tensions culminated in unexpected mass protests that suddenly undermined the positions of the old elite and paved the way for the new one. In the latter cases, the transition to democracy was not characterized so much by uncontrolled mass protests but by the gradual emergence of democratic political institutions and the parallel rise of a new political elite.

The formation of democratic institutions was a clear sign of the fruitfulness of the marginalized intellectuals' active dissent, but it also confronted them with new challenges. The main problem for the (former) dissenting intellectuals was how to retain their "leading role" in the context of emerging democratic institutions. Without taking into account differences among individual societies, it can be claimed that nonconformist intellectuals as a group were relatively unsuccessful in coping with the new situation. Their failure was significantly related to their political attitudes. At the center of their political dissent was the idea that they voiced the interests of suppressed "society" at large and not particularistic interests. They did not perceive their political dissent as a means to achieve political power but only to undermine the old power structures. Moreover, they did not perceive their activities as political ones, but as "antipolitics" (Mastnak 1990, p. 440).

These notions were most clearly and conspicuously elaborated in the framework of the civil-society project; that is, the theory of civil society was the most elaborated version of the ideology of nonconformist intellectuals. They portrayed themselves, in light of this project, as representatives of the society before the authoritarian state, or at the least as the rousers of the society's suppressed potentials (Ash 1990, p. 31).

This ideology, which was highly operative in the preparatory period of democratization, proved to be inefficient once democratic institutions were gradually being established. This inefficiency was reflected most obviously in the fact that, in comparison with political latecomers, the (former) nonconformist intellectuals were generally quite unsuccessful in establishing firmly organized and competitive political parties. Therefore some nonconformist intellectuals looked with obvious disappointment at the process of democratization by which those parts of "civil society" were mobilized which, in their opinion, "could be described as politically and democratically undeveloped" (Mastnak 1990, p. 449). In their view, these "undeveloped" social forces significantly influenced the further process of democratization and its outcomes. Seeing that "actually existing democracy" is not what democracy should be according to their political ideals, the most active proponents of the civil-society project "retired into a corner and at most got on with some writing" (Šiklova 1990, p. 355).

Thus, the group that had decisively influenced the initial stages of the process disintegrated during the course of democratization. A substantial number of former nonconformist intellectuals, as already indicated, assumed the old "antipolitical" stance, whereas the others entered politics as professional politicians. The new, "postrevolutionary" political elite is in no way composed only of former nonconformist intellectuals; in its ranks, political newcomers prevail, not the veterans of the "fight for democracy."

One may argue that the democratization of former socialist countries has been essentially completed by the establishment of a democratically elected elite. The other former socialist societies that for different reasons are lagging behind should sooner or later follow suit. There is no doubt that the establishment of democratic institutions in former socialist societies, no matter how imperfect they are, is an important evolutionary breakthrough. Nevertheless, it would be premature to say that even the most advanced of these societies are characterized by stable democratic orders. On the contrary—it seems that the new democracies will have to endure many difficult tests. In the context of the present analysis, only two of these will be mentioned. The first one is related to the legitimacy of the postrevolutionary democratic elite, that is, the elite that at present is in power; the second is related to the legitimacy of democratic order as such. The following brief analysis will try to show that these questions are closely linked; nevertheless, they address different problems.

To understand the basic legitimacy problems of the postrevolutionary political elite, one must have in mind how they were constituted. In contrast to the veterans of democratization—nonconformist intellectuals whose activities were inspired by a sophisticated ideology—the newcomers simply promised to abolish the old order. The attractive power of this "program" was closely related to the fact that the socialist elite and the socialist order were rapidly losing the compliance of the masses because of their inability to fulfill the masses' minimal expectations (Rychard 1989). In this context, the promise to abolish the old order implied not only the establishment of a democratic political system, but above all the improvement of the economic well-being of the masses. In other words, in the social consciousness of the majority of the population, political democratization was intrinsically linked to the rapid improvement of its economic condition.

The structure of expectations explains why the emergence of democratic institutions, even though relatively smooth and not related to extensive conflicts, has not led to the pacification of society. The attempts of the new elite to restructure the economy have not resulted in improved economic well-being for large parts of the population. Just the opposite—these attempts have not only led to a further decline in the living standard, but they have also opened a Pandora's box of uncertainties and risks. The inevitable clash between high expectations and unvarnished reality is reflected in the growing disappointment and impatience of the majority of the population.

Under these circumstances, the main task of the new governing elite is the "management of mass disappointment." This new task has significantly changed the role of the new elite as well as its possibilities for action. In general terms, these changes can be characterized as "political disenchantment." This characterization refers to the changes in the actual status of the governing elite as well as to the changes in its self-perception and to the perception of the elite by the majority of voters. The governing elite is no more legitimized by its historical task of abolishing the old order, but it has to gain mass support in the troublesome process of solving everyday political problems. In performing its functions, the governing elite is constantly hindered by parliamentary opposition and the expectations of the masses. These pressures can stimulate the governing elite to seek shortcuts—to try to win the support of the masses by populistic measures outside democratic procedure. It is not unlikely that such attempts would be met favorably by those parts of the population that have been most intensely exposed to the negative effects of economic change.

The burdens to which the governing elite is exposed are multiplied by its "loneliness." As already indicated, the process of political democratization has not been matched by a similar functional specialization of other societal subsystems. This discrepancy is reflected in the fact that the formation of a democratic political elite has not been paralleled by the emergence of other social elites, most notably of an economic elite. Thus the governing elite must act not only as an initiator of economic transformation, which should lead to the formation of a market economy, but also as a sponsor of the formation of an economic elite. This fact has manifold implications both for the legitimacy of the postrevolutionary democratic elite and for the stability of the new democratic order.

The absence of an autonomous economic elite means that the political elite cannot share responsibility for the performance of the economy. That again makes the legitimacy of the governing elite strongly dependent on the economic well-being of the masses. Thus, the current economic decline in postsocialist societies has a direct effect not only on the popularity of the governing elite, but also on the stability of democratic order. The importance of the "economic substratum" for the legitimacy of political power can strongly influence the willingness of the political elite to support wholeheartedly the transformation of the state-run economy to a market economy. For obvious reasons, it is as a rule interested in selective and limited introduction of elements of market economy; that is, it is ready to support only those changes that can possibly strengthen the legitimacy of political power and prevent those with adverse effects. This selective approach to economic changes can also obstruct the rise of an economic elite (owners of productive assets and managers); at the least, it can put an economic elite under the strong patronage of the political elite.

On the basis of the above account of the contradictory effects of the postrevolutionary political elite's endeavor to legitimize its power, a bleak future of democracy in postsocialist societies can be predicted. It seems that this prediction should especially take into account the fact that the side effects of the actions of the new political elite can endanger even its own position as well as block transformations in other societal spheres. Under these circumstances, it would be difficult to establish a relatively unconditional commitment to democratic institutions, one that would be sufficiently independent of the economic situation and other developments in society. Until such firm commitment to democratic institutions is established, the transition to democracy, as some authors suggest, cannot be considered completed (Linz 1990). From this point of view, the processes of transition to democracy in socialist countries are far from their culmination. Moreover, they cannot be considered irreversible.

References

Ash, T.G. 1990. "Opozicija" (Opposition). In Gligorov, V., and Teokarevič, J., eds., *Kriza, razpad i reforma* (Crisis, Desintegration and Reform). Beograd: Stručna knjiga, pp. 29–38.

Bernik, I. 1990. "Dual Society. On Some Systemic Properties of Socialist Societies." *Revista Internacional de Sistemas,* vol. 2, pp. 289–316.

Geiger, T. 1949. *Aufgaben und Stellung der Intelligenz in der Gesellschaft.* Stuttgart: Enke Verlag.

Hankiss, E. 1988. "The 'Second Society': Is There an Alternative Social Model Emerging in Contemporary Hungary?" *Social Research,* vol. 55, pp. 13–42.

Huntington, P.S. 1991–92. "How Countries Democratize." *Political Science Quarterly,* vol. 106, pp. 579–615.

Kolarska-Bobinska, L. 1990. "Civil Society and Social Anomy in Poland." *Acta Sociologica,* vol. 33, pp. 277–88.

Lane, D. 1976. *The Socialist Industrial State.* London: G. Allen & Unwin.

Linz, J.J. 1990. "Transitions to Democracy." *The Washington Quarterly,* vol. 13, pp. 143–64.

Luhmann, N. 1983. *Politische Theorie im Wohlfahrtstaat.* München: Olzog.

Luhmann, N. 1990. *Paradigm lost: Über die ethische Reflexion der Moral.* Frankfurt am Main: Suhrkamp.

Mastnak, T. 1990. "Civilno društvo u Sloveniji: od opozicije do vlasti" (Civil Society in Slovenia: From Opposition to Power) *Sociologija,* vol. 32, pp. 439–52.

Nowak, L. 1991. "The 'Post-Communist Society'? An Attempt at a Theoretical Analysis." In Herzog, D., Pradetto, A., and Wagner, H., eds., *Revolution and Rekonstruktion: Der Aufbau freiheitlicher Demokratien in Ostmitteleuropa* (Ein Konferenzbericht). Berlin: Freie Universität Berlin, pp. 60–85.

Offe, C. 1991. "Das Dilemma der Gleichzeitigkeit. Demokratzisierung und Marktwirtschaft in Osteuropa." *Merkur.*

Pollack, D. 1990. "Das Ende einer Organisationsgesellschaft." *Zeitschrift für Soziologie,* vol. 19, pp. 292–307.
Rakovski, M. 1988. *Vzhodno-evropskemu marksizmu naproti* (Toward an Eastern European Marxism). Ljubljana: Komunist.
Rychard, A. 1989. "Konflikt und Anpassung." In Mayer, G., and Ryska, F., eds., *Die politische Kultur Polens.* Tübingen: Francke Verlag, pp. 287–303.
Staniszkis, J. 1991. "Dilemmata der Demokratie in Osteuropa." In Deppe, R., Dubiel, H., and Rödel, U., eds., *Demokratischer Umbruch in Osteuropa.* Frankfurt am Main: Surkamp, pp. 326–47.
Šiklova, J. 1990. "The 'Gray Zone' and the Future of Dissent in Czechoslovakia." *Social Research,* vol. 57, pp. 347–63.
Willke, H. 1989. *Systemtheorie entwickelter Gesellschaften.* Weinheim: Juventa.

DOMINIQUE SCHNAPPER

The Significance of the Ethnoreligious Field in Nation-building

Sociologists still think about modern societies in terms of the bipolarism described by Robert Nisbet (1966), which can be roughly abstracted to the celebrated dualism *Gemeinschaft vs. Gesellschaft.* This is how sociologists of religion have posited the problem of secularization—a characteristic of *Gesellschaft*—and the New Religious Movements, seen as an unexpected resurgence of *Gemeinschaft.* Sociologists of ethnicity, for their part, have been able to speak about ethnic revival—an instance of *Gemeinschaft*—as against the modern nation, a political form of *Gesellschaft.* In the United States, since Glazer and Moynihan's *Beyond the Melting Pot* (1963), ethnicity has become the dominant paradigm in the thinking about "interethnic relations." In Western Europe, the infranational demand movements that developed in the 1970s have been sympathetically contrasted by a number of sociologists, in many cases militants themselves, with the rationality and abstraction of the nation-state.

True, as Nisbet remarked, our civilization has become urban, democratic, industrial, bureaucratic, and rationalized (Nisbet 1966, p. 392). However, even in democratic-liberal societies, this is a borderline concept or general principle which does not apply uniformly in every dimension of social life. The rationalization or "disenchantment" of the world, to use Weber's famous expression, is not a rectilinear or unambiguous process. It is not a condition, but an unending dialectic between a principle of rationality and the concrete forms taken by personal and political relations that are inevitably marked by affect and passion. The idea of the "rationalization of the world" must be understood as an ideal-type or dominant principle, not as a description of social reality.

This essay will offer a few lines of thought for a comparative analysis of the dialectic between "rationalization" and what can be called, in Weber's terms, the "emotionality" of expressions and demands in the religious and ethnic orders as observed in modern societies.

Religion vs. Ethnicity

The Disenchantment of the World and Survival Theory

In line with the linear conception of social evolution which was dominant until the 1960s, sociologists have analyzed the gradual rationalization of social life and the waning of religious life. In European countries, a general decline of religious observance was perceived, particularly in the cities and in the working class. In the United States, it appeared that the persistence of religious observance masked a weakening of belief. The concept of "secularization" made it possible to describe the reduction of the field of religion in social life (Isambert 1976), the decline in religious callings, and the collapse of some forms of religious observance. American sociologists inquired into "the future of religion and change in a society obliged to function henceforth without any religious legitimation" (Hervieu-Léger 1986, p. 140). More or less influenced by Marxism, the sociologists of this period analyzed the incompatibility of religion and modern society.

Specialists of ethnicity propounded the same kinds of analyses. Despite the efforts of Otto Bauer and the Austro-Marxists to posit the problem of nationhood, albeit in the context of the Austro-Hungarian monarchy, all Marxist thinkers foretold the gradual waning of ethnic attachments. As Sir Isaiah Berlin pointed out, belief in the single, universal advance of history led Marx himself, like some historians, to consider that national and regional loyalties expressed irrational resistance from forms of society rendered obsolete by history (Delannoi and Taguieff 1991, p. 312).

In any case, the Marxist tradition was merely joining up here with other trends of sociological thought. For the sociologists of the Chicago school, the model was what they called "assimilation." Park believed that conflicts between groups would gradually be resolved. Ethnic relations would go through the stages of the "race relations cycle" consisting of contact, competition, conflict, accommodation, and assimilation. At the conclusion of the cycle, the diverse groups would be "assimilated"; that is, they would henceforth settle their conflicts within the same system of norms and values. "Assimilation is a process of interpenetration and fusion in which persons and groups acquire the memories, sentiments and attitudes of other persons or groups, and, by sharing their experience and history, are incorporated with them in a common cultural life. Insofar as assimilation denotes this sharing of tradition, this intimate participation in common experiences, assimilation is central in the historical and cultural processes. . . . The unity thus achieved is not necessarily or even normally like-mindedness; it is rather a unity of experience and of orientation, out of which may develop a community of purpose and action" (Park and Burgess 1969, pp. 735–37). Contrary to what a number of sociologists wrote during the militant phase of the 1970s, the aim was not to obtain from the individual "the suppression of old memories, but their incorporation in his new life" (p. 739). At the conclusion of the cycle, Park believed, the strictly "ethnic" dimension would disappear or, at any rate, become secondary.

The literature on development, which grew and expanded after World War II, also argued from an evolutionist perspective, insofar as it assumed, implicitly or explicitly, that the successive phases of economic development would be matched by a gradual dissemination of the nation and of liberal democracy as the dominant form of political organization. This was the basic paradigm of the literature of the 1950s and 1960s devoted to the economic development of the Third World countries, the simplest and most famous form of which was produced by Rostow (1960). From the economic point of view, societies can be classified into five categories or stages: traditional societies, societies experiencing "the preconditions for take-off," those that have attained "the take-off," those undergoing "the drive to maturity," and those participating in "the age of high mass-consumption." Societies produce different political responses to the eternal problems of collective life, depending on the stage of economic development they have attained (Rostow 1971).

Similarly, anthropologists and sociologists who studied the new nations and the phenomenon of "nation building" in postcolonial countries simultaneously analyzed economic development and the constitution of a political domain that transcended internal differences, in particular the preexisting ethnic groups. As can be read in the preface to the most remarkable of these books: "The new nations are engaged in a form of social change that makes nation-building and material development simultaneous political problems" (Geertz 1963, p. v).

It was the same evolutionist perspective that Karl Deutsch defended when he ascribed "nation building" to the "social mobilization" induced by mass communication networks. The constitution of national entities was to his mind linked with the growing numbers of individuals in communication networks: "A decisive factor in national assimilation of differentiation was found to be the fundamental process of social mobilization which accompanies the growth of markets, industries, and towns, and eventually of literacy and mass communication" (Deutsch and Foltz 1963, p. 188). In this view, national sentiment is the result of the development of communications, which gradually erases ethnic peculiarities and leads to the assimilation of peripheral groups by the dominant group. Deutsch went so far as to define the stages of this process: "Open or latent resistance to political amalgamation into a common national state; minimal integration to the point of passive compliance with the orders of such an amalgamated government; deeper political integration to the point of active support for such a common state but with continuing ethnic or cultural group cohesion and diversity; and, finally, the coincidence of political amalgamation and integration with the assimilation of all groups to a common language and culture—these could be the main stages on the way from tribes to nation" (Deutsch 1966, pp. 7–8).

In more theoretical terms, Talcott Parsons defined "societal communities or nations" in terms of four characteristics: "The societal community presumes a relatively definable population of membership, which at this level we ordinarily call citizens for the modern case, and presumes as well that the collective organization of reference is politically organized on a territorial basis, that is, it maintains normative order and certain political decision-making processes covering the human events which occur within a defined territorial area. Finally, as a third primary criterion, at some level it is characterized by a common cultural tradition" (Glazer and Moynihan 1975, p. 59). This "common cultural tradition," which is specific to each case, is composed of some elements based on "kinship" and others based on "contract." It involves a "diffused, enduring solidarity" (ibid.) that is passed from one generation to the next by means of a common language, the sense of sharing a common history, and a common project for the future. In modern societies, that is, in nations, Parsons claimed, the affirmation of ethnic attachments is a survival from premodern times and is contrary to the spirit of complex, universalist societies in which social roles are decreasingly prescribed and increasingly acquired.

So we find liberal thinkers joining up with Marxists to analyze and foretell the gradual disappearance of ethnic forms. These interpretations, which can roughly be grouped together under the term "survival theory," held that social forms relating to the logic of *Gemeinschaft* are bound to disappear or at least decline correlatively to the development and ascendancy of the logic specific to modernity. This was well and truly the view of certain American sociologists of ethnicity rediscovered in the aftermath of Glazer and Moynihan's book: "Ethnicity is one of the forms of *Gemeinschaft* that has *survived* in a rationalized, bureaucratized society" (Greeley 1974).

It was from the late 1960s onward that the paradigm of the "end of religion" and that of the gradual disappearance of ethnicity were both radically challenged. This was because numerous instances of ethnic revival were observed, despite the global dissemination of the model of nationhood as a historic agent recognized by the international political and legal orders. This ethnic revival gave rise to an abundant literature that is both scientific and militant in nature—in itself an indication of the importance of the phenomenon, at least for the educated classes. The paradigm of the "end of religion" was similarly challenged. It was observed that "popular" religion had not declined and that noninstitutional forms of religion remained vigorous (Luckman 1963). Admittedly, the integrated system of beliefs and observances laid down by churches was seen to be breaking down, but it was observed at the same time that neither religious sentiment nor religious manifestations had disappeared. The emergence of "emotional communities," or New Religious Movements (NRMs), in the 1970s led to the extension of these analyses. The dominant paradigm of the "end of religion" was supplanted by an inquiry into renewed forms of the religious phenomenon in modern democratic society.

The variety of forms taken by religious and ethnic expressions and demands has cast doubt on, or at least complemented, survival theory in order to account for the persistence and even the renewal of identities and social movements linked with religion and ethnicity.

The Contradictions of Modernity, or Compensation Theory

Sociologists of ethnicity, like those of religion, have observed that the religious revival and the ethnic revival are not merely "popular" movements with roots in the poorer social classes or in marginal populations doomed to disappear from society, but that they are also vectored by middle-class populations participating actively in collective life. This simple observation has led to an inquiry into the relationship between modernity and the new forms of religion and ethnicity. Not only are the new forms of religious life not incompatible with modernity, but they might also be hypothesized to be the product of modernity. It is in this perspective that I would like to suggest a few parallel inquiries into these "antirational" movements—on the one hand ethnicity vs. nation; on the other, emotion vs. institution.

In order to analyze the forms of this "new Christianity," Danièle Hervieu-Léger (1986) has extended the Weberian perspective demonstrating the structural irrationality of the rationally disenchanted world. She attempts to show that religious revival is not merely the product of survivals from premodern times, but that it also stems from the contradictions inherent in the specific process of modernity. The development of the New Religious Movements, with their twofold train of contestation and innovation, is made possible by the loosening hold of the dominant logic of rationalization. They exemplify what has been called the "revival of the repressed" (*retour du refoulé*).

This analysis can be read alongside those conducted by Anthony Smith on ethnic revival. To Smith, ethnicity comes first, both chronologically and logically: nations built themselves by reinterpreting and reorganizing the ethnic elements existing previously. He interprets ethnic revival as a compensation for the abstraction of the modern state, which he calls the "scientific state." It is this need for "humanity," which the "scientific state" cannot supply, that explains things such as the infranational demands in the older western nations (Smith 1981; 1986). To Smith, the state is both brutal and inefficient. It tends to deny ethnic ties and yet fails to do so, insofar as the tribe's characteristic core of symbols resists the attempt to level it off. The vitality of "premodern" tribes—the sole social reality—is the reason for their resurgence. Given the dialectic between the demands of rational political centralization and the force of the ethnic sentiments that existed before the building of the nation, tribes are always liable to express themselves anew at the expense of the nation.

Kedourie's interpretation follows the same lines when analyzing the destruction of the structures existing before the modern nation as engendering "an atomized society which seeks in nationalism a substitute for the old order now irrevocably lost" (Kedourie 1971, p. 112), all the more so as Kedourie, like Smith, emphasizes that "European administrative methods in particular, centralized, impersonal, uniform, undiscriminating in their incidence, had a leveling and pulverizing effect on traditional hierarchies and loyalties, traditional ties of dependence which, however capricious and oppressive in their general effects, did yet have about them a warm and personal quality which made power seem approachable and comprehensible to the humblest and most insignificant man" (Kedourie 1970, p. 23).

Daniel Bell's theory subscribes to the same train of thought. He offers an interpretation of ethnic revival as a basis for political action. The building of broad inclusive identities invokes by way of compensation the need for "primordial anchorage," and the weakening of the nation and class solidarities makes ethnic ties more "salient." The development of the welfare state, with its train of hope and consequent disappointment, imposes organization into groups. Ethnicity alone makes it subsequently possible to "combine an interest with an affective tie. . . . *What takes place, then, is the wedding of status issues to political demands through the ethnic groups*. . . . In the recent historical situation ethnic groups, being both expressive and instrumental, become sources of political strength" (author's italics; Glazer and Moynihan 1975, pp. 169, 170–71). To Bell, ethnicity is analyzed both in terms of compensation for some of the characteristics of modernity (abstraction, demands for social rights, and so on) and in terms of political strategies. Despite its claim to universality, however, this analysis is particularly applicable to the United States, as the central idea of the combination of affect and interest in ethnic demands is meaningful only insofar as the ethnic group actually obtains rights and becomes a source of interest. This is the case in the United States, where programs of aid for so-called minority groups have been set up. In European countries, however, where programs of this kind are not generally available, Bell's theory boils down to an elaborate form of compensation theory.

Survivals, Compensations, and Historical Realities

That both types of theory can concurrently account for historical realities can be illustrated by comparing the evolutions of Western and Eastern Europe—not to mention the rest of the world.

Two histories—and two ideas—of the nation have always been contraposed to each other; the history of the building of nations and of national identities has differed between the East and the West (Schnapper 1991). Thinkers have contraposed the civic, voluntary, contractual, or elective nation of Western Europe to the populistic, organic, naturalistic, or ethnic nation of Eastern Europe. The "people of citizens" in the West is opposed to the "people of ancestors" in the East. These are ideas, of course, in the twofold sense of social ideologies and conceptions based on historical experience. But scrutiny of French and German nationality rights shows that these ideas have not lost any of their force, even in the democracies of Western Europe; and the separation between liberal Europe and communist Europe over the last half century has highlighted and dramatized this historical opposition.

The idea of a civic nation based on what Kant called the principle of the equality of free, rational beings came about in the West. It is true that, in its concrete forms, this idea has never been purely "rational": in the days of triumphant nationalism, religions were mobilized to serve the nation, and the sacred was partially transferred onto the nation, as illustrated by the reference in *La Marseillaise* to the "sacred love of the fatherland." However, since the end of World War II, respect for the law-based state, democracy, individualism stemming from personal enrichment, and the protection of the welfare state has resulted in the disinstitutionalization of religious life and the dissemination of quasireligious forms of observance in other sectors of social life. By way of compensation for this general evolution, we are currently witnessing signs of "fundamentalist" revival in the churches and the development of the New Religious Movements.

The "political nation" characteristic of Western Europe, in principle open to all those who participate in common political life, remains the form of political organization, the locus of historical continuity, and the collective expression of identity with the greatest degree of conformity to the values of modernity—even though it has to come to terms with the transnationality of economic organization and exchanges in the form of the legal, economic, and political cooperation being built by the European Economic Community.

The historical experience of Eastern Europe is contraposed to that of the West. In the days of triumphant nationalism, the "ethnic" nation tended to transfer the sacred not so much onto the nation, a political organization founded on the law-based state, as onto the ethnic group, the *Urvolk*, the historicobiological community existing before political organization. The transfer was at times accompanied by religious references but was in itself essentially pagan with frequent appeals to sacralized nature. The experiment in secular religion represented by the communist political order contributed to a process of enforced secularization—though in some cases it unwittingly helped to preserve the ecclesiastical institutions that were persecuted but that offered the *locus* of freedom, as in the case of the Roman Catholic Church in Poland. However, insofar as they were unable to avoid collaborating with the political authorities, the churches also compromised themselves. The collapse of communism resulted in a brutal disinstitutionalization, and religious observance immediately declined in Poland. The sacred was transferred once more onto the ethnic group, not onto the nation—a recent development with no democratic tradition and henceforth associated with communist rule. Now the East European nation, which is more ethnic than political and which tends by definition to be closed, is undoubtedly in contradiction to the demands of modern societies with their bases of multiple exchanges of all kinds and the idea and practice of democracy.

The integration of the Western nations is threatened by depolitization, that is, by the decline of political will apparent in the erosion of national institutions, whether political or ecclesiastic.

The integration of the Eastern nations is threatened by the impossibility of the rapidly achieved and active involvement of individuals in economic life, which is probably the precondition for an integration of modern democratic societies. The churches no longer play an integrating role. All that remains is reference to an ethnic nation, which has no political or civic traditions, which is incompatible with the demands of modernity insofar as it is based on the idea of "belonging" exclusively to a single group with a single culture, and which is incapable of creating and maintaining social ties and founding a political order. In the former Yugoslavia, even though ethnic ties have been manipulated by the Serbian Communists to establish their rule, it has been obvious that the passion generated by such ties is stronger than any form of "Yugoslav nation" in the sense of the Western civic nation.

In the case of the West European nations, applying compensation theory applied to both ethnic and religious revival makes it possible to account for historical realities. In the case of the Eastern nations, room has to be made for both survival theory *and* compensation theory.

Ethnoreligious Revival

Contradictions and Dissatisfactions

The following proposals apply to the Western nations seen as modern societies, with their twofold dimension of economic production coupled with social transfers and democratic observance. No analysis of these subjects can afford to neglect the history of concrete societies.

In the spirit of compensation theory, our analysis can be extended by interpreting religious renewal and ethnic renewal from the standpoint of the contradictions nourished by the rationality, the abstraction, and the ideal of modernity. Modern society engenders dissatisfactions and feelings of failure because of the contradictions that exist between the ideals it posits and the concrete realities of social life. It proclaims the value of equality, but is unable to avoid real-life inequalities: "Modern or industrial societies are simultaneously egalitarian in their aspirations and hierarchical in their organization" (Aron 1965, p. 14). These societies confer absolute value on the individual as such and tend to reduce individuals to their roles in technicobureaucratic organizations: "Just as the individual aspires to equality, he also aspires to personality. He wishes to be himself and not an anonymous, interchangeable being. However, the same affluence which promises the acquisition of personality for all seems to have as its condition and consequence the submission of all to the relentless mechanism of production and economic growth" (ibid). Modern society's evocation is abstract universality, whereas its concrete reality is the persistence of personal, national, religious, and ethnic roots. "The tendency of industrial society to extend to the whole of humanity originates in reason, science and technology. Science of the experimental type is regarded today as the expression of rational thought and as the condition for efficient technology. . . . Humanity will remain divided by the plurality of desires for the independence of states, by inequalities in development, by nationalisms which stress particular difference and by ideologies which claim universality. . . . Industrialization will not erase the diversity of the systems of norms and values" (ibid., pp. 194, 279).

More generally still, modern society fails to give an ultimate meaning to existence. In Weberian terms, it does not answer people's need for a system of explanation that can justify the imperfections of the world and their own unhappiness. Based on technical and intellectual innovation, on the invention of new social forms, and essentially forward-looking, it includes an intrinsic utopian dimension. However, unlike religious utopias (Séguy 1971), this rational utopia is based neither on an account of a bygone Golden Age nor on the perspective of a radically different future. It devalues the past and does not look forward beyond the development and improvement of the rationality of the present. It cannot function actively as did the old dreams of a complete and explicit rupture rooted in the mythology of the past. It cannot give meaning to the collective experience of humanity and the individual destiny of mankind. The void of modern societies leaves the individual with the possibility, responsibility, privilege, and anxiety of choosing the meaning he wishes to give to his existence.

In the collective life of the New Religious Movements or of the "fundamentalist" groups within official church circles—as in the life of militants working in ethnic-demand movements—individuals often find legitimation through their personal involvement. In addition, social differences tend to disappear in these groups, and the individual can rediscover the affective dimension of interpersonal relationships. Whether ethnic or religious in their definitions, such "emotional communities" or "elective fraternities" answer one's fundamental and eternal need to be recognized as a person. These groups enable individuals to find compensation for the rationalization of the world of production and for the abstraction of political society and citizenhood.

By formally extending every possibility to every individual, modern society inevitably drives a large proportion of its population to experience objective failures, and all its members to undergo repeated subjective failure (which can be defined as the relationship between aspiration and achievement). Further, modern society's basis in the ideas of ability and merit (as measured by examinations and social success) make each individual solely responsible for his or her failures and failings; these factors make the "emotional communities" or "elective fraternities" all the more necessary, as emotional commitments to such groups enable individuals to compensate for the failures they cannot avoid experiencing in the life of the larger society.

The individual's fundamental need to be recognized as a person, which implies the establishment of direct relationships, can find an equally successful outlet in religious renewal and ethnic affirmation. It is not by chance that all surveys of the socially deprived show their main demand to be dignity (Paugam 1990), that is, recognition, which can be equally expressed in the revival of fundamentalist forms of religion or in the affirmation of "shared" ethnic ties.

The social functions of ethnic revival and religious revival can be analyzed in the same terms. In a society dominated by a general principle of rationalization and secularization, both of these types of revival can ultimately confer meaning on human suffering and enable the individual to establish direct affective relationships with others. The requirement of meaning and the need to be recognized by others can be satisfied by the emotionality that is present in both religious and ethnic movements. In this sense, a theory positing *compensation for the abstraction and meritocracy of modern society* can also account for the renewal, not of "religion" or "ethnicity" per se, but of the "emotional" forms of religion and the "emotional" forms of ethnicity that are nourished by modernity itself.

Convergence: An Ethnoreligious "Field"?

The fact that the ethnic and the religious revivals have the same compensation functions does not imply that the two do not retain their specificity.

Though it is out of the question to return to a substantialist definition of religion or ethnicity, it is necessary to take account of the real-life experience of individuals. Reference to the transcendental does not have the same meaning as involvement in a historical community or a political project. The experienced meaning of religion is not the same as that of "secular religion." It is an oversimplification to describe nationalism as a substitute for historical supranatural religion, or to state that nationalism has become ersatz religion in which the nation, as understood by the nationalist, is a substitute for God (Delannoi and Taguieff 1991, p. 63). A relationship with the transcendental is not the same kind of experience as political commitment, even when the latter takes an emotional form, and the sociologist must take this specificity into account.

However, it is precisely this specificity that is challenged, insofar as the conception and the very domain of "religion" are no longer defined in the traditional terms formulated by Durkheim. Specifically religious experience is restricted to individuals or small groups. For the mass of the population, whether the reference is to constituted religion or not, the sociology of religion finds a parallel evolution in beliefs and observances: the end of the ecclesiastical institution and the evolution toward ethics.

Like all other institutions of social life, the ecclesiastical institution is given short shrift. The decline of institutional religious observance, the lowered status of the clergy (fewer priests with less influence in society), the symbolization of the physical forms and spiritual content of belief, the out-and-out rejection of certain practices such as confession—all these well-known developments illustrate the fact that individuals are recomposing *ad libitum* forms of belief and observance which they claim is their personal subjective right, in line with the values of modernity.

The notion of a personal God, transcendental reference, and the relationship between human and God are being superseded by a conception that is primarily moral and humanitarian. The personal God, creator of heaven and earth, is being supplanted by exemplary human figures—witness, in France, the consensus about the person of Abbé Pierre. Christ is becoming a "moral ideal" common to believers of all faiths. The "vertical" (transcendental) dimension is being reduced to the "horizontal" ideal of human brotherhood. "Religion" in this moral guise is spreading to nonspecific instances of social life. Faith objects are taking on an increasingly symbolic meaning. This general evolution toward ethics is the primary form of the "modernization of religion." The activity of divines is increasingly akin to social work. Indeed, many members of the clergy leave their churches to become social workers.

By tending toward ethics, religion has to compete with other institutions guided by the same ambition—mediation panels and so on—and this dilutes its specificity. This dilution may eventually transform religion into a kind of humanitarianism, as in the case of the "religion of human rights." Simultaneously, it is becoming apparent that practices perceived as belonging to religion (rituals, adorations, processions, mock passions, and so on) are turning up in other domains. Sports events, mass games, ethnic activities, politics, and media stardom have arguably supplanted organized religion as providers of the needs for meaning and recognition.

For most of the population, the evolution of all religions toward a monotheistic moralism is gradually blurring the distinction between religious and ethnic manifestations and actual experiences. Belonging to a historical community—a kind of historical transcendence reflected in ideas such as "the Jewish people"—enables people to feel they are part of a history that transcends them and also gives meaning to their existence over and above the reference to the transcendental. As ethnicity, like religion, is based on a complex system of symbols and values, it may be asked whether *the two experiences are not becoming increasingly convergent.*

The Scandinavian countries provide an extremely advanced example of this convergence (Hamberg 1992). Declared membership in a religion does not correlate with religious observance: only 3 percent of Scandinavians are regular churchgoers. Further, their worldview is quite different from the fundamental ideas of the Jewish and Christian tradition and its humanism, i.e., the essential split between mankind, created in God's image, and the world of animals and plants. As in deep ecological thinking, there is a rift between man and the animals (Ferry 1992). Good health is the first "value" mentioned by 45 percent of the population. However, 90 percent of Swedish people continue to belong to a church, which to them means demonstrating that they are part of the group and the welfare state (membership in a church being equated with membership in a trade union), and which also provides them with a moral yardstick, partly of Christian origin. Observing the same evolution in Great Britain, Grace Davies discusses the phase of "belonging without believing," which has already supplanted the phase of "believing without belonging." Islam or Judaism, in which historical and religious values are inextricably intertwined, could paradoxically become models, and this would make it possible to discuss "ethnoreligious" and "politicomoral" renewal in similar terms.

Depending on the national tradition, the same aspirations are expressed in a relatively religious form (for example, in the United States with its strong tradition of religiosity) or in a relatively ethnic form (for example, in countries with a marked preference for the nonreligious dimension). This does not mean that all the movements can be reduced to a single form, but that there is a *tendency toward convergence* that makes it possible to analyze the limits of secularization and rationalization afresh and from a different standpoint. Passion and emotion—aspects of *Gemeinschaft*—remain an inherent part of the most modern societies. The modern nation may no longer be able to transcend the various ethnic groups, and the universal Catholic Church may no longer be able to control the various sects and charismatic movements.

What is involved is not merely another review of the historic ties, specific to each political unit, between religious and national identities and the exploitation of one form of identity by the other. The communist authorities manipulated the national identities of the peoples of the Soviet Union to impose their rule. Religion is one of the objective characteristics of a people that justifies ethnic demands and ensures the integration of constituted nations. It is clear that the two dimensions are often inextricably intertwined in the assertion of a specific group's political and cultural rights, as is shown, for instance, by the Jewish, Irish, and Armenian peoples.

What is involved is not even the "secular religion" of communism, which, by proposing a global interpretation of the world and a project for radical change, kept alive in its members the dream of universal reconciliation similar to the dream sustained by religious belief—though communism placed the dream in this world instead of the next. What is involved, beyond the similarity of the two domains and their objective ties, is something quite different: the redefinition of the very domains of religion and ethnicity. Once actual experience ceases to make it possible to distinguish clearly between religious life and ethnic or national commitment—once individuals recompose their forms of commitment *ad libitum* from a stock of memories that can be indiscriminately religious, ethnic, or national—these commitments and identifications belong to an "ethnoreligious" domain.

More broadly speaking, this development is part of the general process of critical debate concerning institutions, values, and traditions that is currently historicizing and relativizing all the concepts of modernity. Further, it constitutes a provisional culmination of secularization, defined as "the constitution of sectors of human activity unaffected by religion, i.e., by constituted religions or by religious forms of thought" (Isambert 1976, p. 575). One expression of the rationalization of modern society has been the autonomy of the various domains of social life. At a time when the "field" concept dominates part of sociology, we might well be witnessing a decrease in the diversity and autonomy of the various fields. This, at any rate, is what is suggested by our analysis of the new forms of religious and ethnic expression.

Religions, as sets of beliefs and observances organized by churches—which have declined along with the other national institutions—have almost ceased to play a role in the production of social ties. The ethnoreligious emotional renewal illustrates and reinforces the essential lack of stability of modern democracy, which invents new models of behavior based on the specific values of modernity: individualism and the search for identity and authenticity. But the manifestations of the "ethnoreligious field," which can always be measured by the yardstick of reality (unlike transcendental reference), may not be as effective in ensuring social integration as the old forms of religious life were. Even from a strictly functionalist point of view, political projects are liable to be challenged by social reality, while the transcendental interpretation of the world is less liable to be proved wrong by events.

Answering the need for identification with a group and the need for recognition—both of which modern society as such fails to supply—ethnoreligious feelings, passions, and demands have a fine future ahead of them in the democratic societies of the West as well as in the uprooted societies of Eastern Europe. With their individualism, their rejection of institutions, and their ethical dimension, the "emotional" revivals are in harmony with a number of the fundamental values of modernity. Far from being doomed to disappear under the dissemination of modernity, they are destined to spawn other forms of renewal. Over and above this compensation analysis, however, what is in question is the very definition of the religious and ethnic fields. Individuals improvise and recompose elements gleaned from the great religions and from the ethnic or national memory to produce a moral code based on religion and history; this moral code provides the foundation for their participation in affective communities or elective brotherhoods. By combining the practical significance of religious experience and of ethnic action, emotion and community feeling in all instances now have a greater impact than reference to a personal God and to membership of a constituted church.

This article was written at the suggestion of Danièl Hervieu-Léger, whose work has been particularly enlightening for me. I extend my thanks to her here.

Translated by Roger Greaves

References

Aron, R. 1965. *Les désillusions du progrès*. Paris: Calmann-Lévy.

Delannoi, G., and P.A. Taguieff, eds. 1991. *Théories du nationalisme, nation, nationalité, ethnicité*. Paris: Kimé.

Deutsch, K.W. 1966. *Nationalism and Social Communication: An Inquiry into the Foundations of Nationality*, 2nd ed. Cambridge, MA: MIT Press.

Deutsch, K.W., and W.J. Foltz, eds. 1963. *Nation-building*. New York: Atherton Press.

Ferry, L. 1992. *Le nouvel ordre écologique: l'arbre, l'animal et l'homme*. Paris: Grasset.

Geertz, C., ed. 1963. *Old Societies and New States. The Quest for Modernity in Asia and Africa*. New York: The Free Press.

Glazer, N., and D.P. Moynihan. 1963. *Beyond the Melting Pot*. Cambridge, MA: Harvard University Press and MIT Press.

Glazer, N., and D.P. Moynihan, eds. 1975. *Ethnicity, Theory and Experience*. Cambridge, MA: Harvard University Press.

Greeley, A.M. 1974. *Ethnicity in the United States: A Preliminary Reconnaissance*. New York: Wiley.

Hamberg, E. 1992. "Religion, Secularization and Value Change in the Welfare State: The Swedish Case." Vienna: First European Conference of Sociology.

Hervieu-Léger, D. (with F. Champion). 1986. *Vers un christianisme nouveau?* Paris: Cerf.

Isambert, F.A. 1976. "La sécularisation interne du christianisme." *Revue Française de sociologie* XVIII–4, pp. 573–89.

Kedourie, E., ed. 1970. *Nationalism in Asia and Africa*. New York: Meridian Book.

Kedourie, E., ed. 1971. *Nationalism*. (Originally issued in 1960.) London: Hutchinson.

Luckman, T. 1963. *The Invisible Religion*. London: Macmillan.
Nisbet, R.A. 1966. *The Sociological Tradition*. New York: Basic Books.
Park, R.E., and E.W. Burgess. 1969. *Introduction to the Science of Sociology*. (Originally issued in 1924.) New York: Greenwood Press.
Paugam, S. 1990. *La disqualification sociale*. Paris: P.U.F.
Rostow, W.W. 1960. *The Stages of Economic Growth: A Non-communist Manifesto*. Cambridge, MA: Cambridge University Press.
Rostow, W.W. 1971. *Politics and the Stages of Growth*. Cambridge, MA: Cambridge University Press.
Schnapper, D. 1991. *La France de l'intégration, sociologie de la nation en 1990*. Paris: Gallimard.
Séguy, J. 1971. "Une sociologie des sociétés imaginées. Monachisme et utopie." *Annales ESC* 2, pp. 328–54.
Smith, A.D. 1981. *The Ethnic Revival*. Cambridge, MA: Cambridge University Press.
Smith, A.D. 1986. *The Ethnic Origins of Nations*. Oxford: Blackwell.

Part III

Toward a United Europe—
Prerequisites, Prospects, and Threats

PETER ESTER AND LOEK HALMAN

Empirical Trends in Religious and Moral Beliefs in Western Europe

Introduction

Modern Western society is a secularized society in which religion has become the concern, primarily, of the individual. As a result of the ongoing process of secularization, religion as a social institution has lost much of its societal relevance (Berger 1967; Luckmann 1967). In premodern societies, religion dominated peoples' lives in all respects. Due to processes of differentiation, specialization, and the accompanying process of individualization in particular, religion was forced to retreat from many important sectors of social life. It has become a highly specialized institution of its own, like other major social institutions such as the family, education, economics, and politics. As a consequence of individualization, individuals are free to choose and practice their own religious convictions, just as they are free to choose their own political ideas, primary relationships, and so on (Beyer 1990). In this chapter we attempt to make an empirical assessment of some major theoretical notions of secularization. Four hypotheses are formulated, each based on the idea that modernization and individualization have continued in Europe in the last decade (1980–90). These hypotheses are empirically tested in ten West European countries using survey data gathered in 1981 and in 1990 by the European Values Group (EVG; see Ester et al. 1993; Halman 1991). It is further explored whether or not changes in basic values manifest themselves throughout modern society or are to be located within specific groups, for example, different age groups (Meulemann 1987). Differences in values may be caused by replacement of generations. Younger generations differ from older generations in many respects, and due to these intergenerational differences, values in society change. The other interpretation is that value changes are related to "life-cycle" or intragenerational changes: as one gets older, one's basic values might change.

Secularization and Individualization: Some Hypotheses

The process of individualization is one of the most profound cultural changes in recent history. The gradual though drastic transformation of traditional and civic values toward values stressing personal interest and individual development is an important aspect of individualization. Increasingly, the individual has become the main point of reference in the shaping of values and attitudes. Self-development and personal fulfillment have become major priorities, whereas values related to traditional social institutions such as the family and the church are declining in importance (Yankelovich 1981). According to Klages, a decline can be observed in traditional *Plicht-* and *Akzeptanzwerte* and an increase in *Selbstenfaltungswerte* (Klages 1985). Meulemann (1987) noticed similar trends, and Inglehart (1990) reported a general shift in basic values from a primarily materialistic toward a predominantly postmaterialistic orientation. Value orientations are no longer a "one-possibility thing," but have become fragmented and open to personal choices. They have become options that individuals may or may not choose out of personal preference. Thus secularization does not necessarily imply that people become less religious, but that religiosity becomes increasingly independent from the church as a social institution. Religiosity is individualized and, to some theorists (see Zijderveld 1983), has become vague, noncommitting, and abstract.

The process of modernization in the religious domain has usually been described by social scientists under the heading of secularization (Wilson 1982). In its most simple form, secularization is indicated by a decline in church participation.[1] As a result of increased individual autonomy and privatization of religion, people no longer feel attracted to its traditional forms. Furthermore, social control by the church over participation in religious services has weakened significantly. Other expressions of the decline of traditional religion may be found in the content of religious beliefs, such as in the strong decline in traditional ways of believing. Ever fewer people share conventional beliefs preached by the church, such as the existence of heaven, hell, and the devil, as well as other orthodox beliefs (Halman 1991). Instead, more and more people believe in what they want to believe, and not what the church tells them to believe (Stufkens 1987; Van Steenbergen 1986). In other words, traditional orthodox beliefs have been replaced by a more modern, personalized way of believing. This personalized and deinstitutionalized way of believing also has resulted in a decline of the dominant role of the church in society. Institutional religion was one of the, if not *the*, most powerful social force guiding people's lives—in all respects—in traditional society. Religion was once the social institution par excellence that, through its encompassing definition of reality, ensured legitimation, plausibility, and solidarity (Berger 1967). But due to increasing individualization, institutional religion has lost its influential role in everyday life and is now only one among many social institutions that provide meaning and explanation. Increasingly, institutional religion has to compete with other systems that also aim at supplying people with meaning and explanation (Luckmann 1967). Religion is no longer the "sacred canopy" influencing everyday life that it had been for so many centuries. The influence of religion on other domains of life, such as sexuality, morality, and politics, has greatly diminished (Berger 1967).

Modern society becomes more and more part of a world community. In almost every social domain, there is a strong tendency toward internationalization or globalization. The activities of major companies are no longer limited to national economies but operate at a global level. Telephones, television, fax machines, and so forth have made the world a global village. Further, the political and economic unification of the European Community has raised the question of whether national cultures in Europe will gradually disappear due to processes of cultural convergence. At the same time, however, dramatic trends toward political, cultural, and economic deunification can be observed, for example, in the former USSR and Yugoslavia. Processes of unification and the globalization of cultural developments may lead to a unification of formerly separate cultures in terms of world views, values, and lifestyles. However, the degree to which unification will take place has to be questioned. According to some social observers and theorists (for example, Featherstone 1990), cultural globalization per se will not lead to cultural unification or cultural convergence, but to an even stronger cultural diversification. Precisely because of the increase of trends toward political, economic, and cultural globalization, people are faced with a global, nameless, anonymous world, which is felt as a threat to social identity and might in turn evoke a counter response toward cultural regionalization or localization.

Based on these theoretical notions, a number of hypotheses are formulated.

The first is related to secularization. Ongoing processes of modernization and individualization diminish the role of traditional religion in modern society (Dobbelaere 1981; Meulemann 1987; Wilson 1982). Secularization can be observed in society in at least three different ways: in individual behaviors such as the decrease in church attendance; in the diminished influence of religion on daily life, reflected by the decline of the social significance of religious institutions, activities, and consciousness (Wilson 1982); and, finally, in the decrease in religious orthodoxy. Against this background, we shall investigate whether secularization has indeed continued to increase in Europe in the last decade. The following hypothesis will be tested:

H_1: At the individual level, secularization has increased between 1981 and 1990 in West European societies.

Likewise, modernization and individualization have resulted in a decreased dominance of traditional moral values, particularly in the realms of sexuality and civic morality. Beliefs about issues such as divorce, homosexuality, and abortion tended to be proscribed by the church. Institutional religion was one of the most powerful social forces guiding people's lives—in all respects—in traditional society (Zijderveld 1979; Adriaansens and Zijderveld 1981). The ongoing process of liberalization and individualization of personal lifestyles has resulted in a decline of the dominant role of the church in society and is assumed to have strengthened permissive attitudes in society and to have weakened attitudes expressing civic morality. For increasing numbers of people, moral and sexual choices are no longer matters of proscription or legitimation by religion or the church but are based on personal decision and lifestyle preferences. The following hypothesis is formulated:

H_2: Social permissiveness has increased and civic morality has decreased between 1981 and 1990 in West European societies.

The third hypothesis regards the issue of the convergence or divergence of basic values in different European societies. In line with existing views about the internationalization or globalization of cultural influences, one may argue that values tend to converge in modern societies (Kerr 1983). Modern communications and mass media rapidly diffuse knowledge about other cultures, resulting in an exchange of ideas, world views, and values. The unification of Western Europe has frightened some politicians and social observers into believing that separate countries will lose their national identities, their national habits, and their cultures. In short, a cross-cultural convergence of value orientations may become reality. On the other hand, however, one may argue that diversification and the rediscovery of regional and local cultures counteract developments such as internationalization or globalization. The trend toward both globalization *and* regionalization or localization of cultures has been labeled by Featherstone (1990) as "the paradox of modern culture." Cosmopolitization of thinking and acting brings about problems of identification. These problems may be solved by a stronger orientation toward regional and local cultures, toward the direct social and physical environment, toward primary cultural "roots." This search for identity may cause a process in which the values of the various countries or even regions will grow apart: a divergence of basic values. We shall test a modified version of the convergence thesis. Previous analyses of the European Values Survey (EVS) 1981 data by Halman (1991) indicate that European countries show similarities in value patterns, *but* that differences in values among these countries also exist. It appears that these differences require nation-specific interpretations, indicating that cultural convergence is not identical with cultural homogenization. Therefore, the following hypothesis will be tested:

H3: Religious and moral patterns did converge in West Europe between 1981 and 1990, but differences that did occur demand nation-specific explanations.

The fourth and final hypothesis is related to the phenomenon of the fragmentation of basic values and norms as suggested by postmodern theory (see, for example, Rosenau 1992), according to which people no longer strive for coherent world views, but instead select their values and norms "a la carte." (Post)modern citizens are believed to "consume" values, beliefs, and attitudes just as they do consumer goods (Ester and Halman 1991). "[W]ith the pervasiveness of the consumer orientation and the sense of autonomy, the individual is more likely to confront the culture and the sacred cosmos as a 'buyer.' Once religion is defined as a 'private affair,' the individual may choose from the assortment of 'ultimate' meanings as he sees fit—guided only by the preferences that are determined by his social biography" (Luckmann 1967, pp. 98–99). To some theorists, this phenomenon is rooted in the very nature of the modern welfare state itself. "One not only consumes the services provided by the welfare state abundantly and noncontemplatively and the many goods of a rich society, one gradually also consumes human relations (marriages, friendships), and ideas and theories (religious and political ideologies). Individual gratification comes first and foremost: if a subject is no longer satisfying, it will be thrown away or exchanged for another" (Zijderveld 1983, p. 149; our translation). In the religious domain, this implies that the interrelationships between religious and moral values have lost their traditional congruence and predictability. Due to processes of the individualization of lifestyles and the pluralization of world views, the codetermination of basic religious and moral norms is assumed to be a disappearing phenomenon in modern society. Thus, believing in a personal God no longer implies that one holds negative attitudes toward abortion, euthanasia, or homosexuality. People look for combinations of those values they feel comfortable with. The issue of the fragmentation of basic values is the subject of the following hypothesis:

H4: The fragmentation of religious and moral norms has increased between 1981 and 1990 in West European societies.

Methods and Measurements

These four hypotheses will be tested using survey data from the European Values Group. This group of social scientists conducted a large-scale survey in all countries of the EC and Spain (at that time not yet a member of the EC) in 1981. Research institutions all over the world who were interested in this value survey joined the project and used the EVS questionnaire in their own countries. As a result of this cooperation, data of the participating non-European countries were exchanged with those of the European Values Group. In this way, comparable surveys became available outside Western Europe—in the Scandinavian countries, Hungary, Malta, the Soviet Union, the United States, Canada, Chili, Argentina, Japan, South Africa, Australia, and New Zealand. A second wave of surveys was fielded in 1990, again in all EC countries (except Greece) and in Hungary, Czechoslovakia, the Scandinavian countries, South Africa, Japan, the United States, and Canada; while in Austria, Switzerland, Poland, Bulgaria, the Baltic States, and the former German Democratic Republic, the survey was conducted for the first time by associated research teams. This chapter will report on value changes between 1981 and 1990 using both EVS surveys.

We have restricted our study here to ten European (EC) countries[2] and to the domains of religiosity and morality. Four religious measures are distinguished: church involvement, religiosity, religious orthodoxy, and confidence in the churches. Two moral measures are distinguished: permissiveness and civic morality (de Moor 1987; Ester and Halman 1990; Halman 1991; Halman and Ester 1991). Various survey questions are indicative for these religious and moral measures. These indicators have been transformed into constructs (for example, factor scores). The same (factor) model has been used for all countries at both times, although previous cross-national analyses of the same data set demonstrated considerable differences in values among countries (Halman 1991). Each country has its own, nation-specific character as far as values are concerned. However, in the comparisons here, it is assumed that all constructs are equally useful and valid in all countries.

A first measure of religiosity is *church involvement*. Secularization manifests itself most obviously with changes in religious behavior. Church attendance and other expressions of active church membership declined, and in some countries—the Netherlands, for example—even church membership decreased. Based on these kinds of indicators, a typology is constructed consisting of five types of churched and unchurched people (Peters and Felling 1981; Halman 1991; Halman and Ester 1991; Halman and de Moor 1993). Three kinds of churched people are distinguished: *core church members* regularly attend religious services and are actively involved in work for the church: *modal members* just as frequently attend religious services but are not otherwise active in and/or for the church;[3] *marginal members* attend religious services irregularly. Two kinds of unchurched people are distinguished.[4] Persons who once were church members but no longer belong to one are called *the unchurched of the first generation*. These persons are distinguished from those who never have been a member of a church: *the unchurched of the second generation*.

Apart from these institutional-church–oriented indicators of religiosity, other measures need to be used. Church membership and religiosity are not to be equated (see Luckmann 1967). Therefore, other measures of religiosity apart from church membership are examined: religiosity, religious orthodoxy, and confidence in the churches. Analyzing the 1981 data yielded these three measures of religiosity (de Moor 1987; Ester and Halman 1990; Halman 1991; Halman and de Moor 1993).

Important indicators of (general) *religiosity* are: being religious, a belief in a personal God, the importance of God in one's life, getting comfort and strength from religion, and taking moments of prayer (Halman and de Moor 1993, p. 50). No specific statements about the content of religiosity are part of this dimension. None of these items refers to the institutional side of religion or to concrete rules and dogmas. Measured in this way, "being religious" may even be applicable to people who do not belong to, or do not feel attracted to, one of the traditional churches (de Moor 1987, p. 22; Ester and Halman 1990, p. 7). *Religious orthodoxy* refers to "some set of beliefs which adherents are expected to ratify" (Stark and Glock 1968). Belief in God, hell, the devil, heaven, and life after death are all indicative for such a dimension of "doctrinal orthodoxy" (Lenski 1961, p. 23). These kinds of beliefs are included in the EVS questionnaire; factor-analyzing these belief statements yielded one clearly interpretable dimension of traditional religious belief (de Moor 1987; Halman 1991; Halman and de Moor 1993). Finally, what Glock (1974, p. 178) has called the "consequential dimension" can be distinguished. The more that religion is integrated into existing social structures, the stronger its influence in daily life. In the EVS questionnaire, it is asked whether the respondents think that their church is giving adequate answers to moral problems, family problems, and spiritual needs. The answers to these items refer to a dimension that could be distinguished from the other religious measures, and that we interpreted as *confidence in the church* (de Moor 1987; Halman 1991; Halman and Ester 1991; Halman and de Moor 1993).

One of our hypotheses (H_2) is that social permissiveness has increased and civic morality has decreased between 1981 and 1990 in West European societies. A large list of items referring to a range of moral issues and behaviors was devised for the EVS survey. In 1981, 20 items were presented; in 1990, the list contained 22 items. For reasons of comparison, the analyses will be limited to the 20 items that were used in 1981. Analyzing the 1981 data showed that there were two basic attitudes or values in the area of moral issues and behaviors (de Moor 1987; Ester and Halman 1990; Halman 1991; Halman and de Moor 1993). More or less the same dimensions appeared in the analyses of the 1990 data (Halman and Vloet 1991). One of these dimensions may be interpreted as permissiveness; the other refers to civic virtues and is therefore labeled *civic morality*. Justification of issues and behaviors such as homosexuality, abortion, prostitution, divorce, and euthanasia appeared to refer to one and the same dimension, which we have labeled *permissiveness*. Common features of these items are sexual and ethical matters regarded as sinful by traditional Christian doctrine and therefore severely sanctioned by society in the past (Harding et al. 1986, p. 11). Justification of behaviors and issues such as buying stolen goods, joyriding, avoiding public transportation fare, and claiming state benefits one is not entitled to refers to a second dimension. A characteristic of this dimension seems to be the emphasis on living a virtuous life. All activities mentioned are against the law in one way or another: "They might be seen as falling into an area of behavior where attempting to 'get away with it' or not

Table 1

Church Attendance in Western Europe, in Percent

	Regular[a]		Irregular		Never	
	1981	1990	1981	1990	1981	1990
France	18	17	25	31	57	52
Great Britain	22	23	31	30	47	46
West Germany	37	34	41	46	22	20
Italy	52	53	27	31	21	15
Spain	54	43	21	28	25	29
Netherlands	40	30	18	27	43	43
Belgium	38	31	26	25	36	44
Denmark	13	11	45	45	43	44
Northern Ireland	68	69	21	18	12	13
Ireland	88	88	8	9	4	4

Source: EVS 1981, 1990
[a] more than once a month

is largely a matter of personal discretion. . . . A second strand . . . involves the idea of personal honesty and dishonesty . . ." (ibid.). Therefore, this dimension is called *civic morality*.

Results

According to the first hypothesis, secularization as measured at the individual level increased in the 1981–90 period in Western Europe. As outlined in the previous section, secularization is quantified by assessing church involvement, religiosity, religious orthodoxy, and confidence in the church. Table 1 shows developments in church attendance between 1981 and 1990 in the ten European countries that are analyzed in this chapter.

Secularization and individualization in the religious domain are reflected in the decreased number of people who frequently attend religious services. The general conclusion from Table 1 is that religious practices in Western Europe have been rather stable over the last ten years. In 1981, the proportions of people frequently attending religious services (at least once a month) were low in Denmark, France, Great Britain, the Netherlands, and Belgium. These proportions remained low or even declined over the last decade. Particularly in the Netherlands, fewer people attend religious services at least once a month. However, this decline is not accompanied by an

Table 2

Percentage Decrease in 1990 in Western Europe

	1981	1990	Difference
France	74	62	–12
Great Britain	91	58	–33
West Germany	91	89	–2
Italy	94	85	–9
Spain	91	87	–4
Netherlands	62	51	–11
Belgium	76	68	–8
Denmark	94	92	–2
Northern Ireland	99	91	–8
Ireland	100	96	–4

Source: EVS 1981, 1990

increase in the number of people who never attend religious services. In fact, with the exception of Belgium, the proportions never attending religious services remained constant in Western Europe over the last decade.

The next issue is related to trends in church membership. According to our hypothesis, membership rates are believed to have decreased in Europe over the last ten years. Table 2 reports on some general trends.

The number of people regarding themselves as church members decreased in all countries, particularly in Great Britain. In 1990, 58 percent of the British affirm they belong to a church, a decrease of no less than 33 percent, whereas 42 percent indicate that they do not (or no longer) belong to a church. The British situation resembles the Dutch in this respect. In the Netherlands, the percentage of churched people decreased by more than 10 percent in the 1981–90 period; in 1990, half the Dutch population appears to be unchurched. Relatively high church membership rates are still observable in South European countries (Italy and Spain) as well as in some West European countries (West Germany, Denmark, and both Irelands). However, being a church member does not necessarily imply a high level of participation, as was observed above. Exceptions to this rule are found in Ireland and Northern Ireland, where church attendance is relatively high.

As a further exploration, Table 3 reports on trends in the typology of churched and unchurched people in Europe. In many countries, but particularly in Denmark, being a church member implies being a marginal church

Table 3

Typology of Churched and Unchurched People in Western Europe (in Percent)

	Churched							
	Core members		Modal members		Marginal members		Unchurched	
	1981	1990	1981	1990	1981	1990	1981	1990
France	4	5	13	12	55	45	29	39
Great Britain	15	14	7	10	68	33	10	43
West Germany	10	12	24	21	57	56	10	11
Italy	5	8	43	42	45	35	7	15
Spain	15	5	37	36	38	46	9	14
Netherlands	26	23	12	6	23	21	40	49
Belgium	8	9	29	25	38	36	25	30
Denmark	3	3	8	7	84	81	6	8
Northern Ireland	43	23	24	44	33	23	—	10
Ireland	29	14	59	73	12	9	—	4

Source: EVS 1981, 1990

member (never or hardly ever attending religious services). Marginal membership was and still is typical for Denmark and for other Scandinavian countries as well. This may be a consequence of the strong relationship between the Lutheran church and the state in these countries (Wilson 1982). Being a church member is almost a citizen's duty and therefore being a marginal church member in these countries is less meaningful than in other countries. The proportion of marginal members is rather stable in Denmark; whereas, in other countries, it is precisely this group of marginal members that decreased during the last decade. It seems as if substantial proportions of marginal members have left the church in the 1981–90 period, which also explains the relatively stable proportions of modal and core members in most countries. In both Irish societies, a shift from core membership toward modal membership is visible. Furthermore, the decrease in marginal members in the two Irish countries is as large as the increase in unchurched people.

It has to be concluded that, as far as behavioral characteristics are concerned, the secularization hypothesis is generally confirmed, though trends differ in different West European societies.

The question now arises whether a similar conclusion holds for the other

Table 4

Religiosity in Western Europe: Mean (Factor) Scores

	1981	1990	Difference
France	–.38	–.49	–.10
Great Britain	–.15	–.18	–.03
West Germany	.05	–.00	–.05
Italy	.33	.51	+.18
Spain	.25	.16	–.09
Netherlands	.01	–.17	–.18
Belgium	.25	–.14	–.39
Denmark	–.30	–.48	–.18
Northern Ireland	.51	.50	–.01
Ireland	.59	.59	—

Source: EVS 1981, 1990

measures of religiosity that we have distinguished. Table 4 shows trends in overall religiosity in Europe.

As can be observed in Table 4, religiosity in general has declined in most countries in Western Europe during the last decade. The only exception to this general rule of decreasing religiosity is found in Italy, but this result is likely a phenomenon of modified item-wording.[5] Particularly in Belgium, and to a lesser extent also in the Netherlands and Denmark, a relatively sharp decline in overall religiosity is observed. Less concise is the decrease in countries such as Ireland and Northern Ireland, which remain the most religious societies in Europe. Apart from a (small) general decline in religiosity, no changes seem to have taken place in the rank order of countries. The Irish remain the most religious people, whereas the French and the Danish, in both 1981 and 1990, are the least religious people.

Table 5 shows trends in religious orthodoxy. The conclusion with respect to developments in orthodox religious beliefs resembles the conclusion on trends in overall religiosity, although in general the decline in orthodoxy is rather limited (and statistically not significant [p = .0296]). However, in Spain and Belgium particularly, the decrease is remarkable. Another surprising finding is that Italians have become more traditional in their beliefs, as the people in Northern Ireland are. In other countries, religious orthodoxy decreased or remained more or less at the same level. The French and Danes still are the least orthodox in their religious beliefs, whereas both

Table 5

Religious Orthodoxy in Western Europe: Mean Scores (Count)

	1981	1990	Difference
France	2.42	2.50	+.08
Great Britain	3.60	3.55	–.05
West Germany	2.94	2.77	–.17
Italy	3.59	3.87	+.28
Spain	3.81	3.42	–.39
Netherlands	2.90	2.71	–.19
Belgium	2.79	2.56	–.23
Denmark	1.82	1.86	+.04
Northern Ireland	5.46	5.67	+.21
Ireland	5.32	5.30	–.02

Source: EVS 1981, 1990

Table 6

Confidence in the Churches in Western Europe: Mean (Factor) Scores

	1981	1990	Difference
France	.00	–.16	–.16
Great Britain	–.04	–.08	–.04
West Germany	.00	–.01	–.01
Italy	.12	.22	+.10
Spain	–.00	.07	.07
Netherlands	–.04	–.11	–.07
Belgium	.05	–.04	–.09
Denmark	–.44	–.49	–.05
Northern Ireland	.30	.40	+.10
Ireland	.29	.02	–.27

Source: EVS 1981, 1990

Irish people are most traditional, as they already were in 1981 (Ester and Halman 1990; Halman 1991; Halman and de Moor 1993).

The final indicator of secularization concerns trends in Europe as to confidence in the churches in the last ten years. Table 6 shows the main results.

Apart from Italy and Northern Ireland, confidence in the churches has declined in all countries. In both Irish societies, the highest confidence in

Table 7

Permissiveness in Western Europe: Mean (Factor) Scores

	1981	1990	Difference
France	.20	.32	+.12
Great Britain	–.13	–.02	+.11
West Germany	.05	.07	+.02
Italy	–.32	–.09	+.23
Spain	–.32	–.16	+.16
Netherlands	.34	.91	+.57
Belgium	–.33	.08	+.41
Denmark	.38	.06	–.32
Northern Ireland	–.69	–.48	+.21
Ireland	–.68	–.45	+.23

Source: EVS 1981, 1990

the church was displayed in 1981. Least confidence was expressed by the Danes. No dramatic changes in church confidence have taken place over the 1981–90 period. The only peculiar change that is observed is that Italians and Northern Irish have become more confident in their churches. In the Irish Republic, the level of confidence in the church decreased. This resembles the findings in other European countries. The Danes still have the least confidence in the church of all Europeans.

The analyses thus far all indicate a general trend of decline in religiosity, whether this is measured in terms of orthodox beliefs, religiosity, or confidence in the churches. This decline in religious convictions is accompanied by a decline in church involvement. On all indicators of religiosity, Italy contradicts these findings. In the 1981–90 period, Italians have become more religious and more orthodox, have put more confidence in their churches, and have displayed higher church attendance (see Note 5). Apart from Italy, *the first hypothesis on increased secularization in European societies is confirmed by our data.*

The second hypothesis assumes an increase in social permissiveness and a decrease in civic morality in West European countries over the last decade. Table 7 reports on trends in permissiveness, and Table 8 shows developments with respect to civic morality.

As far as trends in social permissiveness are concerned, the second hypothesis cannot be rejected on the basis of our analyses. However, the hypothesis is not confirmed in all countries. In some countries, permissiveness indeed increased; in others, there is only a minor increase; and in

Table 8

Civic Morality in Western Europe: Mean (Factor) Scores

	1981	1990	Difference
France	–.27	–.38	–.11
Great Britain	.14	.14	—
West Germany	.13	–.05	–.18
Italy	.36	.06	–.30
Spain	–.16	–.16	—
Netherlands	.07	–.06	–.13
Belgium	.03	–.35	–.38
Denmark	.51	.46	–.05
Northern Ireland	.42	.38	–.04
Ireland	.18	.26	+.08

Source: EVS 1981, 1990

Denmark, a reverse trend is observable. The Danes have become far less permissive in the 1981–90 period and are no longer the most permissive people in Europe that they were in 1981 (Ester and Halman 1990; Halman 1991; Halman and de Moor 1993).[6] In 1990, the Dutch appear to be much more permissive than any other European nation. The French, Belgians, and Germans are also more permissive than the Danes, but not as extreme as the Dutch. However, apart from the Netherlands, the largest increase in social permissiveness can be observed in Belgium, in Italy, and in both Irish societies. The French were already among the more permissive in Western Europe in 1981.

Civic morality decreased in all countries, except Ireland. In that country, civic virtues are slightly more accepted in 1990 than they were in 1981. In Great Britain and Spain, no changes appeared. In Belgium and Italy, a rather strong decline in supporting civic virtues is found. Belgians, together with the French, are the least supportive of civic morality. The Danes remain most in favor of civic virtues of all West Europeans! Apart from observed changes in Italy and Belgium, no substantial trends can be discovered in the remaining European countries.

In general, the conclusion is that civic morality indeed decreased throughout Western Europe, although often the decrease is not very pronounced. On the other hand, permissiveness increased in almost all the countries, except in Denmark, where people have become less permissive. In Belgium, large differences appear with respect to both social permissiveness and civic virtues. In the past decade, Belgians have become less in favor of civic morality, as are the people of other countries except Denmark, and much more socially permissive. Thus, *the second hypothesis is confirmed*, although caution is needed here. The trend in Denmark may become a general trend in other countries as well. In that case, the frequently heard lament that modern society is becoming increasingly immoral or amoral needs to be reformulated.

Convergence of Religious and Moral Values?

The analyses so far support the conclusion that, in general, there is a trend toward less religiosity, less civic morality, and more permissiveness in West European countries. The question is whether this general trend implies that these countries are becoming more similar in their basic religious and moral values, as assumed in the third hypothesis. In this chapter, this question is limited to a simple comparison of scores on the compound variables. No attention is given to a comparison of value patterns, that is, the relationships between manifest and latent variables. We have concluded elsewhere that large differences still remain in these value patterns. In the case of religiosity, however, the conclusion was that this basic value is quite comparable across nations. The other measures or compound variables still need nation-specific interpretations, because the relationships between manifest and latent variables proved to be too different among the various countries to conclude at comparable constructs (Halman 1991; Halman and Vloet 1991).

Despite this empirically based need for nation-specific interpretations, the scores calculated for each country are comparable among countries and across time. The question of convergence or divergence can be answered by measuring the differences among "extreme" countries. If these differences have declined, one may conclude at value convergence. In cases where the differences increased, the trend is toward value divergence.

As can be observed in Tables 1–8, the various West European populations do not converge in their scores on the religious and moral value constructs. On the contrary, the differences in extreme scores appear to have become larger in the 1981–90 period. Thus, the variation among countries is greater for 1990 than it is for 1981 in all five value measures. Despite the unification of Western Europe, neither religious measures nor moral attitudes show converging tendencies. Europe does not at all show a growing unity of basic religious and moral beliefs. The differences seem to become even greater and more in line with the idea that Western Europe in terms of value orientations can be divided in two parts: Northern and Southern Europe. In conclusion, *the hypothesis concerning value convergence (H_3) has to be rejected.*

Another way of "measuring" convergence or divergence is simply by comparing the standard deviations of both survey years. Increased deviations would point at value divergence in Western Europe, whereas decreased deviations would support the idea of value convergence. The results are highly comparable with the findings just presented. The only exception is permissiveness. It seems as if West European societies become more homogeneous in this respect; whereas with respect to measures of religiosity and adherence to civic morality, these societies are becoming more diverse. In other words, a converging trend is observed with regard to social permissiveness, whereas a diverging trend is noticed with respect to religiosity and civic morality. In its present form, *the third hypothesis assuming value convergence has to be rejected.*

What Is True of the Idea of Fragmentation?

Fragmentation implies a general decline in the interrelationships between religious and moral values. Traditionally, there always has been a strong and direct link between religion and morality, most obviously expressed in specific proscriptions such as the Ten Commandments. A diminished relevance of religion will be accompanied by a decline in an "absolutist" perspective on moral values (Wilson 1982). Religion is no longer the prime institution determining moral values. The support for moral values is deinstitutionalized and individualized. Moral values are based on personal choice and preference. "Secularization has led to moral breakdown, interaction based on self-interest rather than any more charitable motive, and the loss of a sense of community. Western civilization as a whole is seen as in jeopardy" (Harding et al. 1986, p. 58). This notion implies a weakening of the relationships between religious and moral values; it is empirically assessed in this chapter by analyzing correlations between the measures of religiosity and moral values as described above. Results are shown in Table 9.

Although the correlations between religious and moral values have not changed dramatically, the trend is in line with our hypothesis (H_4). The correlations between religious beliefs on the one hand and social permissiveness and civic morality on the other have weakened. However, already in 1981 the correlations between religious and moral values were not very strong, ranging between 0.27 and –0.48 (Ester and Halman 1990; Halman 1991; Halman and de Moor 1993). In both 1981 and 1990, religious orientations and beliefs about permissiveness were more strongly interre-

Table 9

Correlations (Pearson) Between Religious and Moral Values in Western Europe

	rel 1981	perm 1990	rel 1981	civ 1990	tra 1981	perm 1990	tra 1981	civ 1990	con 1981	perm 1990	con 1981	civ[a] 1990
France	–.38	–.31	.28	.26	–.27	–.24	.22	.19	–.30	–.25	.27	.18
Great Britain	–.34	–.36	.31	.35	–.21	–.26	.14	.22	–.20	–.20	.12	.15
West Germany	–.48	–.47	.46	.46	–.38	–.30	.28	.28	–.38	–.31	.35	.31
Italy	–.47	–.53	.29	.19	–.37	–.41	.20	.14	–.35	–.45	.20	.23
Spain	–.53	–.49	.44	.29	–.39	–.41	.30	.21	–.40	–.41	.26	.22
Netherlands	–.45	–.47	.28	.29	–.35	–.44	.22	.26	–.25	–.28	.20	.16
Belgium	–.38	–.43	.22	.34	–.17	–.26	.17	.22	–.21	–.22	.18	.16
Denmark	–.47	–.29	.34	.19	–.34	–.21	.21	.08	–.33	–.25	.22	.18
Northern Ireland	–.46	–.37	.32	.32	–.35	–.19	.17	.18	–.35	–.24	.30	.20
Ireland	–.47	–.41	.37	.30	–.36	–.37	.32	.28	–.36	–.32	.25	.21

Source: EVS 1981, 1990

[a] Interpretation of variables:

rel = religiosity

tra = religious orthodoxy

con = confidence in the church

perm = permissiveness

civ = civic morality

lated than religious orientations and beliefs about civic morality. This may be explained by the fact that permissiveness refers to behaviors which in the past were regarded as highly "sinful" in traditional Christian doctrine, and were severely sanctioned by society. Civic morality has more to do with personal integrity and honesty (Harding et al. 1986) and is less uniquely related to traditional Christian doctrine. The conclusion from Table 9 is that fragmentation of religious and moral values has increased in the last decade in West European societies. Again, however, different West European societies show different patterns. In Italy, an increase in the strength of the correlations between religious orientations and permissiveness is observed, whereas the correlations between civic morality and religious orientations decreased. In France, West Germany, Spain, both Irish societies, and Denmark, the strength of the correlations between religious and moral values decreased. A relatively sharp decline of these correlations is particularly observed in Denmark. In Belgium, the Netherlands, and Great Britain the correlations have become (somewhat) stronger. An explanation of the results in these latter societies may be related to the relatively large increase in the number of unchurched people over the last decade. The remaining segment of churched people will be more traditional with respect to both religious and moral values. For them, religion and morality remain closely connected. In Denmark, where the majority are marginal church members, religious convictions hardly influence moral values; religion and morality have little in common in Denmark. The correlations between religious and moral values among the Danes are even weaker than among the French, who in 1981 showed the weakest correlations.

Thus, in many West European societies a decline in the linkage between religion and morality is indeed observable. But in some countries this is not the case. Consequently, *the fourth hypothesis meets with mixed support.*

Life Cycle or Generational Effects?

Our analyses indicated that religiosity and adherence to civic morality declined, whereas permissiveness increased in Western Europe. The question that is yet unanswered is whether these changes manifest themselves in all segments of West European societies or only in specific groups, for instance, in younger age groups. Previous analyses showed that age is one of the most important and powerful variables in explaining differences in values orientations. Older people are much more religious than younger people. They are also more strict and more supportive of civic morality (de Moor 1987; Halman 1991; Halman and de Moor 1993). This raises the question of whether people become less religious as they grow older, or whether older generations are still holding to the religious and moral attitudes they acquired during their formative years. "If there is a life cycle effect, we may expect the age differences to persist and to provide a lasting potential for division. If the explanation is generational, we may expect the differences to fade as younger, more liberal generations replace older, more traditional ones" (Heath and McMahon 1991, p. 15). To answer this question, seven age groups were distinguished for both 1981 and 1990. The youngest generation in 1981 (18–26) has been replaced by another generation of youngest people (18–26) in 1990. Persons aged 18–26 in 1981 are the second youngest generation in 1990 (27–35). The oldest age group in 1981 (72 and over) has been replaced in 1990 by another group of 72 and over that was aged 63–71 in 1981. For each of these age groups, the means for the three religious and two moral values, as well as for church attendance, were calculated. The analyses will be limited to Western Europe as a whole. No distinctions are made for the various countries.

Intergenerational changes are measured by comparing different age groups (in Table 10, indicated as difference 90–81). Analyzing the same cohort over time reveals intergenerational changes (in Table 10, cohort 90–81).

Older generations attend religious services more frequently than younger generations. This still holds for 1990, but the differences between the oldest and youngest generations increased not only as a result of aging but also because of replacement of generations. In getting older, the generations are more frequently attending religious services, whereas younger generations (up to age 35) attend religious services less frequently. The same seems to be true for religiosity and religious orthodoxy, and to a certain extent for confidence in the churches. The younger one is, the less religious and the less orthodox one is and the less confidence one has in the churches. Age is thus positively correlated with these religious orientations. The differences between oldest and youngest age groups increased, except for confidence in the churches, where the differences between oldest and youngest generations decreased somewhat. In getting older, people in all age groups become more religious and orthodox in their beliefs and put more confidence in their churches. These differences within generations appear to be greater than the differences among age groups. So religious orientations seem to be influenced strongly by the fact of one's getting older. Intragenerational changes appear to be stronger than intergenerational changes.

This conclusion does not hold for moral orientations. Getting older is not accompanied by fundamental changes in moral orientation. What is happen-

Table 10

Age and Religious and Moral Orientations in Western Europe

Age group	1981	1990	Difference 90–81	Cohort 90–81
Church attendance				
18–26	3.1450	3.1430	–.0020	
27–35	3.2302	3.0800	–.1502	–.0650
36–44	3.8832	3.4856	–.3976	.2554
45–53	4.0712	4.0756	.0044	.1924
54–62	4.2519	4.2848	.0329	.2136
63–71	4.4509	4.8694	.4185	.6175
72+	4.4385	4.7422	.3037	.2913
Religiosity				
18–26	–.414	–.424	–.010	
27–35	–.280	–.311	–.031	.103
36–44	.008	–.152	–.160	.128
45–53	.168	.131	–.037	.123
54–62	.271	.233	–.038	.065
63–71	.372	.381	.009	.110
72+	.439	.519	.080	.147
Religious orthodoxy				
18–26	2.58	2.68	.10	
27–35	2.74	2.73	–.01	.15
36–44	3.27	2.90	–.37	.16
45–53	3.37	3.28	–.09	.01
54–62	3.63	3.56	–.07	.19
63–71	3.84	3.81	–.03	.18
72+	3.79	4.08	.29	.24
Confidence in the church				
18–26	–.283	–.219	.064	
27–35	–.231	–.238	–.007	.045
36–44	–.036	–.171	–.135	.060
45–53	.118	.032	–.086	.068
54–62	.201	.144	–.057	.026
63–71	.296	.317	.021	.116
72+	.408	.463	.055	.167
Permissiveness				
18–26	.402	.468	.066	
27–35	.298	.414	.116	.012
36–44	–.039	.244	.283	–.054
45–53	–.235	–.032	.203	–.007

(continued)

Table 10 *(continued)*

Age group	1981	1990	Difference 90–81	Cohort 90–81
54–62	–.390	–.232	.158	.003
63–71	–.522	–.373	.149	.017
72+	–.643	–.588	.055	–.066
Civic morality				
18–26	–.527	–.633	–.106	
27–35	–.184	–.318	–.134	.209
36–44	.136	–.101	.035	.083
45–53	.237	.141	–.096	.005
54–62	.378	.212	–.166	–.025
63–71	.474	.342	–.132	–.036
72+	.568	.479	–.089	.005

Source: EVS 1981–1990

ing in the moral domain is that, with replacement of generations, society becomes more morally permissive and will emphasize civic morality less. The differences between the youngest and oldest age groups increased in this respect.

Conclusion

In this chapter, four hypotheses concerning developments in the last decade in religion in modern Western society have been formulated and tested with data from the European Values Surveys (1981, 1990) conducted in ten European countries. The first hypothesis predicts an increase of secularization at the individual level and was confirmed. In all countries, indices for religiosity (church attendance, general religiosity, religious orthodoxy, and confidence in the churches) has decreased during the last decade. An exception to this rule is Italy, where adherence to traditional institutional religiosity has increased. It is not clear how this can be explained (see Note 5).

The second hypothesis concerns an assumed increase in social permissiveness and a decrease in civic morality, and is generally supported. Civic morality indeed declined throughout Western Europe, although the decrease is not very strong. Permissiveness, on the other hand, increased in almost all countries except Denmark, where people have become (far) more strict. It is unclear at this moment whether or not the trend as observed in Denmark will become a general trend in other countries as well.

The third hypothesis assumes a growing convergence of religious and moral values in Western Europe but has to be rejected. The distances among "extreme" countries with respect to religious and moral values increased instead of decreased, and the variation on these dimensions also increased in the 1981–90 period. Both results contradict the hypothesis. Thus, internationalization and the globalization of culture do not necessarily imply value convergence or cultural homogenization. In this respect, the collectively and intensively expressed demand for cultural and political autonomy in East and Central European countries is a case in point.

The fourth and final hypothesis deals with increased fragmentation of religious orientations and moral norms in West European societies. In many countries, a decline in the interrelationships between religious attitudes and moral beliefs is observable. For some countries, however, contrary conclusions have to be drawn. As a general finding, it may be concluded that religious values and moral orientations are less correlated in 1990 than they were in 1981. Thus, there is some fragmentation of religious and secular values.

Finally, inter- and intragenerational value changes have been explored. It is concluded that, in the religious domain, intragenerational changes are more important than intergenerational changes. Accordingly, the younger one is, the less religious is one's world view. Through aging, people become more religious, no matter what measure of religiosity is analyzed. Changes in moral orientations are due mainly to intergenerational differences. Younger generations appear to be less strict in moral beliefs than older generations. Aging hardly affects changes in moral values. Thus, one might predict a further liberalization of moral values and lifestyles in Western Europe due to generational replacement.

As a whole, this chapter confirms conclusions from earlier empirical studies (for instance, Halman 1991; Inglehart 1990), that nation-specific interpretations are indispensable in explaining value change in Europe. It has to be concluded that the globalization of culture facing West European societies does not necessarily imply value convergence. Though at a general level cultures evidently do globalize—especially through the mass media—substantial cultural differences among the various West European societies are likely to persist. As far as basic religious and moral values are concerned, there exists no distinctive "European dimension" in the sense of widely and uniquely shared common values and practices. In this respect Western Europe will stay the melting pot that it has always been.

Notes

1. See Dobbelaere (1981) for a further theoretical and methodological elaboration of the concept of secularization.

2. Each country was weighted to correct for its proportionate population in Europe. The following weight factors were used: France 1981: 4.52, France 1990: 5.63; Great Britain 1981: 4.69, Great Britain 1990: 3.76; West Germany 1981: 4.72, West Germany 1990: 3.01; Italy 1981: 4.19, Italy 1990: 2.86; Spain 1981: 1.64, Spain 1990: 1.48; Netherlands 1981: 1.17, Netherlands 1990: 1.47; Belgium 1981: 0.86, Belgium 1990: 0.35; Denmark 1981: 0.43, Denmark 1990: 0.50; Northern Ireland 1981: 0.50, Northern Ireland 1990: 0.52; Ireland 1981: 0.28, Ireland 1990: 0.35.

3. "Modal" seems to be an incorrect description for this group, as they do not nearly constitute the modal group in secularized society. Marginal members may be described as the new modal group in many if not all Western societies. In the Netherlands, it is better to view the unchurched as the modal group in society (see also Dobbelaere and Voyé 1992).

4. However, in 1981 no information was available about former membership. Therefore, in comparisons in time, only unchurched can be distinguished.

5. This may be due to differences in the wording of the question about belief in a personal god. In 1981, only 28 percent of the Italians believed in such a god. In 1990, this increased to 67 percent! Apparently, the formulation in 1981 was not correct. Personal god was translated as *"Dio come persona"* (Calvaruso and Abbruzzese 1985, p. 216). In 1990, a rewording of the question may have caused this relatively dramatic change in Italy. Now the question was whether one believed that "esiste un Dio." However, figures on other measures of religiosity are in the same line: on all measures the Italians have become more religious!

6. At the panel discussion about the paper on which this chapter is based (at the First European Conference on Sociology; Vienna, Austria, August 26–29, 1992), one leading Danish sociologist of religion suggested the following explanation for decreased permissiveness in Denmark: "We have tried it and it didn't work!"

References

Adriaansens, H.P.M., and A.C. Zijderveld. 1981. *Vrijwillig Initiatief en de Verzorgingsstaat.* Deventer: Van Loghum Slaterus.

Berger, P.L. 1967. *Het Hemels Baldakijn.* Bilthoven: Ambo.

Beyer, P.F. 1990. "Privatization and the Public Influence of Religion in Global Society." In M. Featherstone, ed., *Global Culture: Nationalism, Globalization and Modernity.* London: Sage, pp. 373–95.

Calvaruso, C., and S. Abbruzzese. 1985. *Indagine sui valori in Italia.* Torino: SEI.

de Moor, R. 1987. "Religieuze en Morele Waarden." In L. Halman, F. Heunks, R. de Moor, and H. Zanders, *Traditie, Secularisatie en Individualisering.* Tilburg: Tilburg University Press, pp. 15–49.

Dobbelaere, K. 1981. "Secularization: A Multi-Dimensional Concept," *Current Sociology*, vol. 29, pp. 1–213.

Dobbelaere, K., and L. Voyé. 1992. "Godsdienst en Kerkelijkheid." In J. Kerkhofs, K. Dobbelaere, L. Voyé, and Bawin-Legros, eds., *De Versnelde Ommekeer. De Waarden van Vlamingen, Walen en Brusselaars in de Jaren Negentig.* Tielt: Lannoo, Koning Boudewijnstichting, pp. 115–61.

Ester, P., and L. Halman. 1990. "Basic Values in Western Europe: An Empirical Exploration." Paper presented at the XIIth World Congress of Sociology, Madrid, July 9–13.

Ester, P., and L. Halman. 1991. "Consumptiestijlen en waardenoriëntaties: Een typologische reconstructie." In F. Bronner et al., eds., *Recente Ontwikkelingen in het Marktonderzoek. Jaarboek van de Nederlandse Vereniging van Marktonderzoekers 1990–1991*. Haarlem: Uitgeverij de Vrieseborch, pp. 125–47.

Ester, P., L. Halman, and R. de Moor, eds. 1993. *The Individualizing Society. Value Change in Europe and North America*. Tilburg: Tilburg University Press.

Featherstone, J.M. 1990. *The Paradox of Culture and the Globalization of Diversity*. Utrecht: ISOR.

Glock, C. 1974. "Over het onderzoek van de religiositeit." In K. Dobbelaere and L. Laeyendecker, eds., *Godsdienst, Kerk en Samenleving: Godsdienstsociologische Opstellen*. Rotterdam: Universitaire Pers, pp. 160–85.

Halman, L. 1991. *Waarden in de Westerse Wereld*. Tilburg: Tilburg University Press.

Halman, L., and P. Ester. 1991. "Trends in Individualization in Western Europe, North America, and Scandinavia: Divergence or Convergence of Underlying Values." Paper presented at the symposium Growing into the Future, Stockholm, October 22–23.

Halman, L., and R. de Moor. 1993. "Religion, Churches and Moral Values." In P. Ester, L. Halman, and R. de Moor, eds., *The Individualizing Society. Value Change in Europe and North America*. Tilburg: Tilburg University Press, pp. 37–65.

Halman, L., and A. Vloet. 1991. "Measuring and Comparing Values in 16 Countries of the Western World in 1990 and 1981." Tilburg: IVA, Institute for Social Research and Tilburg University.

Harding, S., D. Phillips, and M. Fogarty. 1986. *Contrasting Values in Western Europe: Unity, Diversity and Change*. London: Macmillan.

Heath, A., and D. McMahon. 1991. "Consensus and Dissensus." In R. Jowell, L. Brook, and B. Taylor, eds., *British Social Attitudes. The 8th Report*. Aldershot, Hants.: Dartmouth, pp. 1–21.

Inglehart, R. 1990. *Culture Shift in Advanced Industrial Society*. Princeton, NJ: Princeton University Press.

Kerr, C. 1983. *The Future of Industrial Society: Convergence or Continuing Diversity?* Cambridge, MA: Harvard University Press.

Klages, H. 1985. *Werturientierungen im Wandel: Rückblick, Gegenwartsanalyse, Prognosen*. Frankfurt/New York: Campus Verlag.

Lasch, C. 1979. *The Culture of Narcissism*. New York: Norton.

Lenski, G. 1961. *The Religious Factor. A Sociological Study of Religion's Impact on Politics, Economics, and Family Life*. New York: Doubleday.

Luckmann, T. 1967. *The Invisible Religion. The Problem of Religion in Modern Society*. New York: Macmillan.

Meulemann, H. 1987. "Religiöse und Politische Werte in Alters- und Bildungsgruppen. Differenzierung und Kristallisation von Wertvorstellungen in der Bundesrepublik Deutschland," *Politische Vierteljahresschrift*, vol. 28, pp. 220–41.

Peters, J., and A. Felling. 1981. "Kerkelijkheid en Onkerkelijkheid: een Onjuiste Tweedeling." In W. Goddijn and G. van Tillo, eds., *Hebben de Kerken nog Toekomst*. Baarn: Ambo, pp. 33–60.

Rosenau, P.M. 1992. *Post-Modernism and the Social Sciences. Insights, Inroads, and Intrusions*. Princeton, NJ: Princeton University Press.

Stark R., and C. Glock. 1968. *American Piety: The Nature of Religious Commitment*. Berkeley, CA: University of California Press.

Stufkens, H. 1987. *Heimwee naar God*. Rotterdam: Lemniscaat.
Van Steenbergen, B. 1986. *Sociale innovatie*. Den Haag: Staatsdrukkerij.
Wilson, B. 1982. *Religion in Sociological Perspective*. Oxford: Oxford University Press.
Yankelovich, D. 1981. *New Rules*. New York: Random House.
Zijderveld, A.C. 1979. "Het Ethos van de Verzorgingsstaat," *Sociale Wetenschappen*, vol. 22, pp. 179–203.
Zijderveld, A.C. 1983. *De Culturele Factor: Een Cultuursociologische Wegwijzer*. Den Haag: VUGA.

JAP DRONKERS

The Causes of Growth of English Education in the Netherlands

Introduction

In December 1989, the then newly appointed minister of education and science announced that he wanted to aim at introducing more teaching in the English language in Dutch universities. Members of the lower house of all political persuasions rushed to attack the minister. Did he think that universities in the Netherlands ought to start using English as their official language? Did he not believe that the Dutch language had an essential place in Dutch culture, or that education in particular played a crucial role in passing on cultural values? Or was there not the danger that the minister's position might lead to the Netherlands' gradual acquisition of a cultural elite which would no longer use primarily the language of the land? Minister Ritzen attempted to calm down the commotion by pointing out that he had no wish to introduce English as the official language or as the only official language in the universities of the Netherlands. He also believed that the use of a foreign language must not be allowed to lead to the loss of the national language. Subsequently, the topic of "English in the Dutch universities" was subjected to extensive criticism in all the daily and weekly newspapers. Most commentators found it a ridiculous idea. After an inquiry into this question by an official committee, the lower house decided to make the use of the Dutch language compulsory by law in Dutch education.

However, there remains the question of how far educational policy directs the extent to which education in the Netherlands becomes internationalized. It is entirely possible that it is not the supply of internationally oriented education, but rather the demand expressed by pupils, students, and parents for internationally oriented education, that determines the degree of

---

The Dutch version of this article was published in *Sociale Wetenschappen* (1991, volume 34: 3); the English version was first published in *European Journal of Education* (1993, volume 28: 3).

internationalization of Dutch education. In that case, all the commotion about statements made by ministers is unjustified. If the internationalization of Dutch education is a demand-driven development, attention should in fact be focused on the emergence of this demand, and not on the relatively unimportant supply side. This paper will focus on the demand for English-language education in the Netherlands. Greater attention needs to be paid to this question, since the main focus of interest in the Dutch debate on education is almost always on the supply side.[1]

To date, the internationalization of Dutch university education has been given equivocal treatment. On the one hand, there is a massive outcry if a minister makes a remark about lectures in the English language and attempts to make the use of the Dutch language in Dutch education compulsory by law. On the other hand, universities, faculties, and teachers are bombarded with government and nongovernment initiatives aiming to increase the international mobility of Dutch students and teachers. The best known example of this is the ERASMUS program, the purpose of which is to encourage visits to other universities in Europe. These government initiatives are not criticized; rather, it is anxiously reported that not all the objectives are being met. The attitude of public opinion in the Netherlands toward internationalization is thus ambiguous; it simultaneously condemns and encourages it.

There is limited information available about the degree of internationalization in the Dutch universities. Researchers will hunt in vain for scientific studies into the background and effects of initiatives promoting internationalization, such as the ERASMUS program. True, it is known that disciplines differ in their degree of international orientation (for example, it is high for theory of functions and low for social administration science; Nederhof 1989). These differences give an indication of the extent to which these disciplines and subdisciplines are focused upon in the Netherlands, but it is not known whether particular changes can be observed in them. The same applies to the international impact of Dutch research within a discipline or subdiscipline, seen in terms of references in the international specialist journals. This impact also varies among countries, and it changes over time. However, changes in this impact need not necessarily indicate internationalization of university research, as no checks are made for other changes affecting this research (greater scope, increased productivity, cutbacks, and so on). In short, a great deal is said about the good and bad sides of the internationalization of Dutch education, but there are almost no reliable analyses of this putative internationalization available.

This also applies to the putative internationalization of secondary education. Now and then, internationalization projects appear in the press, but

Table 1

Growth of English Schools in the Netherlands

	1983	1984	1985	1986	1987	1988	1989	1990
Primary school (ENbo)	—	2	4	6	7	7	7	7
Secondary school (ENvo)	2	5	5	6	7	8	8	8
International Baccalaureate	3	3	4	4	5	6	8	8
Totals	5	10	13	16	19	21	23	23

that is the end of the matter. I do not know of any scientific studies of the developments in English-language secondary education in the Netherlands.[2] And yet this lack of scientific study does not mean that there is a lack of tempestuous developments going on around the internationalization of secondary education in the Netherlands. On the contrary; since the beginning of the 1980s, a number of schools in the Netherlands have been experimenting with international education funded by the government.[3] There are three types of English-language educational programs: ENbo (English/Dutch-language primary education),[4] ENvo (English/Dutch-language secondary education, comparable with the Higher General Secondary Education [HAVO] program),[5] and IB (International Baccalaureate, a two-year program, comparable with the pre-university education [VWO] program).[6] According to the official principles, this English-language education is not for "ordinary" Dutch pupils. It is solely intended for children of foreign nationalities, for Dutch children who have lived abroad and gone to school there, and for Dutch children who are living temporarily in the Netherlands. In spite of these limitations on the types of pupils who can be admitted, the number of schools providing English-language education grew steadily throughout the first half of the 1980s (see Table 1). In the view of the government and of the schools that offer education in the English language, the reason for its growth is the increase in the number of Dutch pupils who belong to the target group for English-language education.

In this essay, I shall look at the background of this growth in English-language education by comparing the backgrounds, motives, and plans for the future expressed by Dutch-speaking pupils in the International Baccalaureate (IB) department with those of the pupils in the pre-university education (VWO) department in the same schools. A comparison of this kind can provide more insight into the causes of the internationalization of education in the Netherlands. Furthermore, since the International Baccalaureate is chiefly a pre-university education course, this comparison can also give some insight into the causes of internationalization in Dutch universities.

Two Viewpoints on the Internationalization of Education

In analyzing the backgrounds, motives, and future plans of Dutch-speaking pupils, I have taken my inspiration from two possible viewpoints on the social background of the internationalization of Dutch education.

The first point of view is taken from Ultee (1989). He analyzes the consequences of the increased cohesion among the member-countries of the European Community in the context of the widening cultural differences between the social classes in the smaller EC countries. Ultee rightly points out that the question whether the individual national cultures will disappear because of the European Community is not a proper question, as isolated cultures have never existed in Europe. He considers that a better question would be to what extent the cultures of the EC countries will become even more markedly intermingled than they already are as a consequence of economic unification. He then goes on to refine this question by pointing out that in stratified societies (and all West European societies are stratified), only each *layer* within countries has a culture: besides the dominant culture of the upper layers of a society, subcultures exist which are associated with the lower rungs of the social ladder. Ultee therefore reformulates the question thus: To what extent are the cultures of the upper layers and the subcultures of the lower layers in the member states growing toward each other as a result of the EC? He then points out that the upper layers of societies always possess a more cosmopolitan culture. Most of all, though, these people will have more contact with foreign countries through their work and will acquire a cultural heritage that fits in with this. This means that cosmopolitanism may grow more strongly in the upper layers of the member states than in the lower layers, which would imply that the EC is causing the cultural differences within countries to grow more extreme. This would then apply all the more for the EC countries that are not cultural leaders, such as the Netherlands. Ultee also points out that the EC will increase social mobility by providing both a more attractive opportunity structure and greater relative mobility. This increase in mobility would be brought about by the creation of supranational institutions staffed by officials who have positions above those of the national civil servants, and by the formation of European companies run by a management that also operates at a level above that of the national companies' managers. Over time, these European officials and directors will become separated from the national upper layers from which most of them come, as a result of their developing cosmopolitan culture. The cultural criterion of these top people will be cosmopolitan, while that of the lower layers is noncosmopolitan in a variety of ways. This gives a small upper crust an advantage over the larger lower layers.

Looked at from this point of view, the growth of English-language education in the Netherlands must be regarded primarily as a consequence of the increased cohesion among the countries of the European Community and the resulting development of a cosmopolitan culture by a part of the Dutch elite. From this point of view, education in the English language is both a way to become a member of this cosmopolitan culture and a symbol that one already regards oneself as belonging to this cosmopolitan culture. Since we are concerned here with a new differentiation within the top social stratum of the Netherlands, it is not the class of the parents but the degree of cosmopolitanism that is the decisive factor in choosing English-language education. This also applies to the objective of English-language education. The key consideration is not the level of education to be achieved but the opportunity to become a member of the cosmopolitan culture. This leads to my first hypothesis: The choice between International Baccalaureate (IB) or pre-university education (VWO) programs will be based principally on the degree of cosmopolitanism of the pupil's family, which will in turn be based on the social class to which that family belongs. This also leads to my second hypothesis: The choice between IB or VWO programs will be made first and foremost with a view to joining the cosmopolitan culture; in other words, with a view to studying outside the Netherlands.

The second viewpoint is taken from Boudon (1979) and Mare (1981). Although they are not concerned with the internationalization of education, an alternative explanation for the growth of English-language education in the Netherlands can nevertheless be drawn from their analyses of inequality of opportunity in education. Boudon and Mare examine the ways in which educational systems vary in their power to preserve differences in educational opportunities for different social classes. They see educational systems as a series of hurdles or decision points (for example, the transition from secondary education to higher education). At each decision point, children from higher social classes have a better chance of making a more advantageous choice than children from lower social classes. Because of the growth in educational participation, but also because of particular educational reforms (the Mammoth Act), the importance of decision points at the beginning of one's school career has diminished because nearly everyone is able to pass that decision point successfully (Dronkers 1990; de Graaf and Ganzeboom 1990). This has meant that the educational advantage enjoyed by children from higher social classes has diminished. One of the ways in which this educational advantage can still be preserved is by the creation of new decision points further along in the school career (for example, the postgraduate stage of university education). The introduction of English-language education can be described as the creation of a new decision point, the aim of which is to preserve the "educational distance" between the upper and lower classes. Dronkers (1987, p. 53) therefore thought that the interest in English-language education stemmed from a fear of the leveling effect of primary education. This point of view leads to my third hypothesis: The choice between IB or VWO programs will be based principally on the social class of the student's family and only to a lesser extent on the family's cosmopolitanism. This also leads to my fourth hypothesis: The choice between IB and VWO programs is made first and foremost with a view to raising the intended level of education, that is, to a university degree course.

Data

These four hypotheses were tested using the data collected by Van der Pluijm (1990; 1991). In 1989, he interviewed 237 pupils at four schools that offered both IB and VWO programs, using a written questionnaire. He confined his study to the Dutch pupils in the first class of the International Baccalaureate program and to the pupils in the fifth class of the pre-university education (VWO) program.[7] In these schools the choice between the International Baccalaureate and VWO programs must be made at the end of the fourth class of pre-university education. Van der Pluijm collected data about the backgrounds, motives, and future plans of these IB and VWO pupils. He concluded from his comparison of the two groups that the foreign background of the pupil's parents is the most important explanation for the choice of English-language education. In turn, social class influences the amount of foreign background that the parents have. Social class also has a slight effect on the choice of English-language education. Van der Pluijm's analysis did not convince everyone because he also included in his analyses 65 Dutch pupils who spoke no Dutch at home or who had gone to school in a foreign country in 1988. For 28 percent of the pupils studied, there was no real choice between the International Baccalaureate and VWO programs. Because of this, van der Pluijm may have overestimated the effect of the parents' foreign background on the choice between IB and VWO at the expense of the effect of social class. In this paper, I shall therefore confine my analysis to the 170 Dutch pupils who speak the Dutch language at home, who attended school in the Netherlands in 1988, and who were in the IB or VWO departments in 1989.[8]

It is true that this analysis involves a small group, but it is specifically in the microcosm of schools with both an IB and a VWO department that we can investigate the social background of the putative internationalization of education in the Netherlands. Macro phenomena, such as the growth of English-language education, must by definition develop as the result of a complicated sum of innumerable individual actions, in this case by comparable parents and pupils in VWO and IB departments. It is therefore important to study the mechanisms which, in this case, lead to the choice between IB and VWO, irrespective of the size of the group and the extent to which the group is representative of the Dutch school population as a whole.

Analysis

Forty-six Dutch pupils (45 percent) in the first IB class spoke Dutch at home and attended school in the Netherlands in 1988. The remaining 57 IB pupils (55 percent) either spoke no Dutch at home, or attended school abroad in 1988. About half of the pupils taking the International Baccalaureate program thus had no other choice than education in the English language. This is not to say that the four schools exceed the admission rules. Ninety-six percent of the first group, the "voluntary" IB pupils, had attended school in a foreign country at some time, and 52 percent had done so for seven years or longer. All the Dutch-speaking "voluntary" IB pupils had lived abroad at some point, and 72 percent had done so for five years or more. This does not mean that the VWO program is taken only by pupils who do not have a foreign background: 10 percent of the VWO pupils had gone to school in a foreign country at one time, and 12 percent of them had lived abroad. However, the relationship between VWO and IB pupils is clear: the latter have a more international background than the former, despite using Dutch as their language at home and having been in the Netherlands in 1988.

This difference in international orientation can also clearly be seen from the reasons most frequently cited by the IB pupils for following education in the English language rather than in Dutch, and from the reasons most frequently cited by VWO pupils for following education in Dutch rather than in English. Table 2 gives a summary of the reasons given most frequently by the pupils.[9]

Despite the fact that the pre-university education (VWO) and International Baccalaureate (IB) pupils studied were Dutch-speaking, and were in the Netherlands in 1988, their preliminary education—in the Dutch or English language—was the reason most frequently cited for choosing the IB or the VWO program. In other words, the international orientation of their

Table 2

Reasons for Attending or Not Attending International Baccalaureate (IB) Program (Percentage of Responses)

A.	VWO Pupils: Reasons for Not Attending (n = 124)	
1.	I have the Dutch nationality; I am Dutch	36%
2/3.	I have an upbringing in the Dutch language	22%
2/3.	I have a previous Dutch education	22%
4.	Never thought about IB	16%
5/6.	The English language is too difficult for education	11%
5/6.	I master the English language insufficiently	11%
B.	IB Pupils: Reasons for Attending (n = 46)	
1.	I have a previous English education	72%
2.	I master the Dutch language insufficiently	33%
3.	I have lived abroad	26%
4.	I want to study abroad	17%
5.	English education gives more opportunities abroad	15%
6.	Switch from English to Dutch language too difficult	13%
7.	IB gives a better international orientation	11%

home background was the most important reason. However, IB pupils also mentioned reasons that relate to their international plans for the future. This supports the two first hypotheses that are based on the viewpoint put forward by Ultee (the degree of cosmopolitanism is an important factor in the choice of IB or VWO). It is noteworthy that the IB pupils hardly mention issues of quality as reasons for their choice, which conflicts with the third and fourth hypotheses that are based on the viewpoint of Boudon and Mare (the choice of IB with an eye to a higher future level of education).

However, this is not the only difference between the "voluntary" IB and VWO pupils. Table 3 shows a number of further differences between these IB and pre-university education (VWO) pupils.

It can clearly be seen from Table 3 that the cultural capital of the parents of IB pupils (as measured by the parents' education and the books they own) is significantly greater than that of the parents of VWO pupils. However, it also appears from this table that both groups of pupils belong to the same social class: Their parents do not differ significantly on Bakker's social distance scale, which is a good indicator of class differences between professions (Bakker 1990). One could thus say that the difference between IB and VWO pupils is primarily a difference within the same class and is related to education and international orientation. Table 3 once again clearly shows this difference in international orientation between VWO and IB pupils: IB pupils and their parents maintain more contacts with foreign

Table 3

Characteristics of Dutch-speaking Pupils in IB and VWO Departments of Four Dutch Schools

	IB			VWO		
	mean	st/dev.	N	mean	st/dev.	N
Social Background						
Gender of pupil[a]	1.40	.50	45	1.49	.50	123
Social status father's occupation[b]	1.51	1.16	46	1.45	1.24	123
Social status mother's occupation[c]	.64	2.01	46	.92	2.10	124
Father's educational level[d]	5.70	.63	44	4.68	1.50	112
Mother's educational level[e]	4.41	1.48	44	3.90	1.32	113
Number of books at home[f]	4.39	.81	44	3.43	1.15	122
International Orientation						
Number holidays abroad[g]	5.02	1.60	46	4.19	1.56	124
Father's foreign trips[h]	4.58	1.70	43	2.60	1.66	119
Time father working abroad[i]	4.88	1.74	42	2.86	1.23	70
Number of visits foreign friends[j]	2.33	.63	46	1.97	.66	119
Siblings in English education[k]	1.50	.51	46	1.01	.09	124
Future Plans						
Further education[l]	2.00	.00	45	1.97	.17	104
University education[m]	1.87	.34	39	1.69	.47	74
Education abroad[n]	1.15	.36	40	1.04	.33	81
English-speaking education[o]	1.21	.41	39	1.03	.16	79

Legend: Underlined mean values show a significant difference between the two groups (two-tailed T-test, $p < .05$). Differences in totals are caused by missing values for some questions.

[a] 0–1 = boy; 1+ = girl.

[b] The professions of the fathers were translated into Bakker's social distance scale for men (1990). This social distance scale closely resembles the better known scales classifying professional prestige, but has a number of significant advantages (distinguishes between men and women; scores for nonworking people).

[c] The professions of the mothers were translated into Bakker's social distance scale for women (1990). This social distance scale closely correlates with the better known scales classifying professional prestige, but has a number of significant advantages: its own scoring system for women's professions and for nonworking people.

[d] The highest educational program completed by the father was categorized according to the CBS standard educational classification.

[e] The highest educational program completed by the mother was categorized according to the CBS standard educational classification.

[f] Categories varied from none or few (1 to 2) to a room or library (501 or more).

[g] Categories varied from never to 21 times or more.

[h] The number of times that the father has to go abroad for the purposes of his work, classified in categories varying from never to 11 or more times per year.

(continued)

Table 3 *(continued)*

[i] The amount of time that the father spends abroad for the purposes of his work, classified in categories varying from 1 day per year to more than 3 months per year.

[j] The number of times that foreign friends, acquaintances, or relatives come to visit; could vary from never to often (10 or more times per year).

[k] Brother(s) and/or sister(s) following English-language education: 1 = no, 2 = yes.

[l] 1= work after secondary education; 2= study after secondary education.

[m] Choice of a university degree course in place of higher vocational education.

[n] Further education abroad rather than in the Netherlands.

[o] Official language at the educational institution where the student wants to continue studying: 1 = Dutch, 2 = English.

countries than do VWO pupils and their parents. The clearest difference between VWO and IB pupils in terms of their plans for the future is that the latter already know more clearly what they want. Their level of ambition is also higher, and they more often want to follow an English-language course of study. These findings completely support Ultee's viewpoint and only partly support Boudon and Mare's. The first and second hypotheses (that the degree of cosmopolitanism is important in the choice between IB and VWO) can be accepted; while of the third and fourth hypotheses, only the fourth (the choice of IB with a view to a higher level of education in the future) can be accepted.

Nevertheless, these results are not yet definitive. It is of course possible that a large part of the international orientation of the IB pupils is the result of their parents' cultural capital, and that therefore the choice between IB and VWO is based more on this cultural capital than on international orientation. It is also possible that, after taking into account the parents' international orientation, the social class of the parents may still play a role in the choice between IB and VWO programs. The following path analysis takes these possible phantom effects into account. In these analyses, the international orientation of the pupil's family is made up of a combination of seven characteristics: the total number of years spent at school in a foreign country; the total number of years lived abroad; the number of times the family goes on holiday abroad; the number of times that the father goes abroad for his work; how long he stays abroad for his work; the number of times that foreign friends, acquaintances, or family members come to visit; and whether brother(s) and/or sister(s) are undergoing education in the English language. This combination of characteristics was calculated using the PRINCALS method.[10] Four characteristics were found to be the most important indicators of an international orientation in the pupil's family: number of years spent at school in a foreign country; number of years lived

Figure 1. **Causal Model of the Relationship Among Social Background, International Orientation, IB or VWO Attendance, and Future Plans**

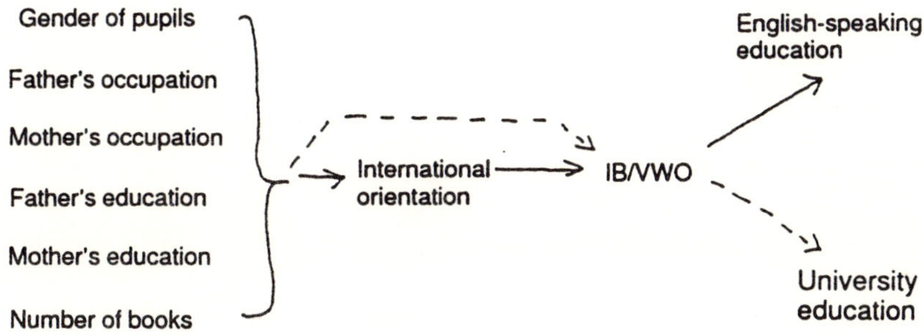

Legend: Broken lines supposed by the perspective of Mare and Boudon; unbroken lines supposed by the perspective of Ultee.

abroad; number of times that the pupil's father goes abroad for his work; and how long he stays abroad.[11]

Figure 1 shows the causal model with which the four hypotheses can be tested.

Table 4 gives the significant standardized regression coefficients that were calculated on the basis of this causal model using multivariate regression analysis.[12]

The first column of Table 4 clearly shows that the international orientation of the pupil's family is dependent on the professional and educational level of the parents, particularly that of the father. This result confirms the first part of the first hypothesis, that the cosmopolitanism of the pupil's family is a consequence of the social class to which the family belongs. This explanation of the variation may be described as satisfactory.

The second column of Table 4 clearly shows that the choice between the International Baccalaureate and pre-university education programs is exclusively predicted by the international orientation of the pupil's family. This

Table 4

Significant Standardized Regression Effects (based on Figure 1)

	International orientation	IB/ VWO	English education	University education
Gender of pupils	—	—	—	—
Father's occupation	.17	—	—	—
Mother's occupation	—	—	—	—
Father's education	.19	—	—	—
Mother's education	—	—	—	—
Number of books	.29	—	—	.34
International orientation		.77	—	—
IB/ VWO			.32	—
Adjusted R^2	.22	.59	.10	.10

confirms the second part of the first hypothesis: that the choice between IB and VWO programs is based chiefly on the degree of cosmopolitanism of the pupil's family. The absence of a significant effect for the parents' professional or educational level confirms the rejection of the third hypothesis, that the choice between the IB and VWO programs is based principally on social class.

The fourth column of Table 4 clearly shows that the choice of the IB program is not related to a greater preference for a university education. That preference is based purely on the cultural background of the pupil's family. The fourth hypothesis, which proposed that the choice of the IB program is made first and foremost with the aim of taking a university degree course, is thus rejected.

Finally, the third column of Table 4 shows that the choice of the IB program is associated with a greater preference for secondary education in the English language. The second hypothesis is confirmed by this finding: The choice between IB and VWO programs is made first and foremost with an eye to joining the cosmopolitan culture.

Discussion

The first two hypotheses are based on the viewpoint that social background and the internationalization of education in the Netherlands are related. By this perspective, the growth of English-language education in the Netherlands is primarily a consequence of the development of the European Community and the concomitant development of a cosmopolitan culture among a section of the Dutch elite. These two hypotheses are confirmed by comparing the backgrounds, motives, and future plans of Dutch pupils in the International Baccalaureate and pre-university education departments in the same schools.

The two hypotheses based on the second perspective, which interprets the growth of English-language education in the Netherlands as stemming primarily from the desire to maintain an "educational distance" between the upper and lower classes, are rejected on the basis of the same comparison.[13] This means that the growth of English-language education in the Netherlands is a consequence of the demand by particular groups of Dutch parents and pupils. This demand is not increased by circumstances internal to the Netherlands but is determined solely by developments outside the Netherlands. The increasing cohesion among the economies of Western Europe is leading to an increasingly strong international orientation among a section of the Dutch elite abroad. In this context, it is useful to bring to mind once again the fact that a father (or mother) working abroad is in itself one of the most important indicators of the international orientation of a pupil's family. At the same time, the close relationship between international orientation and social class means that, for the moment, the entire Dutch educational system will not go over to using the English language. Education in English will form a realistic alternative only for a particular social segment of Dutch parents. However, this segment will be made up of a growing number of Dutch parents, since the increase in mobility in Western Europe will result in increasing numbers of parents and their children meeting the admission requirements for English-language education. With the government-funded experiments in international education, the government has created an opportunity for English-language education to grow, but the question remains whether the government of the Netherlands should be able to reject this possibility, or whether it can still close it again.[14] However, the growth itself appears to stem primarily from the demand from internationally oriented Dutch parents, and it is questionable whether this demand will stabilize.

Seen from this point of view, the uproar occasioned by Minister Ritzen's comments is hypocritical. He does not determine the pressure to internationalize education in the Netherlands. From this study, it would seem rather that the internationalization of one sector of education in the Netherlands results from a demand by the parents and pupils. This demand does not stem from considerations of social classes or differences but from the increased cohesion among the economies of Western Europe, which gives parents and pupils an international orientation despite their use of the Dutch language at home. Members of parliament and commentators must therefore not address their questions to the minister of education and science but to the ministers of foreign affairs and economic affairs. It is much more their policies that are gradually causing the population of the Netherlands to acquire an upper crust that no longer primarily uses the language of the land, than the policies of the minister of education and science.

The "Latinizing" of the church and lay elite of the Celts and the invading Germans was not produced by the broad range of education offered in the Roman language, but by the demand from people wanting to become members of an international elite.

Notes

1. This one-sided interest in the supply side of education is probably the result of the centralized nature of the Dutch educational establishment, which creates the illusion that education can be managed by legislation and policy-making.

2. A possible explanation for the lack of scientific studies into the internationalization of education in the Netherlands is the fact that the bodies that are responsible for research into the workings of Dutch education are dominated by the established educational organizations. Just as these organizations have no real interest in research into the origins and consequences of the continuing compartmentalization of education, also the internationalization of education in the Netherlands is outside their area of interest.

3. In the following paragraphs, I shall make use of the overview offered by Van der Pluijm (1990).

4. ENbo is linked to a normal Dutch primary school as a department, and it can best be characterized as the English/Dutch-language counterpart of Dutch primary education: the areas of education and training covered do not differ in content from those in the Dutch program, and 30 percent of the lessons are taught in Dutch. ENbo departments are funded in the same way as the Dutch primary schools are; the same rules as those for the Dutch primary schools apply to ENbo staff and material facilities.

5. The ENvo is a five-year program of study comparable with the Higher General Secondary Education (HAVO) program. Although 30 percent of the classes must be taught in Dutch, the ENvo program is different from that of Dutch secondary education. Schools are free to develop their own curricula, under certain conditions. The examination that is taken at the end of the ENvo program is usually the English GCE examination at O (ordinary) level. The funding of the ENvo program is also different. A pupil in an ENvo department is not allowed to cost the government more than a pupil enrolled at a HAVO or VWO school. This amounts to 50 percent of the costs. In principle, the remainder of the costs must be covered by third parties.

6. The International Baccalaureate is an international form of education that is offered by 350 schools in 52 countries. The IB certificate is recognized by 600 universities throughout the world, including the universities in the Netherlands. The IB program lasts two years, and the final level reached is comparable with the Dutch pre-university education (VWO) program. Examinations are taken in seven subjects. Besides philosophy, pupils must choose three subjects at a high level (somewhat above the VWO level), and three subjects at a low level (somewhat below the VWO level). It is compulsory to choose two languages, mathematics, one social subject, and one natural sciences subject. The examining office of the International Baccalaureate Organization in Geneva prepares the examinations and awards the certificate. Schools pay for the right to take the

examinations. IB is funded in the same way as regular Dutch education. The extra funds that are needed for the IB program must be provided by interested third parties.

7. Van der Pluijm (1990) defines Dutch pupils as pupils with Dutch nationality.

8. It is possible to object to this selection on the grounds that 88 percent of VWO pupils are not eligible for admission to the IB program because they have never lived abroad, let alone gone to school in a foreign country. Because of this admission rule, there is no real choice for these 109 VWO pupils between education in English and education in Dutch. However, this objection to the selection criterion used here is not valid, because this article is concerned with the differences between comparable IB and VWO pupils. Furthermore, examination of the differences among the characteristics of the VWO pupils who had never lived abroad, the VWO pupils who had lived abroad, and the Dutch-speaking IB pupils revealed that the second group occupies a position between the first and third groups. This reinforces my argument that VWO pupils and IB pupils comprise comparable groups.

9. This question was posed as an open question. All VWO pupils could give a maximum of three reasons for not taking the IB program, and all the IB pupils could give a maximum of three reasons for taking it. These reasons were categorized and subsequently added up.

10. PRINCALS (principal component analysis by means of alternating least squares) can be used where the variables have no interval level and the relationship among these variables is nonlinear. In the present PRINCALS analysis, all the variables were ordinal with the exception of the variable "how much time does the father spend abroad for his work," which was treated as a nominal variable. This was done to cope with the much-used category "not applicable," which does not automatically fit into an ordinal arrangement. However, with PRINCALS, it is possible to calculate coordinators for all categories of a nominal variable.

11. The first dimension used for the PRINCALS analysis has a value of 0.52, while this figure is 0.16 for the unused second dimension. The factor loadings for the seven variables on the first dimension are: total number of years spent at school abroad (0.88); total number of years lived abroad (0.87); number of times family goes on holiday abroad (0.46); number of times that father goes abroad for his work (0.81); how long father stays abroad for his work (0.82); number of times that foreign friends, acquaintances, or family come to visit (0.43); whether brother(s) and/or sister(s) follow English-language education (0.64). The results of the PRINCALS analysis clearly show that all the variables do indeed have an ordinal level, including the variable "amount of time worked abroad by the father," if the category "not applicable" is classified under the category "approximately one day per year."

12. Calculated by the "stepwise forward" method, with $p < 0.05$ as the stop criterion. All variables that appear to the right of the dependent variable concerned in the causal model are treated as independent variables that may possibly have a significant effect on the dependent variable.

13. This result does not differ greatly from that found by Van der Pluijm (1991). The most important difference is the fact that Van der Pluijm also found a small significant effect of the professional level of the father on the choice of the IB program. The more stringent selection of the pupil population used here results in the disappearance of this effect.

14. An interesting parallel will probably be found here between the media establishment and the educational establishment. Foreign broadcasters appear to be able to undermine the bastion of the media establishment, on the basis of European legislation among other things. With the aid of this same European legislation, it will probably be impossible for the government to oppose partly funded English-language education in the Netherlands.

References

Bakker, B.F.M. 1990. "Meten van sociale status in de jaren negentig," *Mens en Maatschappij*, vol. 65, pp. 355–78.

Boudon, R. 1979. *L' inégalité des chances. La mobilité sociale dans les sociétés industrielles*. Paris: Armand Colin.

de Graaf, P.M., and H.B.G. Ganzeboom. 1990. *Family Background and Eucational Attainment in the Netherlands of Birth Cohorts 1891–1960*. Utrecht: Utrecht State University, Department of Social Sciences, Section on Empirical and Theoretical Sociology.

Dronkers, J. 1987. "Ongelijke kansen, schoolloopbanen en reorganisatie van de eerste fase van het voortgezet onderwijs." In Halkes, R., and van Hoek, B., eds., *Basisvorming in onderwijskundige optiek*. Lisse: Swets en Zeitlinger, pp. 39–55.

Dronkers, J. 1990. *The Impact of Parental Occupation and Education on the Transitions in Primary and Secondary School Before and After the Educational Reforms of 1968 in the Netherlands*. Amsterdam: Postdoctoraal Instituut voor de Sociale Wetenschap.

Mare, R.D. 1981. "Change and Stability in Educational Stratification," *American Sociological Review*, vol. 46, pp. 72–87.

Nederhof, A.J. 1989. "Meting van kwaliteit van onderzoek van vakgroepen in de antropologie, bestuurskunde en psychologische functieleer; een empirische benadering," *Mens en Maatschappij*, vol. 64, pp. 166–77.

Ultee, W.C. 1989. *Economische eenwoording, groter wordende sociale afstanden, blijvende culturele verscheidenheid? Afwijkende antwoorden op nieuwe vragen over ongelijkheid en cohesie in de Europese Gemeenschap sins 1957 en na 1992*. Nijmegen: Instituut voor Toegepaste Sociale Wetenschappen.

Van der Pluijm, J. 1990. *Engelstalig onderwijs in Nederland*, Katholieke Universiteit Brabant.

Van der Pluijm, J. 1991. "Engelstalig onderwijs in Nederland." In Dronkers, J., Meijnen, G.W., and Dekkers, H., eds., *ORD'91; Onderwijs en Samenleving*. Amsterdam: Stichting Centrum voor Onderwijsonderzoek, pp. 195–206.

ATTILA ERALP

Turkey and the European Community

Forging New Identities Along Old Lines

Introduction

Questions of modernization have been closely related to issues of identity and therefore of internal order and foreign policy in Turkey ever since the nineteenth century. For Ottoman reformers and their successors in the Turkish Republic, modernization, in turn, has meant the fashioning of the polity along European lines, or "Westernization." This transformation of the land of the infidel and enemy to a societal blueprint to be emulated has brought in its wake serious problems regarding identity and appurtenance. Over a period of a hundred years, the polity has transformed itself from an Eastern empire to a modern nation-state seeking inclusion within the institutional and cultural fold of the West. This makes Turkey an interesting case to look at, especially since in many other countries outside the West, identity has largely been defined in terms of opposition to the West.

The mosaic of ethnic identities that composed the Ottoman Empire had not included Turk as one of the *millets* that served as the building blocks of the administrative framework. The term "Turk" was a derogatory one conferred by the European powers and was used to distinguish Ottoman Muslim subjects from their Christian counterparts. As Europe recast its identity by tracing its ancestry to ancient Greece, "Turk" began to designate the barbarism that, by constituting "the other," could define the civilization whose genealogy was traced out by the nascent Greek nationalism. Turkishness was gradually adopted as a national identity by some of the Ottomans themselves in response to the growing nationalisms within their own boundaries. In contradistinction to the Europeanness that Greek nationalists drew upon, Turkishness was constructed mainly in reference to a Central Asian past. But Turkishness has retained its negative connotations in spite of the attempts by Turkish nationalists to impart it with the glory needed to build a nation. A sense of exclusion and inferiority has therefore haunted

Turkish identity as defined by its elites. Modernization, it was hoped, would redress the balance once and for all.

Turkish foreign policy is itself a key area where it is possible to search for some of the ramifications of this "imagined" identity. For a long time after the establishment of the Turkish Republic, numerous factors including the Depression and the War in Europe prevented the forging of multiple exchange relations with Europe. When Turkey began to seek access to various Western institutions such as the Marshall Plan, the OEEC (later OECD), the Council of Europe, and NATO—all created to cement the Western alliance in the wake of World War II—it did so in an effort to underscore its place within the Western bloc. The grand project of Westernization, it was thought, could not be achieved without the cooperation of Europe and the United States. But at the same time, inclusion in these institutions would also be a measure of Turkey's "Westernness." What it meant to be Turkish could best be understood by looking at who its friends were.

The West, in turn, had been perceived in Turkey as a unitary bloc; the United States and Europe were conceived as the two pillars of what was seen as a progressive and powerful alliance. In the postwar era, Turkish policy makers kept close and balanced relations with both Europe and the United States. Seeking closer relations with the European Economic Community was a logical extension of this approach to foreign policy. The EEC was regarded in Turkey as the economic axis of the Western alliance, supplementing and cementing the political pact. The bipolar world order established after the war goes a long way toward accounting for the ease with which Turkey established itself in the Western alliance. The demise of this international system has prompted a revision of previous assumptions by all parties.

On the Turkish side, this revision has brought the realization that the Western alliance was deeply divided and that cooperation with the United States did not ensure a smooth relationship with Europe as it had done previously. During the course of the 1980s, Turkey found itself progressively distanced from a Europe engaged in redefining its identity and boundaries. Simultaneously, the same period saw a new level of intense cooperation between Turkey and the United States, one based on regional, rather than global, concerns. As the East–West dimension began to lose its strategic importance in determining international events, efforts to formulate a strategic role for Turkey based on a regional dimension have brought a new assessment of identity and appurtenance.

The aim of this paper is to show that questions of identity have always preoccupied the governing elite of the Turkish Republic in their efforts to become part of Europe. The ambiguities posed by the project of Westernization, epitomized by what I shall call for the moment the "Greek factor" (that is, Turkey's concern not to be outflanked by Greece in Western-dominated platforms) have to a large extent traced the course taken by Turkey in its foreign-policy orientations. I shall illustrate these points by analyzing the conditions under which Turkey applied to the European Community for full membership at a time when the chances of its immediate inclusion were at their lowest. I shall argue that such a paradoxical move has triggered a reassessment of Turkey's Europeanness in both Europe and Turkey and resulted in the marginalization of Turkey in the new Europe being created at the moment. The inclusion of Greece, Spain, and Portugal within this new and enlarged Europe has also served to redefine what and who constitute its periphery. It seems that Balkan countries will occupy the space vacated by the nations of southern Europe. Turkey, which has had a special relationship with the Community since the 1960s, seems to be relegated to the outside, albeit with important functions of regional mediation.

Westernization as Foreign Policy

Westernization has always been a dominant factor in the way Turkey's relations with Europe have been perceived. For the elite, closer association with Europe would above all have a civilizing mission, whereby increasingly larger sections of the population would come into contact with Western ways of conducting their affairs, thus spreading the word from the elite downward. But this larger concern has always been mediated by more specific and short-term considerations of a more immediate political and economic nature. For the Turkish elite, the main road toward Westernization was industrialization, which would lead to economic development and therefore greater political stability. Europe and the West were therefore not only models according to which social change could be directed, but also the main source of funds for bringing about this much-desired result. Finally, issues of global strategic importance have always been used as a lever by Turkey and the West in constructing their relations. In spite of changes in all these different parameters over time, the rhetoric on both sides can still be seen to turn around these three axes.

Turkey first applied for membership to the EEC in July 1959, two months after Greece. In the Cold War context of the 1950s, security considerations dominated decisions taken not only in Turkey but in the West as well. Second, the delicate nature of Turkey's relations with Greece required a Turkish presence on each and every platform where the Greeks figured in order to deflect any possible harm that Greece might inflict on Turkey within the Western alliance. Last but not least, there were hopes for an inflow of aid and credit, as had happened in the wake of Turkey's accession to NATO, which could very well save the ailing government from a major defeat at the coming elections. In spite of misgivings in Western Europe regarding the difficulties for full integration posed by the low level of industrial development in Turkey, the strategic position of Turkey and Greece as front-line states prompted the EEC to endorse their applications. Treaties signed with Greece and Turkey (in 1961 and 1963, respectively) envisioned the ultimate full membership of these two countries at a future unspecified date.

After 1960, the exigencies of Turkey's import-substitution industrialization and the first of a series of military takeovers prompted a revision of Turkey's terms of association with Europe. While Turkish industrialists and economic planners began to question the value of a customs union for Turkey's nascent industries, Europe placed the issue of democracy on the agenda by freezing all relations with Turkey until an elected government took office. Within Turkey, flirtations with notions of Third Worldism and independent development further exacerbated the caution with which both parties viewed one another. Only the issue of Turkey's strategic role kept the dialogue going.

By the end of the 1970s the European Community had already defined democracy as a *sine qua non* of membership. It was the processes of first Greek and later Spanish and Portuguese accession that crystallized this change (Tsoukalis 1981). Greece was accepted as a full member after the demise of the junta in 1974, in spite of the unfavorable report on the Greek economy drawn up by the Commission of the European Community. The quick transition to a democratic regime in Greece strengthened the belief that membership in the Community was an important factor in the establishment of democratic regimes in southern Europe. It was this belief that guided responses to the Spanish and Portuguese applications, in the course of which even the technocratic Brussels Commission refrained from delivering negative reports, in spite of the low levels of industrial development in both of these countries.

This shift in European emphasis on democracy, seized upon by the Greeks, the Spanish, and the Portuguese in their speedy bid for membership, was an opportunity that could not be taken advantage of by the Turkish governing elite. Perhaps the single factor that may best account for this inability is the Third Worldist stance that informed the rhetoric of Turkish nationalism, one that very much defined then Prime Minister Ecevit's popularity as a national hero. It was, after all, Ecevit who had stood up against the whole world in order to defend the Cypriot Turks in 1974. Notions of self-reliance described Turkish attitudes toward industrial development as well—attitudes that, although colored in the 1960s with a lot of left-wing rhetoric, could be traced to the conditions under which the Turkish republic had first been established. The Turkish emphasis on independent development served to widen the gulf between Turkey and the countries of southern Europe that actively sought closer economic and political ties to Europe.

The inclusion of southern Europe into the boundaries of the Community brought in its wake a reformulation of its nature. Rather than being a club of northern industrialized countries, the European Community came to define itself in terms broader than economic development, and more in terms of a Europeanness that included above all the promotion of democratic values and human rights. By contrast, Turkish policy makers continued to rely on economic parameters in pressing Turkey's bid for membership, even after the military coup in 1980, which further distanced Europe. The Council of Europe's Parliamentary Assembly suspended Turkey's membership and refused to invite Turkish parliamentarians to its sessions; but it did not go so far as advising the expulsion of Turkey from its Council of Ministers (Birand 1985).

European insistence on democracy and the end of inhuman practices in Turkish courts and jails was interpreted by the military government as unwarranted interference in a sovereign country's internal affairs. The then boss of Turkey's economy, Turgut Özal, tried to counter these arguments by pointing to the greater integration of the Turkish economy in world markets as a result of a radical change in economic policy. But relations with Europe no longer centered on the economy, a fact that was completely bypassed by Turkish policy makers at the time.

The relationship between Europe and Turkey continued to unfold in terms of competing definitions of democracy. For example, the European Community refused to regard the 1983 general elections as a sign of a transition toward democracy. Questions of human rights abuses, party closures, and the restriction of political participation to a few carefully screened figures kept souring relations throughout the 1980s. In spite of attempts by Özal, who was elected to office in 1983, to normalize relations, several unresolved issues other than democracy continued to plague the EEC–Turkey dialogue. Among these, three deserve mention: the volume of Turkish textile exports to the Community; the resumption of the financial aid (the Fourth Financial Protocol) that had been blocked in 1981; and the free movement of Turkish workers in Community countries as of December 1986. Added to these was the obstruction by the Greek lobby, which became much more effective after Greek accession.

Turkey's Application

In view of the many differences that set Turkey and Europe apart, the decision taken by Prime Minister Özal to apply to the Community for full membership in 1987 came as a surprise to many observers inside and outside Turkey. Westernization, the traditional factor shaping Turkish foreign policy, contributed greatly to this decision. By the middle of the 1980s, another identity, that of Islam, had already mounted a considerable opposition to ideas of Westernization. A radical Islamic discourse articulating the anti-Western feelings and the aspirations of a provincial and bazaar population bred on Islamic precepts (Mardin 1989, p. 177) had already managed to challenge the hegemony enjoyed by the ideology of Westernization. Özal and his acolytes represented the technicist, pragmatic, non–Third Worldist section of this revival of Islamic identity (Göle 1990) and, as such, tried to strike a balance between the Western-oriented traditional elites and a newly arising Islamist elite. Thus declarations of Turkish officials to the effect that Turkey's membership in all Western institutions prevented its exclusion from the European Community should be seen more as part of this balancing act engaged in by the Özal government.

In the meantime, the reintroduction of an Islamic and hence "Eastern" identity in Turkish political discourse began to show its effects in foreign-policy decisions. Closer links with Middle Eastern countries were established both at the governmental level and by private entrepreneurs, and Turkey began to take a more active role in the Islamic Conference and increased its economic ties with the Islamic world. The decline in the volume of trade with Western Europe was accompanied in the early 1980s by an increase in trade with the Middle East, and the government encouraged the proliferation of joint Turkish–Arab banks and trading companies. During the Iran–Iraq war, Turkey adopted what its policy makers called an attitude of "active neutrality," which effectively meant that, contrary to many Western and especially U.S. policies, the Turkish state did not pursue an overt or covert anti-Iran policy. Finally, Turkey was among the first countries to recognize the state of Palestine.

This rapprochement between Turkey and the Arab world was circumscribed by both internal and external considerations. The volatility of Middle Eastern markets caused entrepreneurs to turn once again to the comparatively more stable European markets. Secondly, the pro-Arab stance in foreign policy raised a number of concerns in the minds of Turkey's more traditional allies such as the United States, concerns that were exacerbated by Turkey's refusal to follow U.S. policy with regard to Libya. But stronger ties with the Arab world engendered serious opposition within Turkey itself. The country's secularist intelligentsia, the traditional elite to date, met these moves with extreme suspicion and strongly contested any attempt to revise the Westernized secular identity of the Turkish Republic.

A combination of economic and political short-term difficulties in the international arena that seemed to be amplified in the wake of the accession of south European countries were the immediate factors that finally prompted the decision to apply for full membership. These countries with whom Turkey shared a similar export portfolio had gained important advantages over Turkey, both through the funds they received and as a result of the ease with which they could reach European markets. Access to reliable markets and financial benefits were key issues for an economy that had begun to rely on exports as its main source of revenue. This contrasted sharply with the economic calculation of the 1960s and 1970s that had produced a slowing down of Turkey's process of accession. Furthermore, Turkey was having increasing difficulties in international platforms with regard to its protracted conflict with Greece over the Cyprus and Aegean questions.

These issues had already brought Turkey to the brink of isolation in the international arena and furthered her dependence on U.S. backing in economic as well as political matters. Regaining economic and political respectability for Turkey internationally had in fact been one of Özal's election platforms. Full membership rather than association, as it was argued by Turkey's minister for foreign affairs, could circumvent the problems of a customs union by bringing overriding advantages (Yılmaz 1988). This view was shared by Turkey's leading industrialists, whose apprehensions regarding a customs union had been quite effective in the past in stalling the association agreement (Eczacıbaşı 1988; Koç 1988).

The year 1987 also marked the adoption in Europe of the Single European Act, which accepted as a concrete short-term strategy the creation of a single market within Europe by the end of 1992. This, combined with efforts to speed up the process of decision making within the Community, prompted a consolidation of European integration in the course of which the addition of new members would not be that easy. Predictably, the Commission of the European Community, after a two-year delay, proposed to reactivate the association agreement rather than open accession negotiations. It further proposed a set of economic, political, and cultural measures designed to increase interdependence between the Community and Turkey. The Community's Council of Ministers ratified the report without change, adding to it what was called a "package of cooperation" that detailed the nature of the economic, technological, and other areas where cooperation between the two parties was expected. What it failed to deliver was the announcement of a date on which negotiations for full membership would resume. In a sense, the Community was asking Turkey to stay on the fringe for an unspecified period without any certainty of finally gaining accession to the Community.

This decision was greeted with much confusion in Turkey, and interpretations as to the "real" message involved occupied the headlines for a long time. What the decision prompted, in effect, was a public debate on Turkey's Europeanness for the first time since Turkey had declared its aspirations toward Westernization. Turkish officials preferred to see these proposals as part of a comprehensive program that would eventually lead Turkey to full membership. The religious right saw it as a slap in the face that would hopefully demonstrate once and for all that the European Community was nothing more than a Christian association and that Turkey should not seek to emulate an identity that it did not share. The left intelligentsia, hitherto strongly opposed to Turkey's membership—which they had seen as yet another way of furthering dependency and underdevelopment—were deeply disappointed for having missed the chance to establish a truly democratic regime. But for the majority in the center-right and center-left of the political spectrum, as well as the governing economic and political elite, this decision brought home the realization that Europe did not consider Turkey as one of its own, and that Westernization had not been accomplished as they had hitherto believed.

This process also confirmed the critical role played by Greece in defining Turkey's place in relation to Europe. Full membership had accorded Greece the possibility of defining the nature of its conflict with Turkey much more forcefully. Playing on the image of a small country being victimized by a brutal enemy, Greece successfully managed to link the resolution of the Cyprus issue to the improvement of Turkey's relations with the Community. By using its veto power, Greece effectively postponed the resumption of financial cooperation between Turkey and Western Europe. The Fourth Financial Protocol, which became the symbol of the nature of relations between Turkey and the European Community, has still not been concluded as a result of the Greek veto. Contrary to its role in alleviating tensions between other traditional enemies such as France and Germany, the Community has found itself increasingly drawn into the Greek–Turkish dispute on the side of Greece. Moreover, the Greek veto has also given Community members who had reservations about Turkey's membership the possibility of not having to pronounce themselves on the issue. Thus, Turkish–Greek relations have also served as a touchstone defining the boundaries of the European world. This protracted conflict allows Greece to remain as the outpost of the civilization that is constantly threatened, now as in the past, by the invasion of the Eastern hordes. The reality of this threat in the popular European imagination continues to put in doubt the Europeanness that the Turkish Republic seeks to have affirmed.

The Search for Alternatives

The bitter disappointment with regard to Turkey's claims to European identity prompted a search in earnest for a sustainable alternative. Identities other than Western, which had been articulated in nationalist, religious, and leftist discourses, began to circulate more widely among Turkey's traditional elites. The economic integration (including a customs union, the bone of contention during the 1970s) proposed in the package of cooperation now seemed to offer too little in terms of the political and cultural cooperation sought by the Westernized elite. By contrast, for the pragmatically oriented ruling party, economic cooperation was quite an acceptable solution, since it would allow Turkey to endorse a more *sui-generis* identity with which it could try both to find a space for itself in the changing world order and to create a new basis of consensus needed to secure social peace domestically, all the while enjoying the economic benefits of association that Turkey's precarious finances needed.

In this context, the United States emerged as an alternative model to be emulated, an alternative that was acceptable to politicians of both the center-right and the center-left in Turkey. During the 1980s, Turkish political leaders in the army and the bureaucracy who had hitherto been the mainstay of Turkey's Westernization project began to recognize the divisions that existed between Europe and the United States with regard to their attitudes toward association with Turkey. While Europe insisted on dictating reforms of the legal and institutional framework that were still unacceptable to Turkish state traditions, the United States appeared to provide support without being unduly concerned with domestic issues as long as Turkey remained its ally in regional affairs. In addition, U.S. backing of Islamic regimes in the Middle East strengthened Özal's attempts to promote a form of modernization in Turkey that did not necessarily entail adopting a Western identity. The model of American democracy, along with U.S. emphasis on clientelistic politics and promises of greater social mobility, was increasingly perceived to be more desirable for Turkey. Only the traditional, Kemalist elite and some social democrats remained doubtful about this model on the grounds that Americanization would immerse Turkey into further particularisms based on the further constitution and politicization of ethnic and religious identities.

Changes in the world order made this alternative seem increasingly more feasible. Events in Eastern Europe and the demise of the bipolar world order made the fashioning of a new role for Turkey in the international arena seem necessary. Turkey's geopolitical position as a front-line state lost its significance, and it seemed for a while that Turkey would no longer have a bargaining position in international platforms. It was the Gulf War that allowed Turkish policy makers to realize that the West was no longer an undifferentiated entity, and that this provided them with more room to maneuver. At a time when the European Community was preoccupied with the transformation of East European countries and unable to act effectively in a crisis so nearby, Turkish leaders opted to side with the United States and back its intervention in the region. The concept of "strategic importance," the main principle guiding Turkish foreign policy, was replaced with the concept of "strategic cooperation," which defined the development of a special relationship between Turkey and the United States.

The new international role that strategic cooperation implied was to immerse Turkey in regional affairs more than ever before. On the basis of his success in wedding Islamic identity with Western modernity, Özal hoped to act as a role model and become a viable broker for Western interests in the region, as a consequence of which Turkey might obtain the financial and political support of the West. The promotion of trade as a way of minimizing political tensions was the final axis that made up this package. But as it transpired in the aftermath of the Gulf War, Arab nations proved to be unwilling to give Turkey a greater say in regional issues, and Turkey has had to revise its rather ambitious plans (Eralp forthcoming).

Turkey thus seemed at an impasse with regard to its efforts to obtain regional prominence. Not only did Arab nations reject her bid for a key role in the Middle East, but it also seemed that such a role would increasingly immerse Turkey in a painful process of questioning its assumed Westernness, an identity already challenged by the Islamic revival in her large cities. It is the disintegration of the Soviet empire that finally seems to have helped Turkey out of this impasse, by conferring on her a key role in regional matters without Turkey having to renounce totally her claim to a Western identity. The newly independent Turkic Republics of the former Soviet Union, as well as the inclusion of Balkan states in world trade and political institutions, have opened up a new "region" wherein Turkey seeks to insert itself as a key actor. Based on a common linguistic as well as ancestral heritage, Turkey is now trying to export its political model, entrepreneurial know-how, and consumer goods to the Central Asian steppe. For the moment, it seems that acting as a mediator in relations between Central Asia and the West, increasingly identified with the United States, may not necessitate a domestic revision of identity. Other regional links, such as the Black Sea Cooperation Project and improved relations with Balkan countries, appear to have set Turkey firmly on the regional course presaged by the Gulf crisis.

This new regionalism in which Turkey seems to be immersed has removed the issue of full membership in the European Community from the agenda of the governing elite in Turkey. Suggestions that regional projects might provide Turkey with a negotiating card in its bid for membership have been set aside. The fact that the European Community largely endorses this position means that a new model of cooperation between the parties will have to emerge, one that will now entail the exclusion of Turkey from European boundaries. The disappearance of strategic considerations that had maintained the possibility of Turkey's future inclusion within Europe goes a long way toward explaining this new position. Westernization has become a contested issue within Turkey and as such is no longer essential to the promotion of social order. Funds needed to sustain Turkey's development seem to depend much more on U.S. cooperation than that of a Europe engaged in consolidating its boundaries. Thus it looks as if the short-term parameters that converged to make accession to the European Community a viable strategy for Turkey are all pointing in different directions.

Conclusion

This essay has shown the extent to which the creation of national as well as supranational identity is relational and therefore linked to processes of transformation in the international world order. To this end, it has tried to demonstrate how Turkey's bid to become a Western nation has been revised in relation to Europe's own self-definition. The construction of a new Europe prompted by the Atlantic competition and speeded up by the disintegration of the East–West axis in organizing international relations has ushered a revision of what constitutes Europeanness. It is this process that largely informs the search for alternatives that Turkey has embarked upon.

The emphasis on the degree of development that defined identity in the period of the Cold War has been gradually replaced by a rhetoric of identity that prioritizes qualitative difference. To the extent that the creation of any identity involves the identification of significant "others," whose very exclusion will serve to delimit the nature and boundaries of the included, it seems that Turkey has moved into a new position vis-à-vis Western Europe. The emphasis in Europe on a common heritage in defining its identity has prompted a reconsideration of history, including the history of common enmities. It is in this context that the Greek factor becomes operative in reminding Europeans of the specter of the Turk, now in the guise of an army of unemployed and unskilled workers. The large number of Turkish "guest" workers in Germany—the outsiders within—only serves to exacerbate this image of essential difference in spite of the rhetoric of "diversity within unity" that is being articulated in Europe. If it is indeed European insistence on a democratic heritage that has brought down the Berlin Wall, it now seems to be trying to erect new ones perhaps more difficult to topple.

As long as the degree of development was the main criterion for ranking countries, the Turkish governing elite was ready to wait until differences of degree had been eradicated before they were accepted as Europeans. As the Common Market gradually transformed itself into a European Community and a union and political and cultural criteria rather than simply economic ones began to designate Europeanness, it became increasingly difficult to sustain a project of Westernization. The experience of exclusion, which has been related graphically by returning migrants as well as by politicians on international platforms, has given more credibility to existing discourses articulating Turkish and/or Muslim identities. Simultaneously, cultural differences, relegated to insignificance under Republican ideology and contained within the discourse of economic development during the 1960s and 1970s, have resurfaced within Turkey as well. The importance of this for the future of Turkey's democracy remains to be seen.

Finally, the Turkish experience prompts a revision of the concept of periphery, to the extent that this has been defined mainly in economic terms. The process described above implies much more than peripheralization, and the politics of identity that is now being played out seems to reduce economic development as well as politics to questions of culture and heritage. Just as the disappearance of the "second world" prompts a rethinking of the notion of "Third World," the predicament that Europe's others now find themselves in might instigate a rethinking of the notion of Europeanness itself. Over the past fifty years, Turkey has moved from being on the periphery of Europe to becoming its intimate stranger. Thus new concepts linking cultural and political issues to economic ones are now needed to comprehend the novel ways in which Turkey and Europe will continue to define one another.

Note

I would like to express my gratitude to Nukhet Sirman for her help and comments on this paper.

References

Birand, M.A. 1985. *Türkiye'nin Ortak Pazar Macerası 1959–1985*. Istanbul: Milliyet yayınları.

Ezacıbaşı, N. 1988. "Ankara Antlaşmasının 25. Yılında Türkiye AT Ilişkileri," *Iktisadi Kalkınma Vakfı Dergisi*, Ankara Antlaşması 25. Yıl Özel Sayısı, no. 59 (September), pp. 31–33.

Eralp, A. Forthcoming. "Turkey in the Changing Post-War World Order: Strategies of Development and Westernisation." In Ç. Keyder, S. Ibrahim, and A. Öncü (eds.), *Socio-Economic Transformation and the State in Egypt and Turkey*.

Göle, N. 1990. "Ingénieurs islamistes et étudiantes voilées en Turquie: entre le totalitarisme et l'individualisme." In Gilles Kepel and Yann Richard (eds.), *Intellectuels et militants de l'Islam contemporain*. Paris: Seuil, pp. 167–92.

Koç, V. 1988. "25. Yılında Türkiye-AT Ortaklık Ilişkileri," *Iktisadi Kalkınma Vakfı Dergisi*, Ankara Antlaşması 25. Yıl Özel Sayısı, no. 59 (September), pp. 24–26.

Mardin, S. 1989. "Culture and Religion: Towards the Year 2000. In *Turkey in the Year 2000*, Ankara: Turkish Political Science Association publication, pp. 165–86.

Tsoukalis, L. 1981. *The European Community and Its Mediterranean Enlargement*. London: George Allen and Unwin.

Yılmaz, M. 1988. "Ankara Antlaşmasının Siyasi Yönü ve Dış Ilişkilerimiz Bakımından Değerlendirilmesi," *Iktisadi Kalkınma Vakfı Dergisi*, Ankara Antlaşması 25. Yıl Özel Sayısı, no. 59 (September), pp. 9–11.

JOHAN GALTUNG

The Emerging European Supernationalism

Conceiving Nationalism

The term "conceiving" is used here in both senses: both laying the basis for nationalism's birth, and coming to terms with the idea, explicating its meaning and getting used to the idea of supernationalism, not only nationalism and subnationalism.

Nationalism is a state of the individual and collective mind, usually subconscious, retrievable on occasion by leaders and others, calling for identification with say, Britain, France, or Spain (or, more precisely, with what elites of those countries may be up to). So is supernationalism, which differs from nationalism only by relating to a larger, supernational entity usually thought of as a federation or a superstate, such as the European Union that is now emerging from the confederal European Community. So is subnationalism, which identifies with subnational entities such as Wales, Corsica, or Catalonia. The object of identification is a national, a cultural entity, the sum total of language, religion, shared myths of traumas and glories; and the people who are the carriers of the culture in space and through time. The nation-state doctrine concretizes further, identifying with territory, demanding coincidence between territorial and cultural borders. At the very center are institutions such as the state, and personifications: emperor, king, president, and so on.

Above nationalism has been linked to culture. As such it embodies assumptions about reality; some of them, heavily value loaded. As all nationalisms are cultures but not all cultures are nationalisms, some characteristics of nationalist cultures, mapping reality like all cultures do, should be spelled out.

Two axes span nationalism: Self–Other and Good–Bad. The Self is, of course, the (super-, sub-) national, collective Self; the Other is the rest of the world, the non-Self. "Good" is cathexis, positive attachment; "Bad" is negative cathexis. With this fourfold table, the ground is prepared for a guide to the positive and negative aspects of Self and of Other. But the nationalist map is as eloquently silent on the negative aspects of Self as it is on the positive aspects of Other, and as Cartesian-blind to the bad in the Good as it is to the good in the Bad. The more empty these cells, and the more inflated the evaluation of Self and deflated the evaluation of Other, the steeper by definition the Self–Other gradient. Deeply rooted in the collective subconscious, that gradient becomes a powerful social force, preparing people for acts of heroic compassion and solidarity with Self as well as for the rejection, including the extermination, of Other. In short, here is some of the raw material out of which history is made, *la grande narration.*

But nationalism, carried in the individual/collective (sub)conscious as *cultures*, is also embedded in concrete social reality, meaning social *structures* in domestic and/or global space with concrete interests that nationalism may serve, and social *institutions* around which nationalist cultures or, perhaps better, ideologies *may* crystallize.

The interplay between these three—cultures, structures, and institutions—is essential for understanding nationalism. To these might be added personality, or character, as a fourth pillar. But the centerpiece of a discourse analyzing the interests served, the institutions that are the objects of identification, and the character traits compatible with certain nationalisms, particularly the more pathological ones, remains nationalism as culture in general, and as ideology in particular. The other two or three are subsidiary, however indispensable for a concrete understanding of any particular nationalism and any process of emerging nationalism.

Euronationalism as Culture

A nationalist culture may profitably be analyzed at two different levels, as surface culture or ideology, consciously held, and as deep culture or cosmology, subconsciously held.

At the manifest level, easily accessible with such social-science techniques as interviews and questionnaires, we would encounter the typical social distance of verbal and physical reactions in the Bogardus tradition (whom you could and whom you could not imagine to marry, have as a friend, a colleague, a neighbor, an immigrant to your country, and so on). Nationalism as here conceived, a Self–Other gradient, would have prejudice and its concomitant action, discrimination, as offshoots. In the more extreme cases—maximum nationalism, with total inflation of Self and deflation of Other to the point of genocide—we are clearly dealing with sociocultural pathologies, possibly drawing on individual pathologies.

But not all nationalisms are pathological; there are also softer and incomplete versions.

A focus on the positive Self, neglecting negative aspects and neglecting Other completely, is far from social realism, but also far from pathological nationalism. Add to that a positive image of Other, and what we have is a Pollyanna whitewashing of the whole human condition. Turn it around to a focus only on the negative Self and the negative Other, and the Cassandra black-painting is there, the *misanthrope* image. Keep the negative Self, add a positive Other, and the inverted nationalism of unreflected xenophilia emerges—structurally, simply the inverse of the perverted maxinationalism of the unreflected xenophobia of positive Self and negative Other.

There are many variations to be gleaned from this fourfold table, but only the complete version, unfiltered by blinkers, represents a mature view of the human condition. Nationalism is an infantilism, as are other ways of biased images of Self and Other, such as speciesism, sexism and ageism, and racism and classism, found in so much common discourse.

If we now turn to the latent level below the manifest discourse of likes and dislikes, we find aspects of the general culture that may be productive or counterproductive in forging the Self–Other gradients between national groups, here seen as the very essence of nationalism. And at the still deeper level, Subbasement Two (–2) in the deep culture, we would find epistemologies underlying the production of such aspects, the deeper *mentalities*. Without the inclusion of the two latent, not directly observable levels in the social cosmology, an analysis of nationalism is doomed to remain superficial, fit for marketing research, "barometers," Gallup poll summaries in newspapers, and so forth. Important, sometimes useful, but shallow.

If we now start at level –2 with epistemology, we find at the very root of European culture the Manichean dichotomy (or Bogomilean dichotomy for the Russian version). Two mental forms coalesce here: *twoness,* the idea that the world can be seen in terms of two categories (of classes, forces, and so on), and *evaluation,* the idea that one category is totally good and the other totally bad. History is not seen as balance but at best as the process of good overcoming evil, ushering in a final stage, an *Endzustand* (today sometimes called the "end of history"); at worst as the process of evil overcoming good, with a bland undecided in-between, "the struggle is still on."

To this could be added a third and fourth idea in European (or, better said, Occidental) epistemology: a God, transcendent, male, with an abode somewhere above, balanced by a transcendent Satan, also male with an abode somewhere below; and a humanity chosen and choosing by and between the two, thus heavily polarized between good and evil. Add to this the idea of approximate parity in strength between God and Satan, and two occidental archetypes emerge clearly: *balance of power* (making a choice between the two—free will—matters); and *drama* (because the outcome—who wins—is unpredictable).

Both ideas can easily be grafted onto the Manichean dichotomy (as indeed they were) and be used as a general cognitive mold. See Self as chosen by God, and the "Chosen People" emerges as the Judeo-Christian archetype. The conclusion, *God's Unchosen People is Satan's Chosen People*, does not follow by strict Aristotelian logic, but it is very close. The result is nationalism of a quite vicious, theologically rooted, kind.

If we now move up from level –2 to level –1, bringing with us the epistemological archetypes, we enter history as seen through these epistemological filters. It is interesting to note how so many of the shining and guiding lights of Western civilization have seen history in that light. To Plato (The Republic) and Aristotle there were correlates of the Greek/civilized/free–Barbarian/uncivilized/unfree divide, such as manliness (as opposed to the effeminate Persians), tenacity/frugality (as opposed to indulgence), dynamism (as opposed to the assumed stasis of non-Greek societies). Montesquieu plays on the same chords in his Lettres Persanes; Marx and Engels, in their views of the ahistorical societies. The whole tradition of orientalism, as Edward Said has pointed out in Orientalism, is full of this.

These are the neighbors of the Europeans, from Maghreb via Mashreq to the Turkish domain, fading into the Russian steppes; from Casablanca via Suez to Murmansk in the extreme versions. Four Others are defined by the designs of History in Eurasian space: the Arabs/Muslims, the Turks/Ottomans, the Russians/Soviets and, less proximate, the Yellow Peril (Attila and Genghis Khan; later on, the Japanese). The Russians are ambiguous, being Indo-European but Slavic with Cyrillic script to boot; being Christian but then Orthodox and on top of that insisting that theirs is real Christianity and that the Greek Orthodox are sell-outs to the Roman Catholics.

Or are the Russians simply uncomfortably big in land and numbers? Or, even more simply, too far to the East? Like the Arabs, too far to the South, and the Turks too? If the center of Europe is in the northwest of the five Protestantisms, from Scotland/England via Germany to Switzerland/Czechoslovakia, then Southern and Eastern Europe are already suspect. And ultra-South (beyond the Mediterranean), and ultra-East (beyond the Bosporus) are even highly suspect as Satan's instruments: Reagan's Evil Empire in his 8 March 1983 Orlando speech to American Christian evangelists.

Oriental despotism became the catch-all formula, incorporating the Sultan (Satan) in his harem with highly refined tastes enjoying boundless luxury, including more women than any crude king raping peasant daughters at night could ever hope for. It meant the arbitrary rule of rulers as opposed to the rule of law, with no separation between state and dynasty, no concept of private property, let alone using private property to (be)get more private property.

The only redeeming characteristic of this arch of indulgent despotism were the *exotica,* artifacts dutifully excavated and collected, catalogued, and removed to safer places, such as the British Museum. The ultimate conquest of Other, *muse-ization,* incorporation forever by, not in, Self.

Archetypes such as these—so simple, so strong—are not easily undone. Remove an Other from the scene, as recently happened with the Soviet Union, and rather than modifying the inflated image of Self, another Other that meets the bill will be found. The place to look is obvious: *the Orient* again, taking one's choice from among the traditional four Others.

This is not quite the same as being in search of enemies, as the United States, rightly or wrongly, is supposed to be doing. The search is broader, not only for something to fear, but also for something to hate and/or despise. But above all, this is a search to complete a configuration, a powerful *Gestalt,* with a truly positive Self not existing unless a negative Other is present in the configuration. And vice versa.

The candidates for the vacancy of Other are lining up with their credentials (only candidates from the Arch need apply). With the Russians out for the time being, the choice is easy—between Turks and Arabs, with Japan lurking in the background. However, a Slavic-speaking, Orthodox Christian substitute for Russia can also be accepted if it is located to the east, is relatively big, was communist with a record of anti-European (Austria, Germany, Italy) behavior: *the Serbs.* The most perfect candidate, however, was of course *Iraq,* its despotism certainly not only being in the mind of the Self. The general readiness of Europeans, and not only in the EC/EU member-states, to kill 200,000 Arabs and to recognize Croatia in utter disregard for the highly traumatized Serbian minority are good examples of supra-European nationalism at work. The basic point is not only the extreme stereotyping involved, filtering out Self-negative and Other-positive aspects, but also the ease with which anti-Serb and anti-Iraq policies could be engaged in, drawing on deep cultural residues. The ideological, or manifest, has to be argued as there may be counterideologies around. The cosmological is in no need of underpinning since it is shared, at least in the mainstream.

By all reasonable counts, the Turks should come up for a beating fairly soon now. Beaten in World War I, they have not been beaten for a long time, having been overshadowed by the other two, the Russians and the Arabs. As Muslims, their place in Other Evil is secured. Membership in the EC/EU for Turkey is, of course, ruled out as a contamination of the Christian

Self. Turkey as NATO ally is quite all right: that is, using Turkey as an instrument for balance of power, even a battlefield, is entirely compatible with fear and contempt. The same held for the more limited use of Serbia/Yugoslavia in the Cold War against the Soviet Union, and indeed for the use of Iraq against Iran, Turkey against Iraq, and the FLN against the FIS in Algeria.

The pattern of using Orient against Orient, playing one against the other yet keeping them at a distance from Western Europe, has a long pedigree much antedating Lord Palmerston. With the fall of Acre in 1291, two centuries of the Crusades, a France–England–led coalition legitimated by the Pope in the 1095 Clermont speech, was over. A stark aspect of the Crusades was the alliance with Genghis Khan's grandson Hulagu in the sacking of Baghdad in 1258 (the Yellow Peril against the Muslims).

Abbe Pierre Dubois's peace plan came in 1306, fifteen years after Acre. *De recuperations de Terrae Sanctae* expresses clearly what Europe means by "peace": either an alliance/union of Christian/European princes/nations against Arabs/Muslims, Turks, and/or Russians, or a more universal plan (like the League of Nations or the United Nations) but based on western concepts and dominated by the West, definitely non-Oriental and presumably nondespotic. EC/EU is of the first type.

When the U.S.-led coalition legitimated by Security Council Resolution 678 managed "with all necessary means" to evict Iraq from Kuwait—in no way conceding that there might be room for doubt and negotiation, killing at least 200,000 Arabs in the process—all archetypes had already coincided in the creation of a pathologically solid Self–Other gradient. Killing came easy. European supernationalism was at work from one corner of official Europe to the other, including a Czechoslovakia understanding that proven anti-Oriental despotism would weigh heavily when the credentials for EU membership were lined up.

Would this have happened without the United States playing the old leadership role from Cold War days? The answer is probably that it would have been easier for the EC to find a common ground when unrivaled by the United States, and that the common ground would have been based on that millennium-old Self–Other gradient, undistorted by any anti-U.S. sentiments of more recent date. This is seen more clearly in anti-Serbian EC politics, which used the Yugoslav crisis as raw material for foreign-policy "unity" before Maastricht, with the United States on the sidelines. But then Europe is EC turf just like the Middle East is U.S. turf. That the EC was unopposed and the United States was opposed is probably due to the changing EC–U.S. power equation.

So the raw material for European supernationalism is all there and has been present for a very long time; 4,000 years (Judaism); 2,500 years

(Manus and Plato, the two rather similar); 2,000 years (Christianity); the last centuries (Montesquieu, Marx/Engels, the ideology of Oriental despotism). Nothing new is needed, only some variations.

Euronationalism and Structure

The European construction as domestic, European, and world structure is based on three solid center–periphery gradients, all of them defining clear material interests.

Inside the societies there is class, at present with bureaucrats, intellectuals/professionals, and capitalists on the top and citizens, clients, and customers at the bottom. The same individual may be both: the present structure defies Marxist reductionism. Material and nonmaterial value flow toward the top. There are castles upon the hills; many.

At some point close to the year 1500, an explosive growth started in the Northwest of a relatively homogeneous Europe, marginalizing the South and the East in a process eventually leading to the defenses of the twentieth century: fascism in the South and communism in the East with both, in that order so far, in Southeastern Europe. The gradient from center to periphery ran eastward and southward. The European Community became the embodiment of the Center, with some resistance in the peripheral North, incorporating a South that had merely been fascist, not to mention a Nazi Germany; but hesitant in front of an East that had been communist, drawing a sharp demarcation line between Latin-Catholic-Western Croatia and Cyrillic-Orthodox-Eastern Serbia. Fewer castles, more slums.

And finally, the gradient separating Europe from the Arch of Oriental Despotism; with the Yellow Peril lurking behind the Arch as Attila the Hun, Genghis Khan, and the Japanese of 1904–05, 1931–45, and recent years. In short, a social periphery, an inner periphery, and an outer periphery.

The interests are obvious: the Center wants to maintain the gradients, the Periphery to change them. Value must continue to flow toward the Center, making the castles ever more shiny, on ever higher hills. This is done concretely by division of labor, casting the Periphery in the classical roles of providers of goods and services with low value and consumers of the imported, sophisticated, and expensive. Fascism and communism were also about this; not necessarily to turn the flow but to stop it through self-reliant economic policies. Is repression the price for antiexploitation?

The three concentric circles, with inner Europe (EC/EU), outer Europe (essentially in Central and Eastern Europe), and non-Europe, make for more structural variation than only two circles would. Inner Europe can tie outer Europe through vague promises of membership sometime in the future;

pending that status, as associate member. Outer Europe can also be invited to share the spoils from exploiting non-Europe, for instance as *entrepôts* doing semiprocessing of raw materials from the Arch and so forth. But when the chips are down and there are Arabs, Turks, or Russians to be killed, then Central and Eastern Europe are supposed to know where they stand: solidly against Oriental despotism. Eastern European NATO membership is the logical conclusion, but Turkish membership is confusing. And the Russians are even more confusing, but the Baltics are not.

The obvious counterstrategy—an alliance of the inner and outer peripheries—is what the Soviet Union tried and the Untied States and European Community were afraid of. But Turkey was in NATO, the Arabs were divided, and so was Eastern Europe, all awaiting their reward.

In very concrete terms, the highly differential treatment comes out very clearly as the difference between the freedoms of mobility for goods and services, capital, and labor inside the EC/EU, as distinct from the freedom of mobility for goods and services and capital but not labor for the two peripheries. Inside the club, the citizens can seek work anywhere; outsiders can enter only when invited to do so. The result is obvious: Capital flows back to the Center, making the castles even more shiny; the workers partly responsible for the added value are stopped at the gates. They will knock on the gates; they will try to get around, below, above; they may try to knock them down or at least will be suspected of trying to do so. The rest is EC/EU coordination of police and military protection.

Turkish and Arab workers try to climb the gradient into the German and French wings of the castle. Of course the EC/EU will not extend the crucial fourth freedom—for labor to move—to 57 million Turks; not because they are that many (three of the Big Four in the EC/EU are of the same size; so was West Germany). The key reason for blocking the Turks is found in European supernationalism. Thus the cultural Self–Other gradient parallels the structural Center Periphery gradient, legitimating the use of the Turks for menial social labor and relegating them to the peripheries when no longer needed.

The Turkish reaction is painfully obvious: to seek eastward, to the nearly 60 million in six of the former Soviet Republics (and in some parts of Russia). If the West Europeans are recreating Charlemagne and Napoleon, why should the Turks not try and recreate the Ottoman Empire?

Euronationalism and Institutions

We are almost 700 years beyond *De Recuperatione de Terrae Sanctae* ; 500 more years beyond Charlemagne. In no way can this part of European macrohistory be seen as a linear move toward the West European superstate. Even the move toward nation-states with coinciding cultural and territorial borders is far from linear; the maps are changing all the time as any historical atlas will illustrate. Much more constant is the general Self–Other gradient, nourished by the Arab conquest of Spain (except Asturias) in 712 and the Umayyad Caliphate of Cordoba (the drive onward halted by Charles Martel in 732), by the Crusades and the Ottoman expansion before and after 1453 including the Turkish sieges of Vienna in 1529 and again in 1683. Easily forgotten is the earlier Greco-Roman expansionism.

But serious supra-European institution building—beyond the many calls for union presented as "peace plans" in the European sense—is a latecomer on the scene, dating from May 9, 1950, the birthday of the European Community, now to become the European Union. To confuse institution building with Euronationalism is to confuse quite different conceptual categories. The depth and extent of Euronationalism cannot be measured by the scope and domain of supra-European institutions. That there will be disagreement in the EC/EU for years to come (particularly over its construction), that the institutions will not necessarily speak with one voice, that there will be leads and lags among member-states and functional areas, are trivialities when an operation so complex as forging a superstate is being undertaken.

But European nations have been able to initiate concerted action backed by considerable nationalism in spite of disagreement between, say, the English and the Scots, the northern and the southern French, the Castilians and the Catalonians. One reason is simple: the elite's ability, using normative, contractual, and coercive power, to invoke a super-Self (Great Britain, France, and Spain) when confronted with and by a super-Other, that is, the other two countries.

In the same vein, as argued above, the basic Self–Other gradient can be used to mobilize against the Arabs, Turkey, and Russia. It also worked against Serbia because recent World War II and Cold War history could be grafted upon the old tree of European/non-European history, casting Serbia in the role of Russia the German-killer and Communist. It is remarkable, how easily it worked, with hardly any discussion in the West European press, the anti-Serbian bias being (as is argued here) in the cosmology, not in the ideology.

Of course, hardly anyone today would like to die for the European Commission-Court-Council of Ministers-Parliament or the fifth institution, the European Council; nor for passport, hymn, or flag. But the argument here is that this is basically unnecessary; Euronationalism is age-old. *What we are dealing with is European supernationalism in search of institutions, rather than supra-European institutions in search of nationalism.* The debate over details in the institutions of the EC/EU is less remarkable than the speed and ease with which the EC/EU process is proceeding, and the lack of debate over goals. The former is ideology; the latter, cosmology.

The interesting, nontrivial point to be explained is why there nevertheless is this institutional lag when cultural values and structural interests coincide so beautifully that Self–Other and Center–Periphery gradients become almost identical. Why are the plans 700 years old and institution building only 40-plus? One formula for the answer might be given in terms of the communication and transportation deficits of earlier times—hardly a strong argument given the scope and domain of the Roman Empire, the domain if not scope of the Carolingian and Holy Roman constructions, not to mention India and China, the latter already a superstate for more than 2,200 years.

A much better answer, of course, is that nationalisms and subnationalisms have been standing in the way. Countless examples can be listed. With nation-state building by no means being completed because of the many subnationalisms still around, how could we expect supernationalism to succeed overnight, given the many nationalisms?

Answer: Because those nationalisms were exposed to three powerful transforming shocks during the course of only two political generations: the two world wars, and the real or imagined threat posed by the Soviet Union to Western Europe. The same political leaders experienced Nazism and Communism and mobilized accordingly. A formula had to be found, as they say, to keep the Germans down and the Russians out by bringing the Americans in. Alone, the Europeans were unable to do so. The Germans got the message: only by being supranational could they again become national, making the EC/EU, practically speaking, a taboo topic in their debate.

The political class of Western Europe got institutional training in the European Communities and NATO. But the latter had one disadvantage: The Americans were dominant. As the Cold War subsided, long before 1989 (with the completion of the CSCE and the Final Act of Helsinki in 1975), the ambitious plans for the EC/EU, already there from the beginning, were given new life by the French, who combined their talents for long-term planning, state building, and supra-Europeanism with a French accent—a certain talent for blackmailing the Germans into paying. Today it is rather obvious that the Americans have done their job (keeping the Germans down and forcing the West Europeans into cooperation; the Russians were hardly coming anyhow). Time for the Americans to leave.

For all these reasons, the nationalisms were fading, at least for the time being. Like the subnationalisms, they were cut from the same basic model, coming out of the same Western civilization with the same sharp dichotomies and strong evaluations, the same ideas of chosenness, balance of power, and drama. But having proven so counterproductive in two devastating wars during only 31 years (1914–45, possibly between Germany and the United States to succeed Britain as the world economic power, as Arrighi argued; a war won by Japan), something else was needed. This makes the EC/EU and the subnationalisms natural allies with a common enemy: member-state nationalism. The current idea of subsidiarity and a Europe of the Regions is a sign of the vigor attributed to the subnationalisms, and a clever *divide et impera;* problematic for the *United* Kingdom of *Great* Britain and Northern Ireland.

But this is only one reason why the United Kingdom is lagging behind in the entire process. Another is the understandable pride in not having been beaten, in neither the first, nor the second, world war. A third is its alleged special relationship to the NATO superpower, a cooperation between equals; no submissiveness there. A fourth reason may be even more important: the British never fully understood what the EC was about; they interpreted all the talk about "an ever closer union" as so much continental rhetoric easily dissolved in a heavy dose of British pragmatism, and ended up in Maastricht with that "ever closer union" and the meager comfort that the word "federalism" was not there (only the corresponding reality).

They then opted out of what makes capitalism palatable to the social periphery (not to the two geographical peripheries; they are not covered by social charters), not understanding that the Europeans on the continent did not bother so much as to keep them in. Four studies in insular reality, and mentality.

How will this process continue? Some trivial hypotheses:

1. Institution building will continue according to the timetable, giving full birth to the European Union as a federation by, say, May 9, 2000, the fiftieth anniversary.
2. The United Kingdom will bend to this process rather than vice versa, giving power to those politicians who can bring about that transformation, including accepting social charters.
3. There will be a Europe of the regions, a blooming of subnationalisms, also institutionally with greater autonomy.
4. There will be increasingly military postures against the peripheries.
5. There will be a reawakening of nationalisms, with threats of civil wars.

The Production of Euronationalism: Jean-Baptiste Duroselle's *L'Europe: Historie de ses Peuples*

Given the basic thesis that the history of European institution building is a (super-)nationalism in search of institutions rather than the other way around, it might sound as if no deliberate work to foster a European nationalism that could legitimate the emerging European Union is needed. That may actually be the case. Any conscious effort would lift nationalism from the collective subconscious; the cosmology, into the consciously held ideology as something that could be contested by counter- and anti-ideologies. If sleeping dogs do the job, let them sleep. The Self–Other gradient works better when not mentioned; when mentioned, it looks, well, nationalist, Eurocentric, racist, bigoted—negative.

And yet it is almost inevitable that this will happen. When ants make a formicary, they complete it, given time and circumstances, because they are coded to do so; when Europeans make a superstate, they do so the same for the same reason. They make flag and hymn and standardized passports; of course, they will also try to produce explicit Euronationalism.

In doing so, they have to debunk the nationalism, just like the nation builders had to debunk the subnationalisms, casting them as tribal and counterproductive rather than as sources of positive identity. History has to be presented as nationalism triumphant when subnationalisms no longer stood in the way, leading, for instance, to *la grande nation.*

But at the same time, great care has to be exercised not to offend anyone, making all (sub)nationalisms appear as equal.

In Duroselle's *L'Europe: Histoire de ses peuples,* one nation is more equal than the others—his own—with four of the 19 chapters explicitly centering on France. For this reason, it was published in only eight of the nine EC/EU languages, Greece being the only EC/EU country to reject it. But this is precisely the low-level type of critique one might expect when someone tries to write a "Eurohistory for the United European": "Why is he in it more than I am; why am I not mentioned?" That type of critique fails to see the nature of the forest, focusing on a missing tree or on one tree overshadowing others in its struggle for visibility.

And that forest satisfies the four characteristics of nationalism very neatly: positive not negative aspects of the European Self, negative not positive aspects of the Other surrounding Europe, the "Orient." In a short introductory summary, Duroselle sees individualism and dynamism as outstanding positive characteristics of Europe. Imagine this to be true: "individualism" even close to a tautology, given Europe as the abode of the three Christianities believing in an individual and unperishable soul. But is it obvious that this combination is only positive? Could it lead to humans that are innovative but also alienated, cut off from others in space by individualism—and in time by dynamism—less capable of compassion, highly capable of inconsiderateness? But the yin–yang nature of bad in the Good and good in the Bad is not in Duroselle's Cartesian discourse. "Despite all its errors and horrors Europe is the homeland that has the most pity for man, and where justice is the least bad."

How does Duroselle handle such major errors and horrors as the Spanish inquisition and slavery? They enter via names, such as Torquenada (*la repression qu'il conduisit demeurera tristement célèbre;* p. 145), and Wilberforce (*éminent adversaire de l'esclavage*), and that is about all that is said about these two institutions. Colonialism is narrated essentially as discovery in the conventional European manner, never as seen and experienced by the Other (pp. 124–29). The working class in Europe is seen as *"l'envers du decor"* (p. 297) and given one page, mainly on trade unionism. "Errors and horrors" enter Duroselle's supra-European history when they are over or solved. The book is silent on how Europe today exploits Africa, on the exploitation of Nature, not to mention on the important hypothesis that Hitler may not be an atypical European except in one point: the genocide that others (the nine colonial-power members of the EC/EU) did "overseas" Hitler did in Europe, against Slavs, gypsies, and Jews.

The index, with its endless lists of kings and statesmen, is eloquent evidence of what a conventional history this is, untouched by the *Annales* tradition. Here are no old people, no children, and hardly any women. One page (p. 421) in the index, chosen at random, lists 366 names, out of which 16 are women, four percent (one of them is Lucie, the oldest skeletal remnants).

But there are reflections on why Charlemagne, Napoleon, and Hitler did not embody the right Europeanism, whereas the EC/EU does; the latter is embraced in a totally uncritical manner. A beautifully produced example of *the new distortion*, to be followed up by a collectively produced textbook for schools.

Conclusion: Whither European Supernationalism?

At present, the EC/EU has twelve member states, a Germanic group of three, a Latin group of six, and three marginals (England, Ireland, and Greece). With one exception, they are all West European countries; with seven exceptions (Iceland, Norway, Sweden, Finland, Austria, Switzerland, and Malta), all West European countries are members (at present four of them are applying). With three exceptions (Ireland, Greece, and Luxembourg, though it may be argued that Luxembourg was riding piggy-back on Belgium), they are all recent colonial powers, from this century, most of them actively engaged in slavery and slave-trade in the last century. Like other civilizations, they have much to be proud of in art, science and technology, and social constructions based on rules rather than rulers, with liberty from popes and emperors and more democracy. But they have disproportionately much to be ashamed of in their relations toward the unchosen Europeans and other unchosen Others.

The formula for creating supra-European nationalism out of this is exactly the same as it is for creating a European superpower: focus all attention on writing history acceptable to all European nations and on improving relations among old enemies; focus no attention on the least common denominator of all these nationalisms shared by many Europeans; and focus on the emergence of a new superpower actor on the world scene. Of course, the formula cannot be based on adding up all existing nationalisms. But it can be based on what they have in common, and perhaps better kept at the unconscious than at the conscious level. And that is essentially what is happening.

MAX HALLER

Epilogue

Europe as a New Nation or a Community of Nations?

A general reconsideration is necessary here in order to evaluate and integrate the different contributions. In this epilogue, I would like to discuss the concept of "nation," the different models of nation-states, and the structures and processes supporting their development. These considerations are then applied to the context of Europe. Here I investigate both the structural changes and the actors and interests that have lain behind the strong process of integration of Western Europe since World War II. The question is whether it is realistic to expect—as the outcome of this process—the emergence of something like a "European nation." I will argue that a new type of a "Community of Nations" might be a more adequate model for a future United Europe. In the final section some of the institutional prerequisites for such a Community are discussed.

Sociological Considerations on the Concepts of Nation and National Identity

The Concept of "Nation" as "Political Community"—Linking Civil Society and State

In assessing the potential for Europe to become the focus of a new type of (supra-) national identification, let us first make clear what we mean by "nation" and "national identity."

Two central aspects must be distinguished here. First, when speaking about "nation," we have to distinguish between the subjective, consciousness-related aspect on the one hand, and the objective, system-related aspect on the other. (See also Reiterer 1988, 88.)

The first, *subjective aspect* is that discussed mostly in scientific and public discourse under the headings of "national identity," "nationalism," and so forth. National identity in this sense refers to a certain attitude of mind, a weaker or stronger attachment of individuals to a larger sociopolitical unit (usually a state). The existence of a nation presupposes an attitude that "obliges individuals to the highest degree of faithfulness towards the nation state" (Kohn 1964, 15; see also Rejai 1991). Nationalism can be defined, as Galtung does in his contribution to this volume, as "a state of the individual and collective mind, usually subconscious, retrievable on occasion by leaders and others, calling for identification with, say, Britain, France, or Spain. . . ."

There also exists, however, nation in an *objective sense*, as a certain social unit or system; nation in this sense relates to the specific structural, institutional, and ideological conditions that lie behind the attachment of individuals to their nation. From such a point of view, Anthony D. Smith defines a nation as "a named human population sharing an historic territory, common myths and historical memories, a mass, public culture, a common economy and common legal rights and duties for all members" (Smith 1991, 14). This is the Western concept of nation, which is distinct from an Eastern concept in which supposed genealogy and social descent, common language, customs, and traditions are more important.

What is often missing in these discussions, however, is a clear distinction between the level of subjective consciousness and the level of objective social, political, and cultural processes and structures. So, in another important book on the subject, "nation" is defined as "a large collection of men such that its members identify with the collectivity without being acquainted with its other members" (Gellner 1987, 6). This distinction is also connected to the further differentiation between "nation" and "state." I would argue that "nation" and "state" are not, as often held, more or less identical with each other, but designate clearly different facts—though it is true that they usually grow together "like Siamese twins" (Friedrich 1969, 21; see also Flora 1983).

I would argue that we should understand the concept of "nation" as constituting a connecting link between civil society and its institutions on the one hand (family, private associations, private ownership, markets, and so forth) and the state as a political organization or apparatus on the other. Thus the "nation" designates the specific character of the "*political community*," a uniting that partly "will be by emotional attachment and partly by subjection to common rules" (Friedrich 1969, 23). Particularly those authors who foresee the emergence of a "European nation" have insisted rightly on the fact that a "nation" as a political community does not presuppose linguistic or cultural homogeneity (as the case of Switzerland proves), but nevertheless constitutes "a togetherness of persons who are united by having in common some of their values, interests, ideas (including ideologies), myths, utopias and their symbols, religions and its rituals" (ibid.; Coudenhove-Kalergi 1953).

The fact that modern states are based on national integration in this sense is quite important. It was only the modern nation state that had the power to integrate its peoples politically, to create a political order and society, and to confer a meaningful "citizenship" to its peoples (Drucker 1993, 173f). Anthony Smith (1991, 16) in this regard refers to internal functions of national identity; they include the socialization of individuals into national communities, the creation of bonds between individuals and classes through shared values, symbols, and traditions, and the location of individual selves in the world as a whole. The relevance of national integration over and beyond mere political administration and domination is shown, in the negative sense, by the fate of those cases of political systems or state apparatuses where it was or still is absent. So the historic colonial empires could not last because they were unable in their colonies to go beyond the frame of abstract-technical administration and create true "political societies." The same is true for many of the successor states to the colonial empires founded during the 1940s, 1950s, and 1960s in the Third World (Knieper 1991).

As far as the function of national identity in the location of individuals in the world is concerned, it is very important to note that national identity must necessarily be in opposition to identifications with other smaller or larger territorial and political units, such as towns and provinces on the one side, Europe, the Western civilization, or humanity as a whole on the other. National identification in a positive sense (often designated as "patriotism") is also clearly distinct from nationalism in the negative, chauvinistic sense that implies a feeling that one's nation is superior to other nations (Kosterman and Feshbach 1989).

Such a concept of "nation" also implies that there exists a certain correspondence or congruity *(Wahlverwandtschaft)* between the structures and values in the civil society and the structure of the political institutions. This must be so because the political institutional processes of a society are within everyone's grasp. Such a close connection between the political institutions and civil society creates a certain social and political context and "climate" which have to be studied carefully before designating new institutions that shall function at all (Bowie and Friedrich 1954).

In considering "nation" as a concept designating the relation between civil society and state, we can define a nation as an aggregate of people who (1) feel that they belong to each other not only in social and cultural but also in political terms, and (2) take an active part in the political processes of their state. We could also say that a fully developed nation is a "viable political community" (see also Münch 1982, who points out, in a Parsonian tradition, that a political system must be based on "citizen's love of democracy" and must develop rites and symbols for this aim).

We must be clear in this regard, however, that both the subjective and objective aspects of nation as consciousness and nation as ongoing social relations and processes are *relative concepts*. It is a matter of the degree to which specific individuals, citizens, or social groups are subjectively attached to the nation (so that we can speak of "national identification"), and it is also a matter of the degree to which a politically organized civil society, a "political community," can be designated as a "nation." It has been rightly stated from the comparative point of view that "nationness" (as also "stateness") has to be considered as a *variable*. Only a few states score very high on this dimension as fully developed "nation-states." Significant differences in this regard exist within Europe, but even more so between the Western and the other world societies and cultures. In fact, it may even be an open question whether the European or Western idea of the nation-state can be applied to other continents and cultures in the same way at all. The Western emphasis on the congruity of cultural and political identities seems to make little sense in many countries of the Third World; in the North African Maghreb, there historically were never such clear boundaries between different political-administrative areas (Eisenstadt and Rokkan 1973, 26–30). It has been stated that the idea of national sovereignty was fateful and even disastrous for the postcolonial states. It was often used there to unite peoples according to quite arbitrary criteria (most often the arbitrary colonial frontiers did persist after decolonization) and to set them on each other in so-called liberation wars where all parties were financed and equipped with ideological and material weapons from outside. As a consequence, Africa today, for instance, is one of the politically most fragmented and weak continents (Knieper 1991, 48ff).

Even if nation and national identity have to be conceived of as *relative* social facts from several points of view, they have to be considered as social realities highly relevant from many points of view. In this regard, our approach can be distinguished clearly from other concepts. *"Materialist" approaches* stressing the structural prerequisites of nations, such as political power over a territory, economic penetration, and so on, as well as modern system theories pointing to internal networks of political communication, underestimate the relevance of the often very deep-rooted subjective-emotional relation or attachment of individuals toward their larger (ethnic and other) communities and nations into which they are embedded (Scheff 1992). Because of this, they are unable to explain why nationalism could rise to "the most important ideology of the nineteenth and twentieth centuries" (Rejai 1991, 23; Kohn 1964). The subjective, emotional, and volitional element is central, on the other side, for *voluntaristic-idealistic concepts* of "nation," which define nations primarily by their striving toward unity and political independence. Writings using such a conception, however, often take the political will and intentions of elites for social reality and thus often tend to become political pamphlets (an example are some writings of R. Coudenhove-Kalergi, the founder of the Pan-Europa movement).

The present approach can also be distinguished from the concept of "political culture" (Almond and Verba 1963). The relative disappointment with this concept, which seems quite fascinating at first sight, certainly had to do with the fact that it promised too much, including a strongly evaluative component (Fenner 1983). In this regard, the concepts of "nation" and "national identity" are more specific and less value-laden.

Defining "nation" and "national consciousness" both in subjective/objective terms, and as patterns of relations between civil society and state, we can ask two sets of general sociological questions. The first relates to the *causal preconditions, factors, and processes* that contribute to the development and strengthening of nations and national identity. The second concerns the *social and political consequences* that follow from different kinds of nations and different levels of national identification. These questions can be broken up into four more specific problem areas (see Table 1).

As far as national identity is concerned, my general thesis is that it is a central, yet frequently neglected, determinant of social and political process and integration. National identity is a definite and important aspect of personal and social identity (even if so to a differing degree in different societies) in spite of the fact that it is not rooted so evidently in membership in a specific group as other social identities are (see Gàllenmüller and Wakenhut 1993). We will argue that an economically and politically integrated Europe will be created and endure only if its peoples are able and ready to develop a supranational "European consciousness." Thus, our first and main question is whether it is probable that this will happen.

Structures and Processes Supporting the Development of Nations and National Identity

One of the main issues in discussions about "nation" and "national identification" is the question of their *structural bases*. A conceptual difficulty with the use of this idea arises from the fact that it seems to denominate rather

Table 1

"Nation" and "National Identity" as the Pattern of Objective and Subjective Relations Between Civil Society and State: Levels of Analysis

	Civil Society	State
Objective aspect	Character of civil society (degree of socioeconomic and cultural differentiation and integration)	Character of political institutions, (constitution, form of government, bureaucracy, etc.)
Subjective aspect	Degree of subjective feelings of "belonging together" (communality) because of common culture and descent, interactions within society, etc.	Degree of identification with political institutions, political involvement and participation

elusive social facts. There doubtlessly exist clear *structural roots* for nation building and national identity. A common language or religion, a clearly circumscribed territory, and close economic interactions all are social "facts" whose presence or absence can be established unambiguously. Yet the problem is that no one of them as such is a necessary or a sufficient base for the emergence of a "nation." A nation can be based primarily on religion (as in Israel and partly in Ireland) or on language (as in Greece, Hungary, or Finland), but also on history and politics without a common language or religion (as in Switzerland or Canada) or without being distinguishable in their basis from neighboring countries and nations (as in the cases of Austria and Canada).

It seems misleading, however, to look primarily or exclusively at such "factors" or some combination of them as constituting the decisive basis for the formation of national identity. I assume here that nation building and national-identity formation have to be understood also as a continuous *social process*.

Seen from this perspective, we have to distinguish at least three distinct levels of analysis (see Figure 1).

The first level is comprised of the *ecological-structural preconditions* (or "factors") mentioned before, namely, a common (possibly relatively closed, clearly circumscribed) territory, a common language, a closely integrated economy. These factors, however, only serve to facilitate or hinder the development of a nation but can in no way be considered as constituting autonomous causes or forces leading to its creation. Thus they can be called "instrumental" or ecological-structural preconditions for nation building.

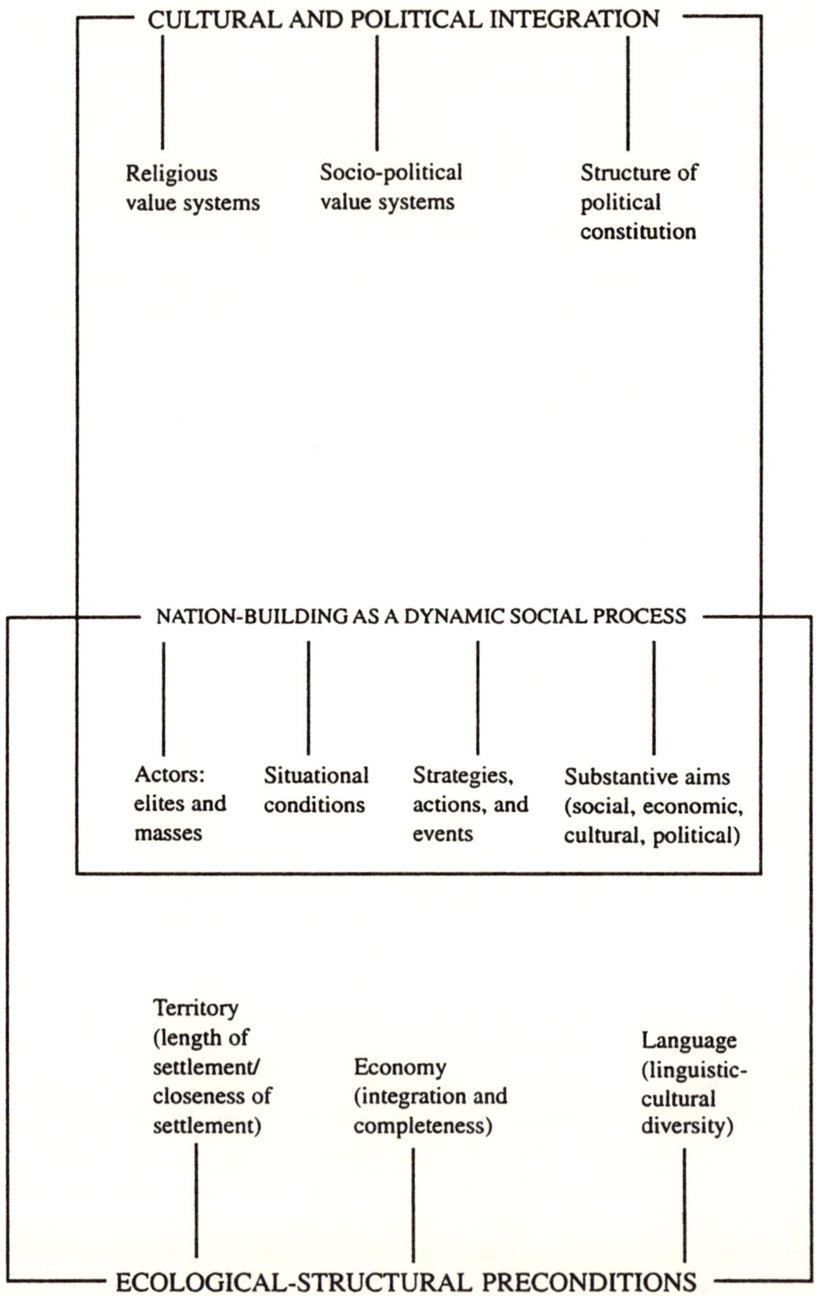
CULTURAL AND POLITICAL INTEGRATION
Religious value systems
Socio-political value systems
Structure of political constitution
NATION-BUILDING AS A DYNAMIC SOCIAL PROCESS
Actors: elites and masses
Situational conditions
Strategies, actions, and events
Substantive aims (social, economic, cultural, political)
Territory (length of settlement/ closeness of settlement)
Economy (integration and completeness)
Language (linguistic-cultural diversity)
ECOLOGICAL-STRUCTURAL PRECONDITIONS

The second level is that of *cultural value systems*, as exemplified particularly in religious systems or secular social and political ideologies (liberalism, socialism, and so forth). While such value systems have a strong power in creating highly persistent social bonds and communities, it is a matter of fact that such communities must not aspire in any case to become politically autonomous units, that is, nations. It is important, however, to look carefully at the content of different religious, philosophical, and political value systems and world explanations because they can be seen as *guiding* the social and political actions that aspire to nation building. I will come back to this issue later when discussing the potential relevance of the religious cleavages within Europe for the emergence of a European nation.

One very important aspect here is the character of the political constitution of a nation. Once a certain constitution has been installed in a country, its character and "spirit" determines to a considerable degree the further political and socioeconomic development, as classic writers like Montesquieu or Alexis de Tocqueville have rightly argued (see Aron 1965). The issue of the constitution as a central institution of society and politics is of primary importance in the case of Europe; I will come back to it in the last section of this epilogue.

There is a third level, which has to be kept separate from these two levels, that is of central importance here. It is concerned with the *process of nation building and national identity formation* itself. It is my thesis that how this process unfolds has important implications and consequences in its own right (Haller 1992b). This process includes at least four specific elements.

The first is comprised of the *actors and leaders* in the process of nation building and identity formation. Two issues are of particular importance here: the kind of relations between national elites and their populations at large, and the kind of relations among and cleavages within different subgroups or types of elites, such economic, political, and cultural elites.

The historical importance of the role of those who act as leaders in the process of nation building can hardly be overestimated. Intellectual and political leaders can be considered as entrepreneurs without whom feelings of national consciousness could hardly develop. Through their actions, national sentiments become awakened and strengthened in such a way that whole regimes may be thrown away. Intellectuals and politicians systematically further this awakening, as it gives them personal influence and power.

Three such groups of leaders might be distinguished: The first is comprised of intellectual and cultural leaders such as historians, writers, and religious leaders who play important roles especially in the early stages of national movements; they often "invent" the idea of a new nation by bringing to light history and myths, by creating literary languages and literatures, and by doing this, they pursue scientific and political aims together. A second group is comprised of politicians who often come to power in the later waves of nationalist movements when it comes time to build up new political power structures. A third group of leaders are economic elites who at first are less concerned with issues of nation building but whose actions and relations nevertheless often set important conditions for this process.

A second element consists of the *situational conditions* surrounding the process of nation building. Probably the most crucial element in this regard is the question of whether a nation's existence is threatened from outside. It is a matter of fact that several of the oldest nations in the Western world have been created just as a reaction to threats that their established rights could become restricted. (This was the case both in the American colonies before the War of Independence and in Switzerland, whose founding cantons fought a successful war against the Habsburgs). Even if there is no such threat from an outside aggressor, the mere existence of a neighbor that is superior in economic power or military force (or both) may lead to the insistence upon one's own peculiarity and independence. For instance, this was and is an important factor in the national self-consciousness of Canadians still today (Berton 1987), and it may play a significant role in the case of some small European nation-states such as Belgium and the Netherlands, Switzerland, and Austria.

A third crucial element is composed of the *strategies, actions, and events* in the processes of nation building. Two aspects are of relevance here.

The first concerns the question of whether these actions have been autonomous and free, or whether they have been induced or enforced externally. Of particular importance in this regard are historical acts of the foundation of nations, such as wars for liberation, revolutions, the passing of constitutions.

The second aspect concerns the role of distrust, hostility, and violence in the process of nation building. Mutual distrust between persons and groups is connected with the fear of being attacked by the other. Actions might be taken to prevent this, which reinforces hostility. Altogether, this may lead to a spiral of distrust and violence (Schelling 1960).

The fourth element in nation building as a process is comprised of the *substantive aims* aspired to by the elites. Here we may distinguish among economic aims implying the preservation or creation of economic rights and privileges; social aims implying the preservation or enhancement of self-esteem and status; cultural aims implying the preservation of a certain language, religion, and so forth; and political aims implying the striving toward political power, autonomy, and independence.

My thesis in regard to these four aspects of the processes of nation building is that the pace and intensiveness of the development of national identity among a population at large will be facilitated to the degree that

- the distances between elites and populations at large, and cleavages within elites, are small;
- the autonomy of a population and its territory are threatened by (probably large) outside powers;
- the strategies and actions in the process of nation building have been autonomous and free and did not involve fundamental distrust or violence;
- the aims aspired to in the process of nation building are comprehensive in the sense that they include all four elements mentioned before (economic, social, cultural, and political).

Looking at the process of nation building and national identity formation from the *historical* or *time perspective*, we can say that this process unfolds as a movement forth and back between two stages:

(1) In revolutionary periods, short-term historical events and processes occur (such as revolutions or wars) which change the whole framework for nation building and set new conditions.

(2) In the longer intermediate time periods, national identity develops as a more continuous and gradual process in the population at large. During these periods, the structural and cultural conditions might also be changed and adapted. This distinction has been made already in the theory of class formation and nation building by the classical Austrian sociologist Ludwig Gumplowicz (a short sketch of it is given in Haller [1992a]). Friedrich (1969, 21ff) refers to it in distinguishing between the phases of building and of growing of nations.

From Individual Nation-States to a European Nation?

On the basis of these general considerations, we can now go on to discuss the different perspectives from which a "European nation" can be seen. We start by developing a typology of different nation-states that are all relevant to Europe. In the following sections, we discuss in detail what the prospects are for a European national identity to emerge.

Different Models of Nation-States in Present-Day Europe

As a starting point, let us begin with a discussion of the different variants of the concept of "nation" or nation-state. An extensive literature as well as present-day social and political reality in Europe enables us to distinguish at least four types of nation-states (see Francis 1976; Lepsius 1988; Eisenstadt and Rokkan 1973; Adam 1993; Smith 1986; 1991; Reiterer 1988; Heckmann 1992; Haller 1992a). All of these have been, and still are, models relevant to different European countries and thus may also influence the shape that a possible "European nation" might take. The main criterion for the distinctions among these types is the degree of coincidence of several distinctive elements or components of the political unit "state" and the degree to which a state can be designated as a "nation."

The first is the *ethnonational state,* characterized by a more or less perfect coincidence of the criterion of "ethnicity" with that of political community (state). "Ethnicity" or "ethnic community" denotes a feeling of communality, of belonging based on common ancestry and history, common language, religion, and culture, and—in most cases—a clearly circumscribed territory inhabited by an ethnic group for a long time. States defined along these lines usually are relatively small, as it is difficult for all the parts of these criteria to be present at once in a larger nation. Examples fulfilling the criteria of the ethnonational state approximately include many of the smaller European states such as Portugal, the Republic of Ireland, Denmark, Norway, Hungary, and—among the new East European states—the Baltic Republics, Slovenia, and others. (It might be added that this type of nation is relevant also for large nations outside Europe; a case in point is Japan).

One large European state, Germany, was historically also part of this group. The historical-theoretical rationale for the characteristic German concept of "culture nation" *(Kulturnation)* was laid down by nineteenth-century "romantic" philosophers, historians, and literary scientists such as Herder and Fichte. They wanted to develop an ideological weapon in the fight for liberty, independence, and unification of the many divided German territories, some under Napoleonic rule. Their ideas soon caught on among intellectuals in Italy and indeed all over Eastern Europe, whose countries and peoples, subjugated under the multinational empires of the Hapsburgs, the Ottoman rulers, and the Russian tsars, found themselves in a similar political situation.

Consequently, the idea of a "culture nation," based on common descent, language, and culture, played a central role in the struggles for political independence and unification of these countries. This principle also entered into their constitutions. It was, in principle, excluded for the first time in the post–World War II constitution of the Federal Republic of Germany, which founded itself explicitly on a "patriotism of constitution" (Lepsius 1988, 250). Nevertheless, even in the Federal Republic one important criterion for the granting of citizenship to foreigners is German ancestry. Therefore, all those people throughout Eastern Europe and Russia who can prove their descent from the "German people" *(Volksdeutsche)* have the right to immigrate to the Federal Republic and to get German citizenship even if they do not speak German anymore. On the other side, Germany today has a large number of new ethnic minorities (in 1991, about 5 million, or 6.4 percent of the population) who are noncitizens. Most of them immigrated as "guest workers," recently also as refugees since the mid-1960s. (In fact, at that time German firms and public authorities were eager to recruit these Southern European workers for reasons of labor-market shortage. Now, while the number of immigrants of German descent *(Volksdeutsche)* who have become new German citizens since World War II goes into the millions, the number of non-nationals (persons originating from non-German, mostly South European cultures) living in Germany who become German citizens is negligible—10,000 to 15,000 annually, that is, only 0.003 percent of the noncitizens living in Germany (Heckmann 1992, 13).

A further important concomitant of this definition of citizenship is a strong tendency (even if it is not expressed openly as an official policy) to assimilate new immigrants into the culture of the receiving country and the unwillingness to grant extensive rights to native ethnic minorities. This is the case in present-day Austria, which in some regards can also be considered as an ethnonational state (even if people feel themselves more and more as citizens of an "Austrian nation"; see Bruckmüller 1984). Among the new states of Eastern Europe, this problem is also highly relevant. The new Republic of Croatia's declaration of its political independence in 1991 and its constitution defining itself as the "State of all Croats" caused deep worries and fears among the large minority of Serbs. This was not the last motive for the outbreak of the bloody war between Serbia and Croatia and the following ethnic "cleansing" and genocide of the Bosnian people.

Another historically and actually relevant type of ethnonation is one based on common religion. In Ireland and Poland, adherence to Roman Catholicism has played a crucial role in the fight for political autonomy and independence. But religion helped to shape the character of state and civil society in other nations, too, and still is a significant determinant of life and cultural patterns, though it operates more in the background. This is the case for Roman Catholicism in most South European countries (for the cases of Spain and Italy, see Giner [1990] and [Gubert] 1992) and for Protestantism in the Scandinavian countries (described there as a private religion, called "protestant humanism" by Rijs [1989]). I will later show that the idea of an "ethnoreligious nation" is of great relevance also at the European level.

The second variant of "nation" is the *demotic-unitarian nation-state,* also characterized by high levels of internal cultural homogeneity. The theoretical rationale of this concept was developed during the French Enlightenment and Revolution and the subsequent constitutional development. Here, the rationale for the cultural assimilation of native minorities and immigrants is not an assumed a priori communality of descent or culture but common political citizenship. The main base for political authority is the "people" (*demos* [see Francis 1976], as against *ethnos*), composed of all those who are living in the territory of the state. Access to citizenship is more open, and the state sees as its central task the provision of equal opportunities for all its citizens. In relation to ethnic-linguistic minorities, this nation-state model also implies strong tendencies to cultural assimilation that are related to a relatively low level of political autonomy granted to regional units (and on the other side of coin, to a high degree of political centralization).

France is the paradigmatic example of a nation-state of this type. It is a historical fact that the high degree of France's linguistic-cultural homogeneity was actually created through a century-long process of unification, centralization, and standardization (see Elias 1976). A similar process, though less consciously planned by the central authorities, unfolded in Great Britain; the still unresolved Irish conflict shows that cultural assimilation processes were also at work in this case (see Hechter 1975). We will show that elements of this concept of "nation" play a significant role in the context of the new Europe.

In the third concept of "nation," the *constitutional nation-state,* political integration and unity is founded primarily on a constitution in which the divisions of rights between political authorities and citizens and between central political power and federal units (which usually have a high degree of autonomy) are clearly delineated. In such nations also, processes of cultural assimilation are at work. These processes are defined, however, as belonging not only to the state proper. A paradigmatic case in point is the United States. Here, public-school education, which is of central importance for the creation of a common language and culture among the immigrants from quite heterogeneous world regions and cultures, is left partly to private associations such as religious communities. Since immigrants are also quickly integrated politically and awarded citizenship, ethnic groups are prevented from becoming self-conscious but the ethnic-cultural hierarchy is nevertheless maintained informally (Adam 1993, 16).

On the other hand, it is in constitutional nation-states where clearly defined "national subgroups" (ethnic communities living on their territory for many generations) have the best chance of preserving their cultural identity by means of a strongly federalistic constitution. Switzerland is the most important European example in this regard; others are Belgium, post-fascist Spain, and Canada. An important characteristic of such states is the fact that they all have federalistic constitutions which grant extensive rights to regional subunits within the state (countries, Kantones, Bundesländer). One can even say that constitutional states typically have developed out of alliances between strong independent regions or countries. This type, obviously, is a very important model for European unification. Relevant also is the fact that the Federal Republic of Germany, now the largest single EC member-state in terms of population and economic power, has a strong federalist constitution and thus provides support for those forces that would like to see European integration to develop along these lines.

A *constitutional state union* is the fourth type that has to be distinguished here. This would be a confederation of independent states whose aim is to create common institutions that would take over parts of the individual states' duties and responsibilities. The difference between this and a constitutional nation-state lies in the fact that the individual member-states in this case retain full autonomy and independence. Such a union becomes an acting unit in its own right with a considerable number of duties. By contrast, a state alliance is a contractual agreement between states that remain fully independent units; the agreement is aimed only at coordination or cooperation along specific, clearly restricted lines (for example, customs unions or defense alliances).

I shall discuss in the last section which of these models seems most feasible for Europe as a whole. First, let us look at the internal structural differences within Europe and their relevance for the emergence of a "European nation."

Transformation and Persistence of Structural Diversity

Following our general discussion in the first section, we shall now discuss, concretely for Europe, how this "culture area" (Jordan 1988) today looks from the viewpoint of its internal structural diversity. Building upon general discussions on this subject (Reiterer 1988; Smith 1991; Heckmann 1992), I assume that at least three structural dimensions are crucial for the development of national identity: a relatively closed territorial basis, a unified economy, and a common culture (including common language, religion, and history). For each of these dimensions, we shall discuss to what degree it is probable, and empirically observable, that "Europe" is approaching a new kind of supra- or multinational unity.

When speaking about the *territorial basis* of a nation, two aspects are relevant. The first refers to the time dimension and history. We can say generally that the longer a certain population is living in a specific territory, the stronger the attachment to it as a kind of homeland *(Heimat)* will be. The second aspect relates to the closeness of the territory. Here, attachment to a certain territory will be facilitated when a population inhabits exclusively a clearly defined territory. This is most probable if the territory is contained within natural borders—such as the sea in the case of islands, or high mountains. Such borders provide a natural protection against military invasions from outside and therefore strongly facilitate the peaceful development of a society within them.

How does the European situation look from this point of view? The first condition for national development is given insofar as nearly all European populations have lived on their present territories now for at least a millennium or even longer. Since the last great migration of nations around 500 A.D., leading to the collapse of the Roman Empire, no further great mass migration has taken place. This fact, seemingly trivial from a within-European perspective, is quite relevant when comparing Europe, for instance, to the "new societies" created by European emigrants in America and Australia. It means that the territorial-local attachment of most Europeans will be rather high (see Strassoldo and Tessarin 1992). This attachment is also due to the fact that, internally, Europe is a highly differentiated "culture area" (Jordan 1988).

From the viewpoint of the emergence of a "European nation," however, the implication of this fact is ambiguous. On the one hand, it may foster a sense of belonging together as good "old neighbors"; on the other, it may foster feelings of being different from one another. It is a matter of fact that during the last centuries many European nation-states (especially the larger ones) were engaged in continuous and bitter fighting and wars against each other. In this regard, the period since World War II in fact marks a wholly new epoch. Mattei Dogan, in his contribution to Part I, argues convincingly that since that time there is a clear shift toward a termination of these hostilities, not only at the level of politics but also at the level of the populations and their mutual perceptions.

As far as Europe as a whole is concerned, it is important that this macroregion is not nearly so clearly defined geographically as is implied by its designation as a "continent." Even if—at first sight—Europe has clear borderlines formed by seas in the north, west, and south, there is no such dividing line in the east, in neither geographical-topological nor anthropological-cultural terms; Russians, a European race, are the main settlers both west and east of the Ural mountains. Modern geographers, therefore, even deny that Europe can be designated as a continent at all (Jordan 1988; Haller 1990). As well, the demarcation in the south by the Mediterranean Sea was not always a dividing line. From antiquity up to the Middle Ages, the world of the Mediterranean Sea constituted a macroregion whose units were closely interrelated in economic, cultural, and political terms.

The issue of the territorial basis for European identity is far from trivial. Rather, one could argue that in fact this is the unique *universal criterion* on which membership in a European Union should be contingent. Here, the main rationale for the establishment of a European Union is that it should contribute to a peaceful coexistence, a high level of economic exchanges, and thus to the economic welfare of all nations and peoples living in a certain geographic area or neighborhood. From this point of view, the main criterion for admission should not be economic maturity or cultural affinity but regional location; that is, neighborhood.

Closely related to the territorial aspect is the dimension of *socioeconomic interdependence and unity* as a base for the development of national identity. This aspect was historically crucial: It was no mere coincidence that the concept and reality of nation in the modern sense developed hand in hand with the spread of the capitalist market economy over Western Europe and the world. A very high and still increasing economic interdependence among towns, regions, and states is one of the main characteristics of this new mode of production (Wallerstein 1974; Giddens 1985). While at one time Europe was characterized in economic terms by a multitude of small, nearly self-contained regions, today it is the macroregion in the world characterized by the largest volume of interregional and interstate trade and commerce. Testimony to the fundamental importance of this growing economic interdependence for the rise of a new European "supranation" is the fact that the European Community gained its main incentive and driving force just from the growth potential it realized in the past and promises for the future (see Volker Bornschier's contribution in Part I).

Yet even in this aspect we should not overlook some facts that may set clear limits to the growth of an economically fully integrated Europe. The first concerns the issue of the free mobility of the four "production factors," goods, services, capital, and labor. In order for an integrated economic area to work effectively, free mobility in *all* these four aspects must be given. It is one of the central aims of the European Community to set up the necessary conditions to make this fully possible. Yet experience shows that this aim has not been achieved. While free movement of capital, goods, and even services already obtains to a considerable degree, the same is not true for labor. Even if by now the necessary legal regulations are more or less fully provided (freedom of access to the labor market for citizens in any other member-country, for example, or widespread recognition of educational certificates), there is still no indication that a Europe-wide free labor market is in the making. Rather, after the massive worker migration from South to Central and North European countries in the 1960s and 1970s, labor mobility within the EC area has decreased significantly. Intracountry mobility in the United States is three times as high as is mobility in EC-Europe.

Moreover, empirical research has shown that even where the exchange of goods and services is concerned, Western Europe is still far from forming a closely integrated economic area. Rather, it seems to be subdivided into a few subregions that have high levels of exchange within them but significantly lower levels of exchange among them. It is highly significant that not only geographical propinquity but also linguistic-cultural affinity seem to be relevant for the emergence of such areas. This is shown by the fact that the three areas are comprised of, first, Great Britain and some Scandinavian countries; second, the German-speaking countries of Central Europe; and third, some Latin countries of Southern Europe (Tichy 1991).

It is in this regard that Europe, after the breakdown of Communism and the Iron Curtain between East and West, has to solve one of its most pressing actual problems. Neither from the viewpoint of geographical propinquity nor from that of economic integration are there any reasons whatsoever why access to the Community should be denied to Central and East European countries. Countries such as Hungary, Czechoslovakia, and Poland have traditionally been strongly connected to Central Europe. Now, however, they face the extremely difficult task of simultaneously transforming their economic and political systems, toward market economies and political democracies, as Georg Vobruba (forthcoming) in his essay "Transnational Social Policy in Processes of Transformation" in the companion volume to this book rightly points out. The central problem arising for these countries today is the fact that their economic reform processes, in essence processes of the liberalization of market forces, must be supplemented by measures of social policy in order to make this economic reform acceptable to the populations; but they do not possess the means to do this alone. According to Vobruba, it is in the interest of the West to aid the Eastern countries in this process. So Western countries, for instance, will increasingly come to recognize that in order to protect themselves from nuclear catastrophes they must assist the East in developing alternative energy resources.

What are the chances of Europe in terms of a *common culture* becoming a new focus of identification for its peoples? Two main subdimensions must be distinguished here. The first is *language*, the basis and primary medium of exchange in any culture. Here, diversity prevails over unity by far: "Linguistically, Europe presents a crazy-quilt pattern surpassed in complexity by few other parts of the world" (Jordan 1988, 89). Some overlapping unity within diversity is given by the fact that most European languages belong to the Indo-European language family. Within this, however, the European languages are further subdivided into the three large groups—Romance, Germanic, and Slavic. There is widespread agreement that this central aspect of European "multiculturality" should in no case be sacrificed to the forced introduction of one or a few common "lingua francas" such as English or French. In this regard, the EC is truly multinational or multicultural in its principles (even if not so in fact, at least in the workings of its central bureaucracies).

Regarding language, two conclusions can be drawn about the potential for the development of a "European nation." The first is that this potential is clearly restricted. The use of at least nine different languages in everyday interaction by most people within only the twelve member states of the present EC means that severe limits exist for the development of a fully free interchange of ideas and people. Moving to a European country with a different language may mean not only language problems for employees in the new working place, but also that their children would have to attend a school where another language than their own is used. The linguistic diversity of Europe also sets clear limits on a free interchange through mass media, newspapers, journals, radio, and television. So far, no attempts at establishing a Europe-wide newspaper or television station have been successful, and no serious plans in this area are in sight. Thus linguistic diversity makes it highly unlikely that, even after the removal of all legal and political barriers, a fully "free market" of capital, goods, and labor and a true political "European public opinion" will unfold. In this matter, Europe will remain fundamentally different from its two economic rivals on the world scene, the United States and Japan, and much more differentiated internally.

One of two things might happen in this regard. The first is that the three big "linguistic" or "culture areas" within Europe (Jordan 1988; Haller 1990; Smith 1991, 172) will gain in importance in the near future. This has already been happening in the German-speaking area since the unification of Germany and the increasing economic interdependence between Germany, Austria, and many of the new small Central and East European countries. Also such tendencies toward a strengthening of linguistic-cultural areas within Europe would counteract rather than strengthen the integration of Europe (Friedrich [1969, 11ff] forecasts a strengthening of linguistic-cultural areas on a worldwide scale).

The second, opposite, tendency here is that English seems to be on the way to becoming de facto the new "lingua franca" in Europe (in view of the increasing competition between Europe and the United States, this appears somewhat ironic). "Multiculturality" in terms of a knowledge of foreign languages and humanistic and literary education and so forth has always been designated as being a strength of Europeans. One of the characteristic "markers" of an educated European in the next century might well become the ability to speak at least two other languages in addition to one's own—that is, English and the language of a neighboring country (see Morin 1987, 200). Both in East/Central and Southern Europe, English is evidently gaining ground as the main second language (at the expense of Russian in the first case, and of French in the second). A common knowledge of English would facilitate, moreover, communication among Europeans and people in other parts of the world.

An interesting case in point is the Netherlands. In this country, not only bi- but even trilingualism has been common among educated people for generations (with German and English as the two foreign languages widely spoken in addition to Dutch). Recently, increasing numbers of parents in this country are sending their children to high schools and universities that teach exclusively in English. Is this the model trend for Europe as a whole? This highly relevant question was investigated by Jap Dronkers in his contribution, "The Causes of Growth of English Education in the Netherlands." He shows that the tendency toward full bilingualism in the Netherlands is clearly restricted to a specific segment of the educated upper classes. The increased spread of English education in Dutch universities can be explained primarily in terms of the demand from parents and students but not as a consequence of some deliberate governmental policy. Particularly well educated parents who have been internationally mobile in their own careers are sending their children to such schools and universities. Thus it can be said that the increasing cohesion among the economies of Europe has led toward an increasingly strong international orientation in the internationally oriented section of the Dutch elite. Doubtless, this is also true for other countries to a large degree. Businessmen and enterprisers had the largest share in building the new European community (Friedrich 1969). From this point of view, however, integration will also contribute to the rise of a new "European elite" and thus to an increasing sociocultural inequality within the single European societies and their national elites.

A stronger case for a traditional but still relevant dimension in which Europe can be seen—at least at first sight—as a cultural unity is *religion*. The Christian religion was traditionally the single most important basis for European cultural identity, especially in the late Middle Ages when faith and culture, Europe and Christianity were almost synonymous (Jordan 1988, 113). The founder of the Pan-Europa movement, R. Coudenhove-Kalergi (1953), has seen here, as have many others, the principal base for the thesis that Europe constitutes a cultural unit of its own. Yet here also Europe today is split up into the three main large groups: Roman Catholicism in the South, Protestantism in the North, and Orthodoxy in the East. Even after long and far-reaching processes of secularization, this split is highly relevant.

The first and oldest internal cultural border in this regard exists between Eastern and Western Christianity. The social, cultural, and political development of Eastern Europe cannot be understood adequately without reference to the profound impact that Greek Orthodox Christianity has had in these regions and countries. Many present-day characteristics of Russia and other Orthodox nations in Eastern Europe are closely related to the cultural-political heritage of Byzantium and Orthodox Christianity, including the close alliance between church and state, a strong hierarchical character, and so forth (Noetzel 1970; Buss 1989). It is very important, however, to understand that East Europeans and others living in countries with Orthodox denominations do not perceive themselves as significantly less "true Europeans" than Westerners, as Elena Bashkirova (1992) has shown with recent survey data. From this point of view, it seems more a one-sided West European perspective (and possibly strategy of exclusion) to see the split between Roman Catholicism/Protestantism and Orthodoxy as another fundamental dividing line in Europe.

One should also not overlook the importance of a second religious dividing line, the one created after the Reformation and distinguishing the Southern and Central Catholic from Northwestern Protestant Europe. Looking at the proportions of people who strongly favor further integration of the European Community, a clear dividing line exists between the Roman Catholic countries, where the proportion is much larger, and the Protestant countries, where it is much lower (Commission of the European Communities 1990). It is a matter of fact that the institutions of the European Community have been strongly influenced by political ideas connected with catholic social thinking; French, Italian, and German (Roman Catholic) politicians, such as Jean Monnet, Robert Schumann, Alcide Degasperi, and Konrad Adenauer, played a leading role in their designation in the early 1950s. Protestant countries have some reasons for showing reservations toward the centralistic tendencies in Brussels, and it is not surprising that they have strongly supported the idea of "subsidiarity" that was brought into the Maastricht treaty. This idea states that the political unit at the highest level should take over only those tasks that cannot be fulfilled better by some lower unit.

Thus there are at least two reasons why the potential of Christianity as a base for a European identity is relatively restricted. The first is that Europe is internally differentiated quite clearly. Peter Ester and Loek Halman in their contribution, "Empirical Trends in Religious and Moral Beliefs in Western Europe," show that this fact is not of decreasing importance even in our age of secularization. By comparing data on religious practices, social permissiveness, and civic morality from the two panels of the "European Value Survey" in 1981 and in 1990, they find that the various West European countries did not converge in these areas. Rather, in several instances the differences among them became even larger. They conclude that Europe does not show a growing unity of basic religious and moral beliefs, but that the differences seem to have become even greater and more in line with the idea that Europe, in terms of value orientations, can be divided into North and South.

Thus it seems doubtful that religion in general and Christianity in particular can constitute an adequate base for a new European identity and nation—even if one objects that religious diversity as such must not inhibit the growth of a nation. (This is shown by the cases of Switzerland, the Netherlands, and Germany, which include both Protestants and Catholics). A further reason for the limited appropriateness of Christianity as an ideological base for a new European nation is the fact that this would imply a concept of Europe as a religious "ethnonation" in the sense discussed in the preceding section. Such a definition would be highly problematic from several points of view. First, there are increasing numbers of Europeans who do not anymore consider themselves "Christians" in the proper sense. In the Netherlands and Great Britain, nearly as much as half of the population does not now formally belong to a Christian church at all (see Ester and Halman in this volume). Second, such a definition of Europe would necessarily lead—as any other ethnonational concept does—to new exclusionary practices.

Within Europe, whole populations not adhering to Christianity—such as the Moslems of Bosnia-Herzegovina and Albania and all the large groups of immigrant workers in France, Germany, and Great Britain of Islamic and other non-Christian religions—would never qualify in the full sense as true Europeans. Furthermore, a new dividing line could be drawn between Europe and its non-Christian neighbors. A highly relevant case regards Turkey. In his contribution to this volume, "Turkey and the European Community," Attila Eralp shows that such processes of social exclusion have already been at work in the recent history of European integration. It seems quite evident that as a concomitant to the redefinition of Europe along historical-cultural lines that invoke ancient Greece and Christianity as ideological foundations, "Turkishness" has increasingly been defined as something alien to European culture. As a consequence, Turkey has been gradually forced to adopt "Turkishness" as a constituent element of its own national identity. This, in consequence, has led to a serious weakening of liberal, democratic, and progressive forces within the country and to a strengthening of those forces that successfully tried to redefine Turkey's geopolitical role as a leader for the Turkish people in the new independent successor states of the Soviet Union in South and Central Asia. Ironically, this redefinition of its role in world political affairs brought Turkey closer to the United States and its power politics in these regions. It is also the reason why Western Europe nowadays has great difficulties when denouncing the violations of human rights by the Turkish governments against its large minority of Kurds. Thus we can conclude that this quite dramatic shift of European politics has had the consequence that Europe has missed one very important occasion for implementing a new kind of peaceful regional neighborhood politics.

We should also discuss here the issue of a *common history* as part of a common culture, even if this dimension cannot be considered as a structural precondition. Here again, there is no immediate potential to build on for a "United Europe." It is typical of all multiethnic and multinational societies that they do not have myths of common descent and history; loyalty to them is invoked rather by symbols like flags, national anthems, and reference to the future opportunities the new "fatherland" will provide (Adam 1993, 15). From this perspective, European history from the late Middle Ages to the midtwentieth century was evidently characterized much more by internal conflicts and wars than by historical events that could be invoked as constituting a common glorious past. However, we must see that history to a large degree is "made" and can be rewritten according to present-day circumstances and interests. Johan Galtung, in his contribution to this volume, rightly points to the potential for a new Euronationalism in this regard. A rewriting of European history, stressing such positive aspects as European individualism and dynamism and leaving out such negative aspects as religious intolerance, colonialism, slavery, and deprivation of minorities and other powerless social groups, seems already to be on its way.

Interests, Actors, and a Changing World Constellation

So far, we have primarily discussed the issue of structural preconditions favoring or inhibiting the possible rise of a supranational European consciousness. One could rightly argue, however, that these factors are only static in nature. Their exclusive consideration could easily lead one to overlook the fact that many structures that have been stable over extended periods are often fundamentally changed in short periods by the actions of charismatic political leaders, social upheavals, and revolutions, and also by evolutionary processes that are less spectacular in their workings but nevertheless can have far-reaching revolutionary effects over time. (In this sense, for instance, H. Mendras [1988] writes about a "second French Revolution" since World War II.) Also in many of the aforementioned structural divisions, processes of assimilation are at work reducing the differences among the single European societies (Kaelble 1987).

Thus the structural or ecological perspective has to be supplemented by a process- and *actor-oriented perspective* that considers the interests and the actions of important personalities, social groups and classes, and organizations and movements. It must further be supplemented by an *institutional perspective*, which holds that there exists a close (even if not deterministic) link between social structures and political constitutions, processes, and outcomes. It is quite clear that this also applies to European integration (Lane and Ersson 1987, 360). Let us also discuss, therefore, the issue of European unification from the viewpoint of nation-building as a dynamic process, as outlined in the first section. The issues shall be discussed in these regards: interests and aims related to integration; actors and their relationships to the population at large; and the fundamental changes in the situational circumstances that have occurred over the course of this century.

Two main kinds of interests and related actors have been of primary importance in the unification process in Western Europe so far. The first are *economic interests*. Bornschier's analysis shows quite clearly, as have many others (for example, Cutler et al. 1989; Scherb and Morawetz 1988), that these interests have played a pivotal role in European unification from the beginning. Two kinds of interests have been particularly relevant in this regard. The first is comprised of the interests of big industry and capital in enlarging the market for goods and services and creating a huge internal market in order to become able to compete with the United States and Japan. The impressive success of the European Community in the removal of trade barriers among its member-states has been achieved to a large degree because of the massive pressure of the big multinational European corporations. In 1983, for instance, a European Round Table of Industrialists convened, which in the successive year published a memorandum. This memorandum, together with a working paper from the leading Philips manager, Wisse Dekker, had a profound influence on a White Book for the Internal Market of the European Commission, published in 1985 (Grün and Foresta 1992). The main intent of this proposal was the creation of a huge internal market of 320 million consumers. There is no doubt that such a market does not profit the consumers alone but also the large and competitive multinational European enterprises.

Later on, and after their success, these interests in the enlargement of markets for goods and services were joined by what we may call *economic growth-and-development interests*. Today, national governments increasingly justify their participation (or application for membership) in the community with the argument that, by remaining outside of it, their growth potential will be severely restricted. It is also for this reason that the attitudes toward further integration are most positive in the less developed countries of the European periphery in the South, in Ireland, and in Eastern Europe. Here, we have a type of identification with Europe which by analogy to the concept of "consumer nationalism" (Adam 1993)—may be called a "consumer Europeanism." It may be hypothesized that this kind of identification will be strongly dependent on Europe's future economic prosperity. This identification may be severely undermined in periods of economic stagnation and crisis (as is already observable). It can also be undermined if the outcomes of economic growth in the long run remain as unequally distributed as they have until now, leaving large gaps in development between the central, economically strong and prosperous EC nations and the peripheral countries and regions. What we can observe in the latter are extremely high levels of unemployment (in October 1993 more than 20 percent in Spain, 17 percent in Ireland), depopulation of large rural areas, and increasing social problems in urban agglomerations. Trends of this kind evidently undermine European unity in economic terms. It seems that the earlier European structure, composed of several more or less independent larger regions with their own centers, is increasingly becoming replaced by a new, Europe-wide structure of center and periphery (Haller 1993; Gallino 1993; Haller and Höllinger 1994).

It certainly would be a simplification to try to explain West European integration by economic motives alone. The second class of interests in the unification of Europe is related to *politics* proper. A look at the motives of those who were most active in the integration process in its beginnings quite clearly shows that political interests also played a pivotal role. Leading postwar European politicians such as Winston Churchill, Charles de Gaulle, and Konrad Adenauer were fully conscious of the fact that their countries were no longer able to play a primary role in world politics. Thus they saw the creation of a European Community (which in fact in its first stage was devised so as to become a military and defense union) as a means of giving back to Europe its proper role as a *political world power*. In doing so, they were reacting to the new bipartite world power structure between the Western bloc, led by the United States, and the Communist bloc, led by the Soviet Union. In the immediate postwar years of the Cold War, the latter was doubtlessly perceived by many Europeans as a real threat. In the writings of the founder of the Pan-Europa movement, R. Coudenhove-Kalergi, this motive for European unification—as a bulwark against Soviet Communism—played a central role. Meanwhile, after the breakdown of communism in Eastern Europe, the dissolution of the Warsaw Pact, and the massive economic weakening of Russia, this threat is felt much less in Central and Western Europe.

Thus, since its beginnings, the unification of Europe in political terms was also a reaction to large concentrations of power in the world as a whole. It might well be that in most recent times, since the collapse of the main enemy—the communist regimes in Eastern Europe—a newly motivated, active *European power politics* of its own is gaining ground. Such a motive is often—even if seldom openly—invoked when pointing to the great discrepancy between the economic strength and the political weakness of (Western) Europe. This interest in power politics, obviously, is also connected closely to the interests of large corporations that wish to have the backing of a politically stable and secure environment for their economic undertakings. One could also hypothesize that the decreasing nationalism *within* Europe, demonstrated so convincingly by Mattei Dogan, was a concomitant to these changes going on in the larger arena of world power politics (see also Morin 1987, 144). From such a view, the decrease of single-state nationalism within Europe must by no means be meant to imply a general decline of nationalism. On the contrary, it would be quite compatible with increasing European supranationalism, as pointed out by Johan Galtung.

The rise of such a new (West) European military superpower would doubtless be perceived as a threat by Eastern and Southern Europe. Thus not only Russia but also the Turkish-Arab countries of the Middle East could organize similar alliances leading to new tensions and conflicts. (Efforts in this direction are already being made by Turkey, the former Soviet Islamic republics, and some other Middle East Islamic countries).

We can ask why the aforementioned interests were able to become so influential in the process of European unification. Evidently, other fundamental social, economic, and political interests had much less influence in this matter. One could think here of the interests for a just and equal distribution of economic wealth and power, for full-scale political participation of citizens, for more regional autonomy and power against the national states. All these interests together could be summarized in the formula that Europe should become a new kind of peaceful "civil power" (Kohnstamm and Hager 1973; Senghaas 1990), instead of an additional big economic-military bloc. We think that one key for the answer to these questions can be found by looking at the main *actors* in the European integration process. It is evident that this process has been and still is promoted overwhelmingly by *economic and political elites*. Two facts are highly significant in this regard; both are related to the issues of the relative involvement of different kinds of elites and the relationships between elites and their populations.

The first is the remarkably widespread absence of elites other than economic and political ones, such as writers, historians, and social scientists, from the discussions of and developments in the process of the unification of Western Europe and the European Community. In the late nineteenth and early twentieth centuries, intellectuals constituted a strategic group in nation building in all the single countries, and they participated actively in the discussions about the project of a United Europe as well—as they already had in the French and American revolutions.

Today, many of these intellectuals seem to be voiceless observers of the seemingly so successful process of integration (see Morin 1987, 183ff). This is strikingly parallel to some other historical processes of nation building in which intellectuals contributed quite actively in the early stages—by opposing political suppression and devising models for national unification and integration—but were soon replaced by "political men," leaders who were much more experienced in the usurpation and the management of political power (Smith 1991, 95ff). Such was the case in the process of German unification in the nineteenth century when Bismarck's successful

Realpolitik soon pushed aside the democratic ideas of intellectuals and idealists in the national assembly of the Frankfurter Paulskirche some decades ago. Such was the more recent case in the postcommunist Central and East European states where, in many cases, the persons coming to power were not the intellectuals who had played decisive roles in the subversion of the totalitarian regimes, but political leaders who had already learned their "craft" as Communist leaders. The political disintegration of several of the former multinational or multiethnic states must also be seen as a strategy of these political leaders to gain more power and influence in a new small, but independent state (Haller 1992b). In Czechoslovakia, for instance, opinion polls continually showed a majority of the population to be in favor of the continuation of state unity; in Croatia, the regime in power found it necessary to conduct a big advertising campaign to convince the population to vote yes in the referendum on political independence.

A second significant fact in the postwar unification of Western Europe is the deep *split* that is observable in many West European countries today between economic-political elites on the one side, and the populations at large on the other. This split became evident in the 1991 referendum in Switzerland on membership in the "European Economic Area"; practically all the large parties and interest groups supported membership strongly but the population voted against it, even if only by a small margin. It is evident in Great Britain and most Scandinavian countries, where opinion polls show that the opponents to EC membership and the deepening of EC integration along the lines of the Maastricht treaty are in a clear majority. Here again, it is the elites who strongly favor membership or further integration. In a paradoxical analogy to the corresponding situation in the new small East European countries, the political elites in West European countries deny the population the right to decide this fundamental issue in national referendums. A Eurobarometer poll in the late 1980s showed that nearly 90 percent of those interviewed wanted such a referendum (Commission of the European Community 1990).

There is a third important issue to be considered when speaking about nation building as a dynamic process. This is the question of the circumstances, or the *situation,* within which strategies for European integration are formulated and pursued.

The relevance of this aspect is quite evident in the case of the unification of (Western) Europe. In the recent history of this continent, plans and efforts at unification have always been formulated in periods after big and bloody internal conflicts. Thus after both world wars—essentially European wars—efforts at political pacification and integration of Europe flourished. But it was only after World War II that the ideas of the interwar period (such as the Pan-Europa movement) took on a concrete form. This was facilitated by a fundamental shift in world power that reduced even the largest West European states to second class, behind the emerging superpowers of the United States and the Soviet Union. The late 1980s brought a further fundamental change in this regard. With the breakdown of communism in Eastern Europe and the Soviet Union, the essential West European model of political integration lost one of its reasons to exist, namely that of forming a strong united power against the Communist bloc. (This motive was central, for instance, for the founder of the Pan-Europa movement, R. Coudenhove-Kalergi.) With this fundamental change, the hitherto clear dividing line between Western and Eastern Europe became blurred. It can already be observed today, that the loss of the big enemy in the East is weakening the impetus for European unification even among some of its most enthusiastic proponents. As a consequence, a new decision lies before Europe: that of the intensification of West European integration along the lines of the Maastricht treaty, or that of the extension of membership to the smaller, economically crisis-laden postcommunist East and Central European states. A decision between these two alternatives will be contingent upon the general possibility for Europe to become a new nation of its own. Let us turn to this issue in the concluding section.

The First New "Community of Nations"? Constitutional Perspectives for a United Europe

What conclusions can be drawn from the foregoing considerations of nation building and the constitutional foundation of a United Europe? In discussing this issue, I start by pointing to two empirical facts related to processes within the (West) European Community, the most successful enterprise of European unification so far.

The first concerns the interest and participation of the citizens of the member-states of the European Community in community affairs as such. Here, all the data concerning active political interest, participation, and involvement of citizens in European political affairs give an unambiguous picture showing that political participation and interest at the European level is much lower than it is at the national level. For instance, in six out of the twelve member-states, only about half or less of the voters participated in the 1989 elections to the European parliament (Lane and Ersson 1987, 39; see also Lepsius 1991). This has to do with, first, the sheer size and diversity of the European Community. Each of the large nation-states has the problem that political participation of its citizens in national affairs is considerably lower than it is in the small states (Kohr 1986). This problem might arise in a United Europe on a massive scale. Issues that are highly relevant in, say, Denmark or Norway may be rather irrelevant in Spain or Italy. Issues that are considered to be of great impor-tance by Germans (as, for instance, environmental pollution) may appear irrelevant to citizens in France or Italy. It would simply overcharge people's information-processing capacities to be interested in and follow all important events in other member-states.

The low level of citizen participation in European affairs is further linked directly to the workings of the "Eurocracy" as sketched out in the contribution by Maurizio Bach in Part I. Citizens' interest in European politics as such remains restricted in the single nation-states because of both the high degree of informality and confidentiality of EC politics and the frequent substitution of public political discussion and action by administrative decisions (see Hancock 1993).

The second empirical issue concerns the aims that European politicians really are pursuing in regard to the European Community. It seems to be a fact that the substantive aim of the leading politicians in the member-states is not, as frequently assumed, the creation of a nation-state in the sense of a fully integrated, centralized political unit. What they are aspiring to in reality is better described as some kind of supranational, federative arrangement. Evidence of this thesis is the fact that the prime ministers of the member-countries are quite set on not giving up their power of independent decision making to the Council of Ministers, including the right to veto decisions that are of "vital impor-tance" to individual countries (Arnold 1993). The Council of Ministers so far remains the single most powerful, quasi-monopolistic deciding body of the EC, with the European Commission as the nonelected, executive organ (Lane and Ersson 1987; Lepsius 1991; Hancock 1993).

It seems somewhat paradoxical that the principle of strong superiority for the Council of Ministers over the competences of the directly elected European parliament often provides small member-states with an overproportional degree of power in decision-making processes. Luxembourg, for example, was able to influence EC decisions on taxation and capital markets in a way that strongly favored the powerful banking sector of this ministate. (It may also be that the interests of the banking sector in Luxembourg often coincide with the interests of big capital in other EC countries). In another recent example, Greece's position and actions contributed considerably to the inability of the EC to impose an efficient blockade against

Serbia after its military aggression against the other republics of former Yugoslavia. As the latter example shows, this principle leads directly to the often bemoaned inability of the EC to arrive at clear and prompt decisions on pressing political issues. The ambivalent and often contradictory declarations of the EC and its member-states on international disputes over tariff and trade regulations during the Gulf and Yugoslav wars are testimonies to this fact. It is also shown by the recurring fundamental crises of the European monetary system, which in no way have been solved so far.

This inability of the leading European politicians to realize what they have stated as their aim in many festive declarations, namely, a truly integrated political community—a nation in the classic sense—should be no surprise given the fundamental and persistent internal differentiations within Europe outlined above. What is the conclusion to be drawn from these facts? Should the project of a United Europe be abandoned altogether? I think that this would be premature. There are also pervasive trends that strongly support the claim for the necessity of European unification. We might mention here the increasing internal interlocking of this continent in terms of capital and goods, scientific and cultural exchange, travel and tourism, and so forth (see Friedrich 1969). The impressive and undeniable success of European integration through the European Community, as well as the increasing interest by nonmember-states in Western and Eastern Europe in joining the EC, also has to be mentioned here. It is of primary importance to be entirely clear, therefore, about the real possibilities of unification.

In discussing the question of what kind of constitutional framework would be feasible for a United Europe, let us follow here the distinctions among the four types of nation-states outlined above.

It is evident that the *ethnonational state* is unthinkable for Europe as a whole given its extreme cultural differentiation. Yet this concept played and continues to play a significant role, as pointed out in the foregoing section. Not only the founder of the Pan-Europa movement, but also many present-day Christian and conservative political and intellectual leaders, conceive of a United Europe as a continuation of the idea of the "Christian occident" (*christliches Abendland*; see Faber [1979] for an discussion of this idea; certainly one of the great European personalities of our time, Pope John Paul II, was inspired by it). Such a conception, however, would imply some highly problematic consequences. Among them, we might mention the possible exclusion of the Slavic, Orthodox Christian countries of Eastern Europe from a properly defined Europe; a rigid politic of exclusion of non-Christian immigrants and new minorities within many single countries (see Noiriel [1991] for an impressive account of the forms and consequences of closing nation-states against refugees); and a hostile and potentially aggressive front line against non-Christian countries and civilizations. One should also note in this regard that today in some European countries (for example, the Netherlands, Great Britain) as much as 40 percent of the population does not belong to any Christian denomination at all. We must not deny that, historically, Europe owes a lot to Christianity. A United Europe, however, can take over from it only those values that are truly universal across cultures, such as the insistence on the dignity of human individuality and personality, equality, freedom, and so forth.

A positive aspect of the second model, the *constitutional nation-state*, is that it is here where the constitution lies at the heart of national identity. This should certainly be the case for a United Europe as well. We can say that one of the most important and lasting achievements of European unification so far has been the formulation and securing of universal citizenship rights, backed by the pathbreaking institution of the European Court for Human Rights where these rights become usable. Many observers consider the creation of laws and legal orders as the most important achievement and resource of the European Community so far (Joerges 1991).

The idea of Europe becoming a constitutional nation-state seems to underlie the strategies of many politicians as well as the social-scientific analyses that envision a United Europe as a kind of "state." (For instance, Lepsius [1988], following Francis [1965], speaks of a "state of nationalities" as a true alternative to a "nation-state"; see also Friedrich 1969.) In my opinion, there are two reasons why the model of a true "state" seems not to be appropriate for Europe. The first is that the creation of a state apparatus in the last instance would lead to a gigantic new bureaucracy that would be—given the size and internal heterogeneity of Europe—quite far removed from ordinary citizens. Today it is already a characteristic of international organizations that they tend to develop relatively detached functional elites and expert groups (Lepsius 1991). If a European bureaucracy and government would come into being, problems of administrative waste, economic and political corruption, and so on would arise on a grand scale, especially as long as different laws are valid in different countries (Kapteyn 1993). The fact that most constitutional nation-states tend to standardize their populations culturally is also relevant here.

We should not overlook the possibility, in this regard, that a hidden cultural standardization and leveling of Europe could develop in spite of the preservation of the autonomy of the many language and cultural areas.

Today, most national European television programs are already flooded by standardized "Euroamerican" mass entertainment and political information. (A case in point was the information during the Gulf War, which was practically exclusively dominated by the view of U.S. television companies; as is well known, the news reports that these companies were able to transmit from the theater of war were themselves submitted to censorship by the U.S. military leaders.) This standardization is furthered greatly by the fact that in the area of the modern electronic mass media large profits are possible and strong processes of concentration are going on in Europe as well (Fabris 1988).

It seems quite clear what remains as the only feasible constitutional model for a United Europe. I would call it a constitutional "Community of Nations" or "Community of Nation-States." This vision, even if somewhat less ambitious than that of a true state, would be unique and pathbreaking from a comparative and historical perspective. In fact, European unification could serve as a model for the many other attempts presently going on in North America, Eastern Asia, and Africa at making agreements and "marriages" between adjacent groups or "families of nations" (Therborn 1993). In contrast to mere international *alliances* for specific purposes (such as defense alliances, customs unions, and so forth), such a community would oblige its member-states to coordinate their aims and activities in many fields of politics and for a long time. It would reach this aim, however, not by establishing a central government proper, but by establishing community bodies that in principle have only the right to enact general laws and regulations (as well as to impose penalties in the case of their violation).

Considered from a substantive point of view, two requirements would be important for such a Community of Nation-States. The first concerns its actions in substantive fields of politics such as the economy, welfare services, and so forth. It is widely recognized today that the creation of free factor markets (of capital, goods, services, and labor) throughout the Community makes it necessary to introduce explicit measures to counteract the necessarily arising new social and economic disequilibrium and inequalities (see Room 1990; Busch 1991). EC regional and social policy is a first step in this direction. In my opinion, however, it would be absolutely necessary to look for mechanisms that would enable an indirect, more or less automatic redistribution that would not necessitate day-to-day interventions of governmental agencies which, as can be seen already today, would open the door for myriad uncontrollable wastes, embezzlement, and corruption. A central aspect of a more or less "automatic," indirect redistribution, however, would be a coordination of the systems of taxation and a system of financial adjustment among countries and regions with very differing economic power.

A second point concerns the relevance and meaning of a European citizenship in this sense against national and subnational memberships and loyalties on the one side and international loyalties on the other.

I have already pointed out that there must be no contradiction between the development of a new "European" identity and the persistence of loyalty to one's own nation-state. However, the rise of a European identity certainly would have its effect on national identity. This could, however, have a welcome effect, namely, the weakening, or a "specification," of the meaning of national identity. Recent discussions of the change in the role and relevance of the nation-state rightly point to its weakening from several points of view (Urry 1990; Knieper 1991; Galli 1991; Drucker 1993; Hankel 1993). On the one side, the nation-state comes under pressure from worldwide economic integration. This is most evident in the case of currency politics, in which single nation-states increasingly are unable to act with real autonomy. So many small nations have de facto refused to carry out an independent politics at all. But today, even large nations are increasingly unable to counteract the actions of worldwide capital and money speculations, which move immense amounts of money every day. Moreover, the actions of the multinational corporations undermine the autonomy of single nation-states because they can transfer their investments and profits to just those countries that provide the best opportunities for them.

On the other side, the modern nation-state comes under question from subnational agents and units such as organized ethnic and national minorities and regional movements. This happens particularly in the strongly centralized European nation-states such as Italy, France, and Great Britain (Kruse 1990; Fix 1993).

From this perspective, the rise of a European consciousness and citizenship should also be seen as part of the general advance of *multiple social and political identities* in the modern world. This tendency would also make necessary a wholly *new conception of citizenship:* Citizenship would be seen as a socially embedded set of rights and duties; it would not emanate "from above," from membership in one single and exclusive nation-state, but "from below," from the several social relations, associations, and communities whose members are individual persons. The highly differentiated structure of European society, in regional, cultural, and political terms, would be subdivided in this way into many "universalistic autonomous spheres" of citizenship (Donati 1993; Turner 1990).

The development of multiple identities and a corresponding differentiated conception of "social citizenship" can only be welcomed, as it would help to defuse the danger historically associated with nationalism as the only form of sociopolitical identity. It would also correspond to trends in international law that question the practice of seeing only and exclusively the existing nation-states as autonomous acting units ("persons" in the juridical sense). From a more universal point of view, there seems to be no reason why individual persons, organizations, minorities, and other groups should not also be able to act on the international scene on their own behalf as up to now only states are permitted to do (Knieper 1991). Only when it is also possible for these units to act on their own will it become possible to enforce the full rights of individuals all over the world. As is well known, this often applies to individuals even within their own nation-states.

In this case, this process would certainly have to be considered as a process of social closure. Thus it is essential to conceive the project of European unification not only as an internal European issue. Rather, European unification must fit into the demand of a worldwide process of internationalization and globalization—a demand already formulated very clearly by G.H. Mead (1983) during World War I (see also Luhmann 1975).

Seen from this perspective, European unification should not close our minds to the fact that the most pressing actual issues of humanity—control of armaments, poverty in the Third World, environment pollution—are not specifically European, but are worldwide problems. The idea and purposes of European integration must, in the last instance, be evaluated against the question of whether it does contribute to a solution of these issues. At present, the impression is often that (West) European nation-states aim at coming more closely together only in order to better isolate their continent from these global problems.

References

Adam, H. 1993. *The Politics of Identity: Nationalism, Patriotism, and Multiculturalism. Policy, Theory and Practice.*

Almond, G., and S. Verba. 1963. *The Civic Culture.* Princeton, NJ: Princeton University Press.

Arnold, H. 1993. *Europa am Ende? Die Auflösung von EG und NATO.* Munich/Zurich: Piper.

Aron, R. 1965. *Main Currents in Sociological Thought.* New York: Basic Books.

Bashkirova, E. 1992. "Russian Public Opinion about European Identity." Paper presented at the First European Conference of Sociology, Vienna.

The author would like to thank Albert F. Reiterer (Vienna) for very useful comments on a first version of this chapter.

Berton, P. 1987. *Why We Act Like Canadians: A Personal Exploration of Our National Character.* Harmondsworth, Middlesex: Penguin Books.

Bornschier, V. 1988. *Westliche Gesellschaft im Wandel.* Frankfurt/New York: Campus.

Bowie, R.R., and C.J. Friedrich. 1954. *Probleme einer europäischen Staatengemeinschaft.* Frankfurt: Institut für Europäische Politik und Wirtschaft.

Bruckmüller, E. 1984. *Nation Österreich. Sozialhistorische Aspekte ihrer Ent-wicklung.* Vienna/Cologne/Graz: Böhlau.

Busch, K. 1991. *Umbruch in Europa. Die öknomischen, ökologischen und sozialen Perspektiven des einheitlichen Binnenmarktes.* Cologne: Bund Verlag.

Buss, A. 1989. "The Economic Ethics of Russian-Orthodox Christianity. Part I." *International Sociology*, vol. 4, pp. 235–58.

Commission of the European Communities. 1990. *Eurobarometer: Public Opinion in the European Community* (Summary). No. 33, June.

Coudenhove-Kalergi, R. 1953. *Die europäische Nation.* Stuttgart: Deutsche Verlags-Anstalt.

Cutler, T., et al. 1989. *1992: The Struggle for Europe. A Critical Evaluation of the European Community.* New York/Oxford/Munich: Berg.

Donati, P.P. 1993. *La cittadinanza societaria.* Rome/Bari: Laterza.

Drucker, P. 1993. *Post-Capitalist Society.* New York: Harper Collins.

Eisenstadt, S.N., and S. Rokkan, eds. 1973. *Building States and Nations*, 2 vols. Beverly Hills, CA: Sage.

Elias, N. 1976. *Über den Prozeß der Zivilisation,* 2 vols. Frankfurt: Suhrkamp.

Faber, R. 1979. *Abendland. Ein politischer Kampfbegriff.* Hildesheim: Gerstenberg Verlag.

Fabris, H.H. 1988. "Statistenrolle reserviert? EG-Anbindung, Medien- und Telekommunikationspolitik in Europa." In M. Scherb and I. Morawetz, eds., *Der un-heimliche Anschluß. Österreich und die EG.* Vienna: Verlag für Gesellschaftskritik.

Fenner, C. 1983. "Politische Kultur." In M.G. Schmidt, ed., *Westliche Industriegesellschaften. Pipers Wörterbuch zur Politik*, Bd. 2. Munich/Zurich: R. Piper, pp. 343–50.

Fix, E. 1993. "Participation in Regional Movements as 'Rational Choice,' Based on Unequal Distribution of Resources in the Process of Nation-Building." Paper presented at the ÖGS-Conference "Foci of Societal Development," Innsbruck.

Flora, P. 1983. "Introduction: Stein Rokkan's Macro-Model of Europe." In P. Flora, ed., *State, Economy, and Society in Western Europe 1815–1975*, vol. 1. Frankfurt/London/Chicago: Campus/Macmillan/St. James Press.

Francis, E.K. 1965. *Ethnos und Demos. Beiträge zur Volkstheorie.* Berlin: Duncker & Humblot.

Francis, E.K. 1976. *Interethnic Relations. An Essay in Sociological Theory.* New York/Oxford/Amsterdam: Allen & Unwin.

Friedrich, C.J. 1969. *Europe. An Emergent Nation.* New York/Evanston, IL: Harper & Row.

Gallenmüller, J., and R. Wakenhut. 1993. "The Conceptualization and Development of a Questionnaire for Analyzing Consciousness of National Affiliation." In M. Martini, ed., *National Consciousness.* Special Issue of *Ricerche di Psychologia*, no. 4, pp. 9–28.

Galli, R. 1991. *Globale/Locale.* Milan: ISEDI.

Gallino, L. 1993. *Disuguaglianze ed Equità in Europa.* Rome/Bari: Laterza.

Galtung, J. 1973. *The European Community. A Superpower in the Making.* Oslo: Universitetsforlaget.

Gellner, E. 1987. *Culture, Identity, and Politics.* Cambridge: Cambridge University Press.

Giddens, A. 1985. *The Nation State and Violence.* Cambridge: Polity Press.

Giner, S., ed. 1990. *Espana. Sociedad y Politica.* Madrid: Escasa-Calpe.

Grün, M., and R. Foresta. 1992. *Warnung vor EG-Europa. Argumente gegen eine Weltordnung.* Salzburg: Unipress.

Gubert, R., ed. 1992. *Persistenze e Mutamenti dei Valori degli Italiani nel Contesto Europeo.* Trento: Riverdito Edizioni.

Haller, M. 1990. "The Challenge for Comparative Sociology in the Transformation of Europe." *International Sociology*, vol. 5, pp. 183–204.

Haller, M. 1992a. "Class and Nation as Competing Bases for Collective Identity and Action." *International Journal of Group Tensions*, vol. 22, pp. 229–64.

Haller, M. 1992b. "New Societies or Social Anomie in the Europe of Tomorrow?" *Schweizerische Zeitschrift für Soziologie*, vol. 3, pp. 635–56.

Haller, M. 1993. "Significato e dimensioni delle disuguaglianze." In L. Gallino, ed., *Disuguaglianze ed equità in Europa.* Rome/Bari: Laterza, pp. 3–44.

Haller, M., and F. Höllinger. (1994). "Zentren und Peripherien in Europa." In S. Immerfall and P. Steinbach, eds., *Historisch-vergleichende Makrosoziologie: Stein Rokkan—der Beitrag eines Kosmopoliten aus der Peripherie.*

Hancock, M.D. 1993. *Politics in Western Europe.* Houndsmill, Basingstoke/London: Macmillan.

Hankel, W. 1993. *Die sieben Todsünden der Vereinigung.* Berlin: Siedler.

Hechter, M. 1975. *Internal Colonialism. The Celtic Fringe in British National Development 1536–1966.* London.

Heckmann, F. 1992. *Ethnische Minderheiten, Volk und Nation. Soziologie interethnischer Beziehungen.* Stuttgart: Enke.

Holland, S. 1980. *Uncommon Market. Capital, Class and Power in the European Community.* London: Macmillan.

Joerges, C. 1991. "Die Europäische Integration und das Recht." In W. Zapf, ed., *Die Modernisierung moderner Gesellschaften.* Frankfurt/New York: Campus, pp. 331–36.

Jordan, T.G. 1988. *The European Culture Area. A Systematic Geography.* Cambridge: Harper & Row.

Kaelble, H. 1987. *Auf dem Weg zu einer europäischen Gesellschaft. Eine Sozialgeschichte Westeuropas 1880–1980.* Munich: C.H. Beck.

Kapteyn, P. 1993. "'Kulturgerecht Verhandeln': Über nationale Zivilisationen und europäische Integration." In R. Blomert, H. Kuzmics, and A. Treibel, eds., *Transformationen des Wir-Gefühls. Studien zum nationalen Habitus.* Frankfurt: Suhrkamp, pp. 85–117.

Knieper, R. 1991. *Nationale Souveränität. Versuch über Anfang und Ende einer Weltordnung.* Frankfurt: Fischer Taschenbuch Verlag.

Kohn, H. 1964. *Von Machiavelli zu Nehru. Zur Problemgeschichte des Nationalismus.* Freiburg/Vienna: Herder.

Kohnstamm, M., and R. Hager. 1973. *Zivilmacht Europa.* Frankfurt: Suhrkamp.

Kohr, L. 1986. *Das Ende der Großen.* Vienna: Orac.

Kosterman, R., and S. Feshbach. 1989. "Toward a Measure of Nationalistic and Patriotic Attitudes." *Political Psychology*, vol. 10, pp. 257–73.

Krejci, J. 1978. "Ethnic Problems in Europe." In S. Giner and M. Archer, eds., *Contemporary Europe. Social Structures and Cultural Patterns.* London/Henley/Boston: Routledge & Kegan Paul, pp. 124–71.

Kruse, H. 1990. *Reform durch Regionalisierung.* Frankfurt/New York: Campus.

Lane, J.E., and S.O. Ersson. 1987. *Politics and Society in Western Europe.* London/Newbury Park/New Delhi: Sage.

Lepsius, R.M. 1988. *Interessen, Ideen und Institutionen.* Opladen: West-deutscher Verlag.

Lepsius, R.M. 1991. "Die Europäische Gemeinschaft: Rationalitätskriterien der Regimebildung." In W. Zapf, ed., *Die Modernisierung moderner Gesellschaften. Verhandlungen des 25. Deutschen Soziologentages in Frankfurt am Main 1990.* Frankfurt/New York: Campus, pp. 309–17.

Luhmann, N. 1975. "Die Weltgesellschaft." In N. Luhmann, *Soziologische Aufklärung,* Bd. 2. Opladen: Westdeutscher Verlag, pp. 51–71.

Mead, G.H. 1983. "Die psychologischen Grundlagen des Internationalismus." In G.H. Mead, *Gesammelte Aufsätze,* Bd. 2. Frankfurt: Suhrkamp, pp. 424–39 (orig. published 1914/15).

Mendras, H. 1988. *La Seconde Revolution Francaise 1965–1984.* Paris: Gallimard (English ed.: Cambridge University Press).

Morin, E. 1987. *Penser L'Europe.* Paris: Gallimard.

Münch, R. 1982. *Basale Soziologie: Soziologie der Politi.* Opladen: Westdeutscher Verlag.

Noetzel, K. 1970. *Die Grundlagen des geistigen Rußland. Versuch einer Psychologie des russischen Geisteslebens.* Hildesheim/New York: G. Olms (orig. published 1923).

Noiriel, G. 1991. *La Tyrannie du National. Le droit d'asyle en Europe (1793–1993).* Paris: Calman-Levy.

Reiterer, A.F. 1988. *Die unvermeidbare Nation. Ethnizität, Nation und nachnationale Gesellschaft.* Frankfurt/New York: Campus Verlag.

Rejai, M. 1991. *Political Ideologies: A Comparative Approach.* Armonk, NY/London: M.E. Sharpe.

Rijs, O. 1989. "The Role of Religion in Legitimating the Modern Structuration of Society." In *Acta Sociologica,* vol. 32, pp. 137–53.

Rokkan, S. 1980. "Eine Familie von Modellen für die vergleichende Geschichte Europas." In *Zeitschrift für Soziologie,* vol. 9, pp. 118–28.

Room, G. 1990. *"New Poverty" in the European Community.* Houndsmill, Basingstoke/London: Macmillan.

Scheff, T. 1992. "Emotions and Identity. A Theory of Ethnic Nationalism." Paper presented at the ASA-Miniconference on Theory, Pittsburgh.

Schelling, T.C. 1960. *The Strategy of Conflict.* Oxford/London/New York: Oxford University Press.

Scherb, M., and I. Morawetz, eds. 1988. *Der un-heimliche Anschluß. Österreich und die EG.* Vienna: Verlag für Gesellschaftskritik.

Senghaas, D. 1990. *Europa 2000. Ein Friedensplan.* Frankfurt: Suhrkamp.

Smith, A.D. 1986. *The Ethnic Origins of Nations.* Oxford: Basil Blackwell.

Smith, A.D. 1991. *National Identity.* London: Penguin.

Strassoldo, R., and N. Tessarin. 1992. *Le Radici del Localismo. Indagine sociologica sull'appartenenza territorial in Friuli.* Trento: Riverdito Edizioni.

Therborn, G. 1993. "Beyond the Lonely Nation States." In F. Castles, ed., *Families of Nations.* Philadelphia: Gordon & Breach.

Tichy, G. 1991. "Is Europe an Optimum Integration Area?" Unpublished manuscript, University of Graz.

Turner, B. 1990. "Outline of a Theory of Citizenship." *Sociology,* vol. 24, pp. 189–217.

Urry, J. 1990. "Globalisation, Localisation and the Nation-State." Lancaster Regionalism Group, Working Paper 40.

Vobruba, G. Forthcoming. "Transnational Social Policy in Processes of Transformation." In T.P. Boje, ed., *A Changing Europe: Trends in Welfare State and Labor Market.* Armonk, NY: M.E. Sharpe.

Vogler, C. 1985. *The Nation-State: The Neglected Dimension of Class.* Aldershot, Hants.: Gower.

Wallerstein, I. 1974. *The Modern World System.* New York/San Francisco/London: Academic Press.

Index

F